MEMOIRS OF A
WHITE CROW INDIAN

MEMOIRS OF A
WHITE CROW INDIAN

(THOMAS H. LEFORGE)

AS TOLD BY
THOMAS B. MARQUIS

With an introduction by
JOSEPH MEDICINE CROW and HERMAN J. VIOLA

A
BISON
BOOK

UNIVERSITY OF NEBRASKA PRESS · LINCOLN

77

First Bison Book printing: November 1974

Most recent printing shown by first digit below:
1   2   3   4   5   6   7   8   9   10

Bison Book edition published by arrangement with the copyright holders.

Library of Congress Cataloging in Publication Data

Leforge, Thomas H   1850–1931.
    Memoirs of a White Crow Indian (Thomas H. Leforge)

    Reprint of the ed. published by Century Co., New
York.
    1. Leforge, Thomas H., 1850–1931. 2. Crow
Indians. 3. Indians of North America—Wars—1866–1895.
I. Marquis, Thomas Bailey, 1869–1935, ed. II. Title.
E99.C92L49 1974   970.3 [B]   74–6222
ISBN 0–8032–5800–3

Manufactured in the United States of America

INTRODUCTION

THE CROWS believe that when the First Maker created the earth and placed the Indian people upon it, he gave the Crows the best place. They received a beautiful and wild land, with wooded hills and open meadows that abounded with game; it was neither too hot in the summer nor too cold in the winter. But in giving them such a favored location, the First Maker was testing the courage of the Crows for he surrounded them with several of the most militant Indian tribes of North America. For generations, the greatly outnumbered Crows withstood incursions from the Sioux, the Cheyennes, the Blackfeet. Constant warfare made them a hardy, brave, and cunning people. It also made them embrace the white man as an ally against their traditional enemies and explains why six Crow warriors were riding with Custer and the Seventh Cavalry that fateful day in 1876.

Perhaps because of their friendship for the white man, the Crows have received relatively scant attention from historians. This neglect is puzzling considering their service as scouts for the U.S. Army in the Sioux wars of the 1870s. Certainly few events in American history have captured the scholarly and popular imagination as this tragedy enacted in the

The authors wish to express their appreciation to Deborah A. Harsch, who searched the records at the National Archives for information about Thomas H. Leforge.

Montana and Dakota wilderness as the northern plains tribes lashed out in their last desperate attempt to keep the white man at bay.

Fortunately, someone did tell the story of the Crow scouts. He was Thomas H. Leforge, an Ohioan by birth and an adopted member of the Crow tribe by choice. But for a broken collar bone he would have accompanied the Crow scouts and Custer into the Big Horn valley where, doubtless, he would have joined his friend and fellow scout Mitch Buoyer in death. Had Leforge died in that dramatic affair, history would have been deprived of *Memoirs of a White Crow Indian*, a simple, fascinating story that highlights the little known yet important role of the Crows and the many other Indians like them who served the white armies as guides, scouts, and comrades-in-arms in the exploration and conquest of North America.

Echeen-Akindesh, or the Horse Rider, as the Crows knew Leforge, abandoned his family for the lures of the Indian way of life shortly after the Civil War, when about nineteen years of age. He attached himself with little difficulty to a band of the Crows, whose ways and language he quickly learned. His transition to Indian life became complete when he married a young Crow woman named Cherry, by whom he fathered one child, a son later known as Old Tom Leforge. To keep himself in money, he found employment at the Crow Agency working at such odd jobs as blacksmith, dispatch rider, interpreter, service that is verified by official records. For instance, according to the roster of agency employees, "Thomas Laforgey" worked as a laborer for fifty dollars a month from September 20, 1873, to March 26, 1874. After an absence of three months, he returned to the agency as the night watchman, a position he held for two months.[1] His name does not appear in the official records again, however, until April 10, 1876. On that day, "Eet-seé-dahkh-in-dush, Horse Rider, *alias* Thomas Leforgey," enlisted as a private in the company of Crow scouts being enrolled by Lt. James H. Bradley of the Seventh Infantry. Bradley noted on the muster roll that "these scouts . . . are all members of the Crow tribe of Indians, full blood, except two men [Leforge and Barnard Bravo] allied to the tribe by marriage, adopted therein, and speaking their language." Following his discharge on July 9, Leforge remained unemployed only until September 21, when Lt. Charles E. Hargous, commander of the Crow scouts, hired him as an interpreter.[2] This work must have suited the restless young man because for the better part of a decade thereafter, "Leforgey," "La Farge,"

1. Rosters of Agency Employees, vol. 3, 1870–74, Crow (Mountain) Agency, pp. 164, 165, Record Group 75, Records of the Bureau of Indian Affairs, National Archives. Hereafter cited as RG, NA.

2. "Muster Roll of 1st Lt. James H. Bradley's Detachment of Indian Scouts . . . from the tenth day of April, 1876, to the thirtieth day of April, 1876," Regular Army Muster Rolls, Indian Scouts, Montana, 1867–93, Box 2362, RG 94, Records of the Adjutant General's Office, NA; Charles E. Hargous to E. L. Randall, November 30, 1876, Reports of Persons and Articles Hired, 1818–1913, No. 565-1876, RG 92, Records of the Office of the Quartermaster General, NA.

"La Forgey," or "Leforge" was listed regularly as an interpreter on the roster returns of Forts Keogh and Custer, Montana Territory.

After twenty years as a Crow Indian, Leforge in 1887 decided to try his luck in the white world. His reasons for doing so are unclear. Perhaps it was prompted by his divorce from Magpie Outside, Mitch Buoyer's widow, whom he had married after the Battle of the Little Big Horn and the death of Cherry. Leforge had three children by that marriage, another son, known as Young Tom Leforge, and two daughters, Rosa and Phoebe. He also adopted Buoyer's two children, Mary and James. Whatever the reason, Leforge left the reservation, moving to the Pacific Northwest and Alaska, where he subsequently entered into two unsuccessful marriages with white women before returning to Montana in 1912. Joseph Medicine Crow, official historian and anthropologist of the Crow tribe, personally knew both Leforge and Dr. Thomas B. Marquis, his biographer. He describes his acquaintance with the old man:

I first met Leforge in 1926, when I was about twelve years old. At the time I was in the Federal Indian Hospital at Crow Agency recuperating from an adenoids operation. I awoke one morning to find this strange man in bed across the room. He looked just like a ghost with his bluish-white skin and hooked nose, his toothless, gaping mouth, and his long, tangled white hair and beard. I tumbled out of the room and ran down the long hallway screaming "Ghost! Ghost!" It was some time before the nurses calmed me down enough to bring me back into the room, where the ghost was sitting up in bed vigorously eating his breakfast. When finished, he sat back and looked me over for a long while with his watery blue eyes. Then he said in Crow: "Little boy, whose grandson are you? Do not be afraid of me. I am just an old white man and . . . ." I took off again. If there was anything I considered worse than a ghost, it was a white man, especially one with long beard and hair.

After this harrowing introduction to Horse Rider, we became good roommates and friends. He had known my grandfather, Medicine Crow, and had even gone on the warpath with him several times. He told me many stories about the old days. How I wish I could remember those stories! But because I found some of them so hard to believe, I dismissed them as fantasies, especially when he told me of fish as big and long as our hospital wing. He was, of course, talking about whales he had seen in Alaskan waters, but he was unable to explain himself clearly as there is no word for whale in the Crow language.

Our paths crossed many times in the years before his death, but most often we would meet at the home of his daughter, Mary Laforge Littlenest, where I visited each summer. Littlenest was Medicine Crow's brother and therefore another grandfather to me. Leforge always wanted to tell stories, but we children did not pay much attention. In fact, except for occasional white historians, military people, and Custer buffs who came to him with questions, few people on the reservation had any interest in his stories. Why listen to a white man tell Indian stories when there were many tribal storytellers around? Besides, Jim Beckwourth, Crow Davis, and other squaw men who had lived with the Crows were known for their tall tales. Even Jim Bridger's yarns were lightly regarded by his own people.

Fortunately, the right person heard the stories, otherwise they might never have been recorded. This person was Thomas B. Marquis, a Bureau of Indian Affairs doctor to the Northern Cheyennes at Lame Deer, Montana. For several years the doctor had been interviewing Cheyenne veterans of the Custer battle with the idea of writing a book about it. This book was later published under the title *A Warrior Who Fought Custer*; essentially, it is the autobiography of Wooden Leg.[3] Having completed his research on the Northern Cheyenne Reservation, Marquis moved to the Crow Reservation about 1926, establishing residence at Lodge Grass. His purpose was to interview the Crow scouts and to conduct on-scene study of the battlefield itself, which is on the Crow reservation. Marquis was well suited for the task. A lawyer as well as a physician, he was a thorough and meticulous researcher. Moreover, his proficiency in the use of the Plains Indian sign language enabled him to gain the confidence and friendship of the old Cheyenne and Crow warriors, making him perhaps the first and only white man with whom they talked freely and truthfully.

I first saw the doctor when he came to my home seeking an interview with my grandfather, White Man Runs Him, then the only survivor of Custer's six Crow scouts. Marquis found my father, John, now eighty, most useful and valuable in his sessions with the old scout, who was then thoroughly disgusted with the many white men who came to ask him only leading questions and then would misquote him, ignoring his attempts to tell it like it was. The disbelief of the white historians at his description of the drunken

3. Thomas B. Marquis, interpreter, *A Warrior Who Fought Custer* (Minneapolis: Midwest Company, 1931), reprinted as *Wooden Leg: A Warrior Who Fought Custer* (Lincoln: University of Nebraska Press, 1962).

troopers who had been given whiskey to bolster their courage before the attack on the Sioux village would abruptly end the interviews. Nevertheless, Marquis and my parents became good friends.

Before the doctor moved to Lodge Grass, he would come to our home from Lame Deer by driving over the tortuous dirt roads in his old Model T Ford. Sometimes he would pitch his sheepherder's tent near the spring and stay a few days at a time. When he moved to town, our family camped nearby that winter. "We often visited him," recalls Amy White Man Runs Him, my mother, who is now seventy-seven. "He and John would play checkers till way after midnight. He would serve us hot cocoa and dried bread. He was a vegetarian and had a very restricted diet. Occasionally, he would boil potatoes and eat them by himself." Amy also remembers that in 1929, when she was about to give birth, the doctor pitched his tent at Crow Agency in case he was needed. "After the girl was born," Amy continues, "he came back to Lodge Grass with us and camped with us for over a week and gave us advice in caring for the new baby. He named the girl Minnie Ellen after his daughter."

Periodically, the doctor would visit the Lodge Grass Public School and examine the children. We children, who invariably feared white doctors, nicknamed him "Dr. Boo," the Crow expression for "bogeyman." His kindness and gentleness soon dispelled all fear of him, however, and we grew to enjoy his company, especially when he took our pictures. The doctor was a good photographer. Before he died in 1935, he gave his large camera to my father, who still has it.

I guess in his own way the good doctor was as much a character as Leforge. Rather aloof and always serious, he usually wore tight-fitting trousers or army type leggings; a stiff straw hat of the "eastern dude" variety; a bow tie stuck to a high, rigid collar; and arm bands that held up his long, cuff-linked shirt sleeves. The two friends were often seen together riding about the reservation in the doctor's old Model T, and the spectacle they presented can well be imagined: Marquis with his straw hat and celluloid collar, Leforge in his buckskins, their arms flailing in a lively sign language conversation. One time they were so engrossed in their sign talk, they rammed another car. No matter. They may have been an unlikely pair, but they combined to produce a rare and wonderful story.

Several other members of the Crow tribe now living on their Montana reservation knew the Horse Rider in his declining years, following his return from his twenty-five-year absence in the white world. Once seen, he could not easily be forgotten, for he presented quite a picture with his long white hair and beard, buckskin shirt, and cavalry leggings. When not riding around on his old gray horse, he could be found sitting in the shade telling stories, his favorite pastime. "He liked to talk about old times, hunting, chasing Piegan horse stealers, and scouting for soldiers looking for Sioux and Cheyennes," his granddaughter, Julia Red Wolf, recalls. Francis Laforge, his grandson, remembers people coming to visit him all the time. "Important white men would ask him about various battles between the soldiers and the Sioux and Cheyennes."[4]

Leforge did more than tell stories, however. A good blacksmith and carpenter, he kept busy even as an old

4. Joseph Medicine Crow obtained the statements that are quoted here from members of the Crow tribe.

man by doing odd jobs for his children and grandchildren. He built a bungalow for the Littlenest family and put a brick chimney on the Red Wolf house that is still in use. He also performed an important service by helping the Crow scouts apply for their military pensions. Typical of these efforts is this typewritten letter of July 12, 1922, in the pension application file of Curly, one of the six scouts with Custer at the Little Big Horn:

I, Thomas H. Laforge [sic], being first duly sworn, depose and say that I am 72 years of age; that I am well acquainted with Curley and have known him since about the year 1875; that Curley was enlisted in Co. e, 7th Inf., Walter Clifford, Company Commander, and that Curley enlisted on or about the 10th day of April, 1876, and served until he was honorably discharged in the winter of 1876–77 at Bozeman, Montana, and that he served in campaings [sic] against the Sioux, Cheyenne, and other tribes of Indians.[5]

Nevertheless, the memory of Leforge is a mixed one among the Crow people. To Robert Yellowtail, patriarch of the Crow tribe, Leforge was a typical squaw man, "except he never took part in Indian doings like some squaw men did." His own children did not appreciate his return from Alaska because they felt he had deserted the family. Regardless, with typical Indian generosity, his children and stepchildren opened

5. Certificate No. 10689, Application of Takes-A-Shield, wife of Curley, Pension Application Files, Indian Wars Series, RG 15, Records of the Veterans Administration, NA.

their homes to the old man, caring for him until his death in 1931.

At the time Leforge related his life story, he was in his mid-seventies. Time was robbing him of his sight, but it obviously had not dulled his mind, as can be seen when his version of an incident is compared to the official record; discrepancies may appear but the basic facts are there. A good example is the capture of seven hostile Northern Cheyennes which is described on page 271. For this exploit, which consisted merely of asking the Indians to surrender, the other Crow scouts dubbed Leforge "Captured Seven." He recalls it was a winter campaign, perhaps late December. According to the commandant of Fort Keogh, however, the incident occurred in late August, 1878; otherwise the versions are essentially the same. "Scouts Brengier and 'Horse Road' have returned from across the line bring[ing] five Indians and 2 women and children who formerly belonged to [the] Crazy Horse band," the commandant reported. "Brenghier states that they have come for the purpose of meeting Gen Miles with a reference to a surrender."[6]

Official records confirm at least two other minor incidents mentioned in *Memoirs of a White Crow Indian*: the killing of the Sioux warrior described on pages 296–99 and the skirmish with Piegan horse thieves

6. Commanding Officer to Assistant Adjutant General, September 4, 1878, Fort Keogh Letters Sent, vol. 1, p. 255, RG 393, Records of the United States Army Continental Commands, 1821–1920, NA.

that appears on pages 302–6. According to a Fort Custer muster roll, six Crow scouts, "while on detached service with Troop 'F' 2d Cavalry, captured and killed one Sioux Indian, May 25, 1881, about thirty miles north of Stillwater." Carried on that roll are Three Irons and Red Wing, better known as Riley, both of whom Leforge recalled as being present.[7] The fight with the Piegans, a band of the Blackfeet, occurred on November 8, 1882, and is described on another Fort Custer muster roll: "The Detachment pursued a party of hostile Indians (Piegans) and overtook them near Tullocks Fork M.T. about 20 miles east from this Post, and recaptured the stock stolen from them. One enlisted Indian Scout (Crooked Face) was wounded in the skirmish, two Piegans reported killed."[8] According to Leforge, the only injury on either side was to a Lieutenant Fuller.

What contemporary merit does *Memoirs of a White Crow Indian* have? Not only is it an engrossing story, but as Joseph Medicine Crow writes,

it reveals much about the early history of southern Montana, the conquest of the so-called hostile Indians by the

7. "Muster Roll of a Detachment of U.S. Indian Scouts serving at Fort Custer ... from the 30th day of April, 1881, when last mustered, to the 30th day of June, 1881," Muster Rolls, Box 2363, RG 94, NA.

8. "Muster Roll of a Detachment of U.S. Indian Scouts serving at Fort Custer ... from the 31st day of October, 1882, when last mustered, to the 31st day of December 1882," ibid.; see also Commanding Officer to Assistant Adjutant General, November 14, 1882, Fort Custer Letters Sent, vol. 55, p. 520, RG 393, NA.

U.S. military (including the humiliating defeat of the Seventh Cavalry and Custer), and the federal government's administration of the "reservation system" for Indians. In my opinion this book will be of special value to both students and instructors in the growing and popular Indian studies programs in our schools today.

Leforge claimed that he made his descriptions of Crow activities, customs, and ceremonials as a "casual observer" and he could be wrong about certain things. Except for some minor details about which both he and Marquis were somewhat confused, I find these casual observations to be generally correct and acceptable. For instance, his explanation of the Crow tribal name Absaroka as meaning "forked-tail bird" is not accurate, according to recent conclusions by tribal historians and linquists. The word Absaroka has become obsolete and abstract in the present Crow dialect, but in the dialect of the sister tribe, the Hidatsa of North Dakota, it literally means "children of the large-beaked bird" (Abisa = large-beaked and roka = its children). It is believed that this bird is the raven, a larger species of the crow. In fact, some of the Sioux bands referred to this tribe as "The Raven People" or "Children of the Raven." Leforge's conclusion that the white men misinterpreted the tribal name as Crow is understandable.

The book provides some remarkable insights into Crow history and culture. Young Leforge's courtship of Cherry was his first attempt at adhering to Crow customs, and it turned out very well. He soon married the young maiden, and they became members of the Crow Agency social elite, the interesting community of white squaw men and their Indian wives who lived in a double world. Horse Rider's taking leave from agency employment and turning into a Crow warrior is not only good reading but an accurate ethnological study of Crow military customs. By observing the rules, Leforge attained the rank of "wolf," or scout, and fulfilled at least two of the four required military deeds for attaining chieftancy. This military experience gained for him further and sincere acceptance into the tribe, making him a real Crow.

In the chapters entitled "Life in the Lodges of the Crows" and "Old Crow Indian Customs and Beliefs," Leforge, the self-proclaimed casual observer, proved most observant of Crow ways. These chapters contain rich source material for students of Indian culture. His description of the Crow tribal government is simple and clear; he considered the system sound and effective. His detailed descriptions of camp life also show he was more than a casual observer of Crow life. He understood well the necessity of frequent camp moves and the part played by the Camp Chief and his staff of advisors and security guards. Today's readers should find interesting his description of the daily activities of camp life, the breaking and setting up of camp, and the care and arrangement of the tepee, which served as a combination kitchen, dining, living, and bedroom.

The Horse Rider witnessed a Crow sun dance, and he had no hesitation in becoming a part of the atmosphere of full tribal participation which this most important ceremonial generated. His description of the ceremonial is far from a professional ethnological treatise, but it gives a good layman's view. Apparently, the Indian religion impressed him, for he later performed the vision quest ordeal, which he described as "the old time Indian cleansing penance." He sincerely believed he had received a vision from the First Maker through an animal emissary. He regarded the eagle as his "medicine animal" for the rest of his life. In closing out the telling of his life in a two-dimensional world, the

Horse Rider said, "I worship the Sun and the Big Horn Mountains : . . to me both father and mother. . . . their offspring lands and streams provided me with an abundance of good food and rich raiment. I was born an Ohio American, I shall die a Crow Indian American."

He died the Indian way with Indian thoughts, but he was buried as a white man with military honors at the Custer Battlefield National Cemetery among his comrades Mitch Buoyer, Barney Bravo, Curly, Hairy Moccasin, White Man Runs Him, and others.

Although *Memoirs of a White Crow Indian* was a very worthwhile contribution to the library of Custer Americana and western history, it fared poorly in the literary marketplace. Only 847 copies of the three-dollar book were sold in the six years following its publication in 1928; Marquis alone sold 30 copies. This information comes from the doctor himself, who entered the semiannual returns from the Century Company on a back flyleaf of his personal copy. On a front flyleaf, he wrote: "Do not ask to borrow this book. It is the author's personal copy of the work. April 20, 1928." Below this statement appears Thomas Leforge's signature with the typewritten note: "Above signature was written by Mr. Leforge June 9, 1929. He had become utterly blind by that time.—T.B.M."

This copy of the book, which is in the possession of the Marquis family, contains about two dozen annotations in the doctor's hand. Some correct minor errors, for example changing an officer's rank from captain to lieutenant, or Seventh Infantry to Seventh Cavalry;

others are more significant. For instance, on page 245 the text reads: "If Custer's light-baggage horsemen and pack-mules were being urged into hurried movement, how about Carroll's heavily loaded wagon-trains accompanying Terry?" In the margin next to this statement, Marquis wrote: "No, wagon train did not go to Bighorn. They had pack mules." On page 248, where Marquis states that Curly first relayed the news of Custer's death to General Gibbon, the doctor later noted: "No, he took news to boat [*Far West*] but not to Gibbon. T.B.M. Aug. 1930."

Other comments may be of less historical significance, but they are interesting nonetheless. "I attended this man [Scratch His Face] at his last illness, spring of 1926," the doctor noted at the bottom of page 296. On page 342, he wrote: "I visited two hours or longer with Leforge and Cold Wind together in Little Nest's teepee, July 3, 1927, in Crow 4th-of-July celebration camp at Wyola, Montana." Several are simple statements like these: "I know many descendants of Pierre Chien. All of them are extra bright and extra good Indians" (page 49), and "Tom Stewart's mixed-breed descendants are good Indians; I know several of them. TBM, 1930" (page 50).

The doctor also pasted several news items into the book. One is a postcard dated April 28, 1934, from a Helena reader who wrote: "The following . . . may be of interest to you, in case you have not seen it: 'Married. At the Crow Mission . . . Thomas Leforge and Bah-te-chua (The Cherry). A Cherry by any other name will taste as sweet.' Bozeman Avant Courier, Friday, Jan. 9, 1874." Another is a clipping from the Billings *Gazette* of March 30, 1931, which announced in bold type: "DEATH CLAIMS TOM LA FORGE"—ARMY SCOUT, 'WHITE CROW' SUCCUMBS AT AGENCY." Marquis noted simply: "Death occurred March 28, 1931."

Marquis gave up his medical practice in 1931 and settled in Hardin, a small town near the Crow Reservation. There he opened a little museum crammed with Custer memorabilia given him by his Indian friends; he also took up serious writing. *Memoirs of a White Crow Indian* and *A Warrior Who Fought Custer* were the only books he published, but he produced several other book-length manuscripts and numerous pamphlets, short stories, and magazine articles.[9] For several years his stories appeared weekly in a Montana newspaper syndicate. An untimely heart attack, however, ended his literary career within four years of retirement. He died March 22, 1935, at age sixty-five. Marquis, a World War I veteran, was buried with full military honors at the Custer Battlefield National Cemetery, where he joined the men he helped immortalize.[10]

JOSEPH MEDICINE CROW
HERMAN J. VIOLA

9. His daughters have since reprinted six of the pamphlets in a booklet entitled *Custer on the Little Bighorn* (Lodi, Calif., 1967).

10. Hardin (Montana) *Tribune-Herald*, March 29, 1935.

THE AUTHOR'S STATEMENT

The stories herein are, in essence, just as Mr. Leforge told them to me.

There were many fragmentary and disconnected recountings during the course of dozens of times of visiting with him.

Mine has been the business merely of arranging his tales into consecutive order and of clothing them in suitable verbal dress.

THOMAS B. MARQUIS, M.D.

March, 1928.

CONTENTS

MEMOIRS OF A WHITE CROW INDIAN

MEMOIRS OF A WHITE CROW INDIAN

THE EMIGRATION WESTWARD

My name is Thomas H. Leforge. My paternal ancestors were of the South Carolina French Huguenots. I was born at Portsmouth, Ohio, on July 9th, 1850.

My father moved his family to St. Joseph, Missouri, in 1852. The following year he went on across the Missouri River into Kansas, locating in Doniphan County. Our post-office was at Palermo. Neighboring villages were Ellwood and Wathena. The county-seat was Troy. My father bought a thousand or more acres of land. For this purchase he used war scrip coming to my mother from some ancestral soldier services.

Buffalo were yet roaming along the Big Blue River. The plains westward were full of them. Kickapoo and Pottawatomie Indians lived in our vicinity. Members of other tribes visited there. The

greater number of my playmates were Pottawatomie children. I liked them. The association with
them was so enjoyable that by the time I was twelve
years old I could rattle off the Pottawatomie talk
well enough for all practical purposes.

Gold discoveries in Idaho Territory—or in Montana Territory, as the special region later became
—aroused in my father a desire to go into that
country. We set out in the spring of 1864. Our
family outfit consisted of two wagons with ten head
of cattle to pull them, a spring-wagon drawn by
horses, and one saddle-horse. Six of our cattle were
steers, four of them were cows. These latter yielded
us a small quantity of milk, very welcome to us on
the long overland journey.

Our wagons contained only household goods and
family supplies. My father drove a six-ox team, a
man named Hansen drove a four-ox team, my
mother or one of the boys drove the horses attached to the spring-wagon. Some other wagons
from the eastward joined with us. I particularly
remember the merchant wagons of Beauvais and
Mollette. They came from St. Joseph. These two
men already had been trading among the Indians
along the Platte. To me it was wonderful to see
them converse with the red people by means only
of the sign-talk gestures.

It was Gus Beauvais who was with us. He had a brother, John Beauvais, who operated a trader store at the California crossing of the Platte. John was married to a Sioux Indian woman. Both of the brothers were big and powerful and capable men. I believe they were Canadian French. Jim Bridger used to make one of his homing places at the trader store of John Beauvais.

Soldiers held us several days at the California crossing. We then had altogether about a dozen wagons, and they said this was not a large enough train to venture through the danger zones. Other wagons came. When the number reached twenty-five or thirty we were allowed to proceed. Besides the family groups and the merchant traders, several single men were along, these working their way by serving as drivers.

Quicksands and high water on the South Platte hindered us. We took off wagon-beds, calked them, and used them as ferry-boats to take across the families and the goods. We had with us two brothers who were especially good swimmers and particularly capable as drivers for the cattle in swimming the river. They swam and hung to the tails of the animals, each man carrying a club to urge them forward. They were good "water cowboys." Notwithstanding their skill, our train lost ten or twelve head of cattle and one wagon, drowned or mired in the quicksands and mud.

We saw buffalo along the South Platte. At Fort Kearny I saw for the first time a pile of tanned buffalo-robes at the trader's store. From there on westward we encountered many buffalo. The biggest herd I ever saw, on that trip or afterward, was south of the Bighorn Mountains, in Wyoming. The last of these noble plains animals that I saw on this pioneer journey were on Clark's Fork of the Yellowstone. They were swimming the river there just below us.

Hostile Indians killed people ahead of us and behind us, but we did not lose any members of our party in this way. We attributed our good fortune to the presence of Beauvais and Mollette. On the South Platte we found one day the evidence of Indian raiding. The mortifying and blackened arm of a man was sticking up from a shallow grave beside the trail. Wolves had been at the body. An object was lying near it which I did not recognize then, but which afterward I learned was an Indian warrior's coupstick.* Feathers were hanging upon the sage-brush in a wide circle about the place. Off

* Coupstick (koo'stik). A slender rod, often decorated, used by some North American Indians in counting coup—that is, the striking or touching of an enemy in warfare in such a way as to be counted an act of bravery.

a little distance from this corpse I saw the decaying body of a woman. She had been scalped and her face had been hacked. The outer clothing was gone, and one foot had on its shoe. Our people buried both of these bodies. Other human remains were discovered, but they were too scattered and fragmentary to bury conveniently. Remains of wagons that had been burned were near by. Of course, the wagons had been plundered and the horses and cattle had been driven away. The current talk was that the Sioux committed these depredations, although from my experience of later years I learned that the Northern Cheyennes and Arapahoes also were operating at that time as hostiles in this region.

Our only death loss on the trip over the plains was by means of lightning. Two of our men were killed by it on the South Platte. They were greasing the wagons at the time. Some kind of tar mixture was used for this purpose. Later along the way this lubricator supply was exhausted. Butter then was used as wagon-grease.

A band of Sioux visited us after we had left the South Platte. They were traveling with families and lodges. Mollette knew some of them personally. They remained with us several hours, conducting themselves in a most amicable manner. Perhaps the size of our train deterred them from attacking us, or perhaps the acquaintance with Mollette served as our protection.

We crossed the North Platte at a toll-bridge owned by a man named Richeaux, a half-breed Sioux. In the present day, more than sixty years later, I know some Crow Indian grandchildren of this same Richeaux. They live in the vicinity of Wyola, Montana, my present home. Their present family name is Daylight.

A war-party of Sioux came to us just after we had crossed the North Platte. There were about fifteen of them. They were painted, were wearing their beaded and feathered clothing, and all of them were carrying lances and coupsticks. They stayed an hour or so, made sign-talk with Beauvais and Mollette, then went away peaceably. They told Beauvais and Mollette if we would go by the "Blanket road," the Sioux would not annoy us. "Blanket" was their name for Jim Bridger. At that time there were two trails that separated just west of the North Platte and came together again in Montana where Bridger Creek flows into Clark's Fork of the Yellowstone. The Bridger road went south of the Bighorn Mountains and then through them into Montana. The Bozeman road went north of the Bighorn Mountains. This northern region was claimed by the Sioux as their acknowledged treaty hunting-grounds. It was here that during the next few years they fought so bitterly against the soldiers at Fort Phil Kearny, Fort C. F. Smith, and at other places outside of the claimed territory.

We traveled the Bridger road, "south of the mountains." In fact, our train was not far behind one that was led by Jim Bridger as its guide. Nevertheless, we had some minor attacks by Indians. One night our night herders were shot at, but no damage was done. About noon one day a war-party appeared off on a hill to our right. They fired upon our outriders,—our "jack-rabbit hunters,"—and chased them to the train. We corralled our wagons and prepared for a battle. But after the Indians had lingered and shaken their lances at us for a while they rode away. During the entire journey every man kept himself armed and ready for trouble. Every driver of a wagon kept a loaded rifle strapped by his side.

The notorious Slade, two or three years later hanged by the vigilantes at Virginia City, Montana, was located at the North Platte bridge when we crossed there. He was agent for the mail-route and he was regarded as a very competent man for that position in those desperado days. He was courteous and helpful in his suggestions to the leaders of our train.

Bad water caused the death of eight or ten head of our cattle not long after we left the North Platte. We hastened to drive the remaining cattle away from the harmful spring to other watering and pasture places not far away. The people who had lost their stock were given substitutes by others in the train who had a surplus of animals. In this way and in all other ways our group of emigrants were mutually helpful. I never heard of any quarreling, at any rate not any serious quarreling, among this company of travelers.

A merchant wagon tipped over a grade at the "Devil's Backbone" point on the trail, between Wind River and Stinking Water River. Much of the cargo was lost, though most of it was recovered. The wagon was abandoned. I remember especially the scattering of candy. We children gathered it up, filled our pockets, and some of us ate too much.

Dancing was our usual night amusement. A space would be cleared off, a bonfire built, the fiddler would tune up, the mild revelry would begin. I often saw people dancing barefooted. I went barefooted, and I walked much of the time, all the way from northeastern Kansas into the heart of Montana.

A preacher also was with our train. He held religious services, and these were well attended. He protested against the dancing, but without avail.

At the last part of our migration, near the present site of Livingston, Montana, he became so distressed by what he regarded as the incorrigible wickedness of the company that he announced his determination to turn back. The next day he did so, taking with him his son. But they did not go far. News came to us in a few days that their dead and mangled bodies had been found along the trail. Hostile Indians, who ever were seeking just such opportunities, had pounced upon them as easy prey.

A man named Adams, also, for some reason, detached himself and his wife from our train and lingered a day or so behind when we had arrived on the Stillwater River. His three wagons were loaded with merchant goods, including a rich cargo of silks. One day, after he had dropped behind, he and his man helper came afoot to our train on the Yellowstone. He reported that his wife had been killed, his wagons robbed, and himself chased away by murderous Indians. Close inquiry elicited that he had not actually seen the woman killed, but he supposed she had been killed, since some Indians chased her as she fled.

A body of our men accompanied Adams back to search for his wife. They found her tracks by a creek. They rummaged along the stream, from time to time calling out her name, Lou. Finally, a response came. They found her, very tired and very hungry, but not injured. They then sought the wagons. These they found guarded by a few Crow Indians, not any of the goods in the wagons having been disturbed. It developed that the supposed "attack" was by friendly Crow Indians. In the course of their visit to the small party, one of them playfully displayed his hunting-knife. Either Adams or his helper fired a shot that killed this Indian, Sorrel Horse. Then the three whites scattered themselves to get away, with Crows following after them in an effort to assure them of good intentions. At their request, Adams now gave them presents from his stock, these to compensate them for the killing of their companion.

We met a band of Nez Percés on the upper Yellowstone River. They had come over the Rocky Mountains to hunt buffalo in the Crow country, they being friendly with the Crows and both tribes being on good terms with the whites. In this band was an Indian from some tribe in Kansas who had married a Nez Percés woman. His name was Hill. My father had known him in Kansas, had served with him in the army, and this renewal of acquaintance helped greatly to ease our minds as to possible Indian trouble.

A big wash-day was indulged in at the natural hot

springs now known as Hunter's Hot Springs. We went on then over the Bozeman Pass into the Gallatin valley. This was another point of divergence for the Bozeman and Bridger trails. Bridger's road here took the longer, but more gradual, route up Shields River, up Brackett Creek, and down Bridger Creek to the town of Bozeman.

In this frontier farmer town we stopped a week or so. But most of us were gold-seekers, so we went on to Virginia City. Here my father kept his family during the ensuing autumn and winter. Here I received a few more weeks of schooling that advanced me a few steps beyond the rudimentary acquaintance with primers and spelling-books which I had gained in Kansas. This text-book association at Virginia City ended my career in that kind of educational training.

Beef was very cheap in Virginia City, due to the incoming oxen that were no longer needed to draw the emigrants' wagons. But at times, there was no paper in which to wrap the beef handed out from the butcher's shop. Sharpened sticks were kept in stock for providing customers with a spear on which to carry home their purchases. My first paid job was cutting and sharpening sticks for use in the butcher-shop.

A flour famine occurred here during that winter.

The price ran up as high as $125 per sack. But the people organized and compelled owners of the precious food-stuff to sell at lower prices. My father had brought along an ample supply, more than he needed for the family, and he was urged into putting his surplus stock on the market at fair rates. Salt sold as high as fifty cents a pound, until an additional stock of this important commodity came into the camp. A recollection of mine is that during that winter I heard a great deal of talk about a prize-fight between Con Orem and Hugh O'Neill. It was a bare-knuckle engagement of seventy-two rounds.

Our family returned to Gallatin valley when the spring of 1865 came. My father operated for a time a ferry on the Madison River, then we moved on into Bozeman. This village then had but a few houses, although it was a lively advance-post of civilization. My father built a home for the family and he built also two or three other houses. At this time I came into contact with the Crow Indians. Two Leggings and some other heads of families had their buffalo-skin tepee lodges pitched near the village. I was drawn to them first by curiosity, but afterward by actual liking for their company. I got acquainted with Mitch Buoyer, a half-breed Sioux a few years older than I was. He told me he had

seen me and my people at the North Platte when
we came through there during the previous summer.
He said he had come through on horseback.

Carpentering and contracting of various sorts
kept my father employed for a year or more at
Bozeman. He also joined with Colonel Bogart and
others in promulgating there the first newspaper,
known as "Pick and Plow." I worked at times, but
often I idled away my time or hunted and trapped
with the Indians. My acquaintance with the Crows
extended. Mitch Buoyer became a soldier at Fort
C. F. Smith, but he came often to Bozeman, as a
despatch-rider, to bring and to receive military mes-
sages through this avenue to the civilized world.
On a certain occasion he became somewhat befuddled and disabled by liquor, as was his habit. He
had me get a Crow Indian to carry to Fort Smith
an important despatch he then had. "Big Bat" was
with Mitch when I talked with them in a tepee
lodge. This Big Bat had Baptiste as his surname.
There was another Baptiste famed in the annals of
the West. This other was known as "Little Bat."
They both were of the Canadian French trapper
stock, I believe, but it was my understanding they
were not related.

BAD INDIANS AND BAD WHITE MEN

I JOINED the Montana militia during the summer of
1867. My father then was on the Bozeman-pass
mountain, getting out timber to sell to miners. On
my way into Bozeman one day I met John Evans
and a man named Griggs. They were recruiting for
the militia. Although I was not yet eighteen years
old, they accepted me and swore me in then and
there. I returned and told my parents. They urged
me to retract my vow, but I told them I could not
do so. I went then to the camp of the recruits, on
the Gallatin side of the mountain. The enlistment
was for ninety days.

Our company mutinied a day or two after my in-
duction into the militia. We were being held there
with only our own personal arms, without clothing
or other military accoutrement, without any horses,
without provision for shelter, with scant food, except a little wild game. The specific act of insub-
ordination was our refusal to leave the temporary
camp and go to the Yellowstone, where hostile
Indians were plentiful. Governor Meagher ordered

the entire company to be arrested and brought to him, up where the Northern Pacific tunnel now goes through the mountain's top. When we arrived there, we found companies from Virginia City and Bannack drawn up to receive us. We were headed so as to go between them, but our leading ones turned aside and we went behind them. Governor Meagher stood up and began a lecturing speech to us. Some of the men in the other companies handed guns to men in our companies. A man known as "Chris," a tough, but good-hearted, Mormon, leveled a rifle at the governor and told him we had heard enough. The untamed militiamen of the other companies cheered him, cheered his associate culprits, and shouted, "We are with you, boys!" The governor had to yield the point. The matter soon was settled in a way acceptable to all. Not long afterward we all were on our way to the Yellowstone in search of marauding Indians—or of anything else that might stir up excitement.

While we were camped at the present site of Livingston some of us were sent on an errand back to Bozeman. The Mormon Chris and a man named Spencer got into a quarrel along the way. In Bozeman, drink made the quarrel worse. In the fight that ensued, Chris stabbed to death the unfortunate Spencer. When we got back to our company, Chris was court-martialed. After a scanty inquiry he was acquitted.

We built at the mouth of Shields River a stockade, storehouse, etc., of cottonwood logs. This became the headquarters of the three companies while we skirmished along the Yellowstone and its tributaries. About this time a band of Flatheads came through Gallatin valley on their way to the buffalo country east of the Bridger Mountains. They attacked, or got into an altercation with, a white rancher. He was injured, but not killed. The Flatheads went on through Flathead Pass into the valley of the Shields River, or the Twenty-five-yard River, as it often was called. Our militia received information of the trouble, and a body of us set out to intercept them. We came upon them at the mouth of Brackett Creek. We demanded the man or men who had attacked the Gallatin rancher. Flathead Jack, an English-speaking Indian, responded for them. They designated the man, but they wanted to substitute another Flathead for the coming sacrifice, since the offending Indian was held to be an important one in the tribe. Some parleying was done, but not for long. We seized the principal factor in the intrusion upon white-man rights. In a jiffy he was hanged, or was strangled to death while suspended from the limb of a cottonwood tree. The other Indians were permitted to go on their way. Flathead Jack lingered and said his people were "talking bad," so he feared they might make further trouble. We followed them, bluffed them into acknowledgment of our superiority, and that was the last we heard of them.

This first Montana militia was composed largely of ex-ruffians of the Missouri-Kansas border. As soldiers, they were utterly unruly. One company drowned its first captain. He showed some inclination to disciplinary action, so the bold and unterrified subordinates threw a rope about him and dragged him back and forth through Shields River until life was extinct. Desertion was a matter to be determined merely by personal inclination. One day I met out on the road my own company's captain. He told me he was quitting, and he advised me to do the same. His departure brought about the unofficial disintegration of our company. Only a few of us remained to receive formal discharge-papers. After I left, Captain Hart, of another company, was shot and killed by one of his men. Several men also were killed in a fight among themselves. The deserters scattered here and there. Some went to Nebraska. One went to Wyoming, where he afterward was hanged. A gang of these absconding men raided Fort C. F. Smith, where regular-army soldiers were stationed, although at this time only a few were there. The raiders demanded food and general entertainment, which the commandant of the fort provided, owing to the greatly superior force of the visitors.

The regular-army men of these frontier forts also deserted their posts without much hindrance. A peculiar incident occurred wherein two deserters from Fort Smith were attacked by hostile Indians on the east side of Boulder Creek, near where Big Timber is now situated. A scouting party of Montana militia happened to come upon the scene. Two or three Indians had been killed by the truant soldiers, who had good army guns. The militia attacked and chased away the Indians. It was said they scalped the dead hostiles left on the field of battle. They made no effort to arrest the slacking soldiers. On the contrary, they gave them food and other aid and comfort.

A second set of militiamen were recruited after the melting away of the original organization. This second set were enlisted for four months at a time. They did much better than had our outfit. They built a log barracks and other fort buildings on the site of the present town of Livingston. From here they operated in the punishment of hostile Indians during the remainder of that summer and autumn.

This log building served as a home for our family during the winter of 1867-68. My father was engaged in cutting logs for the building of Fort Ellis, which had been established a few miles out from Bozeman during the summer of 1867. I helped at times in the logging operations on the mountains, but much of my time was occupied in hunting and trapping. The meat obtained from hunting was disposed of mostly at Fort Ellis, and the furs from trapping brought me a comfortable pile of money when spring came. For a month or so during this winter Jim Bridger lived with us. He was naturally a bright and able man, and I learned from him a good deal about trapping. Stories nowadays are told about the drunkenness of Bridger, but in those times I always heard of him as a particularly sober man. I know that during the time he stayed at our place, there was no indication of drunkenness.

Piegan Indians were raiding through that region during this winter and early spring. Colonel Kimball came out from Bozeman in a cart. He was shot as he was in camp near the present Bozeman Tunnel. A man known as Fritzie, who had a special reputation as an astronomer, was shot and killed as he traveled afoot near a cold spring on Fleischman Creek. These enterprising Indians killed four of Story and MacAdow's cattle-herders on Shields

River that winter and took whatever horses and cattle they wanted.

Twelve Piegans came to our log-barrack home on the Yellowstone in early March of 1868. They were afoot, as the Piegans usually traveled when out for war and plunder, their idea of praiseworthy warfare being that they should go out afoot and return to their camp on horseback. These twelve had just swum the Yellowstone when they came to our place. We fed them, and they appeared friendly. Finally, they proposed to my father that he go outside with them. It was just about dusk, and my father refused. This angered them, and one of them grabbed my mother by the shoulders and shook her. My father seized a butcher-knife and slashed at him. The Indians had bows and arrows and flint-lock guns, with the butts, or the barrels, sawed off, such as they used for buffalo hunting. Some, if not all of the Indians, had knives in their belts. But their bowstrings and their guns were wet from their having swum the river, so the fight that followed developed into a scuffle, with our folks all trying to get away. We all got out and fled. There were my father and mother, two brothers, one sister, and myself. The oldest brother, Isaac, had gone hunting up the Yellowstone Cañon the day before.

I got my mother and sister into the cottonwood

timber and took them to a flatboat I had made that winter. With this we started to cross the Yellowstone to where I knew some trappers were encamped. But we gave up this attempt, they hid in the brush, and I swam the river. Slush ice was running, and I was barefooted. I could not find the trappers, so I had to keep myself moving all night to prevent freezing. When morning came I skirted along the river-bank and peeped through the brush. Finally, my father saw me and beckoned to me. I swam back over the river to him. The united family then went to the house whence we had fled the night before. The bedticks and pillows had been emptied of their feathers and the cloth taken away. Many articles had been burned in the open fireplace. We found there some charred remnants of our family Bible. All the bedclothing was gone. They stole also some wagon sheets belonging to Nelson Story which were stored in the building. There were horse tracks about the place next day, which indicated that they stole, or already had hidden away, some horses, which were used to carry off the plunder. Several years later, when Colonel Baker fought these Indians on the Marias River, one of my mother's quilts was found in their camp after the battle.

This same dozen hostiles who robbed us went to

the place of a man named Seabeck who lived a few miles up the Yellowstone. This man they robbed of two hundred dollars in gold-dust. At the frontier home of the Smothers family, living just above Yellowstone Cañon, they plundered the house, assaulted members of the family and broke one boy's shoulder.

Lots of guns, pistols, and even a cannon were stored in the militia-barrack building we were occupying. But there was no ammunition for them. Just a day or so after the raid, though, my brother found what appeared to be a root-house in the brush a hundred yards or so from the building. When we explored it we found stored there eight boxes of ammunition.

Our few horses, mules, and cattle were not quickly obtainable preparatory to leaving that region. Perhaps they had been stolen. At any rate, my parents decided to go back to Bozeman, so the stock was abandoned. Nelson Story came the next day, accompanied by a wagon. He was in a buggy. He had come to look after his cattle interests. His wagon brought supplies for his herders. He let us load our remaining effects into the wagon for removal to Bozeman.

We camped one night on the hill while moving to the Gallatin valley. That night the steers that drew the wagon got scattered. Lee Wyatt, the driver, went the next morning to search for them. After several hours of waiting for his return, Story hitched up his buggy and drove out to seek Wyatt. He found his dead body, evidently shot by the Indians, and he brought it in his buggy into our camp. We put the dead man into the wagon, my father drove the steers, that had been found by one of my brothers, and we continued our way into Bozeman.

My father resumed his work as a building contractor. After a few months he went out and took up a ranch on the West Gallatin River. In the early summer of this year, 1868, I roamed back over to the Yellowstone, attaching myself to some Crow Indians led by Yellow Leggings who were camping just above the Livingston cañon. I became the constant companion of Three Irons, who was a son of Yellow Leggings and about my age.

My Indian name had been Fast Runner, this because of my fleetness on foot. I could outrun all of the Indian youths in short-distance races. But some of them, especially Three Irons, could leave me behind in a long-distance test. My name became changed, though, by reason of a special incident. This was my successful riding of an especially fractious horse that had thrown the Indian riders. I never claimed great capability as a horseman, but on this occasion I made a good ride. Yellow Leggings promptly conferred upon me a new name, "Horse Rider." This name stuck to me. For sixty years since then the Crows have known me in its terms. Even now, among the old Crow Indians, Thomas H. Leforge is a stranger to them, but Horse Rider is a man whom they all know.

Yellow Leggings finally adopted me in formal manner. The ceremony took place at the Crow camp just above the Livingston cañon, where some warm springs create an ever open slough of clear water. Old man Seabeck then was living there. Yellow Leggings invited Indians from neighboring lodges, informed them what was to take place, and a dance was begun. In due time I was brought in. Yellow Leggings said:

"I know this young man's true father and mother. They are my friends; they have eaten at my lodge and I have had food given to me at their home. Now this young man is going to be my son. His name is Horse Rider. There,"—pointing to his squaw wife, "—there is his mother."

As a final act the adopted mother gave me water to drink. Then she spread a feast for the assembled guests. The adopted father gave away many presents to the people, and these in turn gave presents to me. Thus I became a Crow Indian, a brother of

Three Irons and a son of Yellow Leggings, who was a leading counselor of Blackbird, chief of the Mountain Crow tribe.

After Fort Ellis had been established I lingered often about that place. I sold there enough wild-game meat to keep me supplied with the little money I needed. My time was divided between the Crow camps, Fort Ellis, and my parents' home, with the home quarters almost neglected. Hostile Indians still were active, notwithstanding the establishment of the regular army fort. I remember that during the summer of 1868 a man was killed by the Indians only a few miles out from Fort Ellis. I saw his dead body, with many arrows sticking out from the flesh, when they brought it to the fort. A Mexican named Hosea and myself camped and hunted together as partners around Fort Ellis, Bannacks, Nez Percés, and Crows often camped about the fort.

A report of Indian depredations on the Yellowstone and Shields rivers came to Fort Ellis. One company of cavalry, under the command of Captain Cliff, was sent out to that region. I went along as a camp-follower, to hunt and to experience whatever excitement might come. The soldiers encountered a band of warring Indians just above the mouth of Shields River. The Indians boldly charged us.

"Fall back to the next bluff, boys," Captain Cliff ordered.

The Indians again charged us. Although we were better armed, they greatly outnumbered us. They began to crowd us more closely, yet more closely. Again the captain shouted:

"Fall back to the next bluff, boys."

The retreating maneuver was carried out three or four times, but finally we got into a position where we whipped off the Indians and then put them to flight. Nevertheless, the mode of combat and the repeated verbal order gained for Captain Cliff a good nickname. Instead of Captain Cliff, the soldiers among themselves jokingly referred to him as "Captain Bluff."

The escorting of emigrant trains was one of the duties of the soldiers stationed at the forts in the West. The Fort Ellis soldiers were sent out at times on such expeditions. I went occasionally with them —or I went with Mitch Buoyer, who guided them. This young Sioux-Frenchman friend of mine now had become permanently attached to the Crows, and often he was called upon to guide the soldiers as well as other exploring parties over the country he had come to know so well.

Mitch and I had one thrilling experience on the Bridger road, in Wyoming. He was guiding a detachment of cavalry from Fort Ellis. We were a few miles out in front, and we saw an emigrant train coming. We galloped on forward to meet it. As we approached the wagons we found ourselves facing a dozen or more cocked rifles. They had the idea that we were outlaws. They compelled us to dismount, disarmed us, and tied us to wagon-wheels. Our explanations were not believed, and it appeared they were determined to kill us. Soon they untied us, gave us a pick and a spade, and we were set digging a grave for ourselves. Armed men, ready to shoot, stood guard over us while we dug. We tried to work slowly, so as to give our soldiers a chance to arrive, but we were urged to hurry. The only pity manifested was by some women. One old woman brought a Bible and essayed to comfort us by reading aloud from it. She assured us she would see that we had a respectable funeral. They all were in dead earnest, and for a while the situation was to us anything but amusing. The tragedy was averted, though, by the appearance of our soldiers on an adjacent hill-top. Even then, one man insisted they were Indians coming, and he wanted to shoot us as the first act in the expected battle.

I hunted, during a part of these youthful years, with Eckley and Austin, two successful pelt-gathering white men. We spent most of our time in the valley of the Shields River, where we found buffalo, elk, and deer in plenty. The skins from these animals were traded for supplies. It was to me an attractive mode of obtaining a living. I traded them also for cattle, so before I was of age I owned some stock that made a basis for further accumulation of this sort of wealth in future years.

AT THE FIRST CROW AGENCY

THE Crow Indians had been participants in the great treaty council near Fort Laramie, in 1851, where members of many of the old plains tribes assembled and came to agreements with our government representatives. The Yellowstone country from the Big Horn River westward was conceded to the Crows. The Yellowstone River was known to them at that time and ever since as "Elk River." This tribe was divided into two principal subtribes—the River Crows, who roamed north of the Yellowstone, and the Mountain Crows, who stayed on the south side of this stream. My attachment was to the Mountain Crows, particularly to a coterie of them known among themselves as the Kick-in-the-Belly band, this name arising from a certain pugnacious act incident to the quarrel which had split the tribe into the two factions.

Yellow blankets and other presents of a like nature were issued to the Crows in 1869. The distribution was through the military officers at Fort Ellis. They brought the goods in wagons over to the

Yellowstone valley, and the issue took place on the north side of the river and just above the present town of Big Timber.

An agency was established in the spring of 1870. It was located on a bench beside Mission Creek, ten or more miles down the river from the present situation of Livingston. It was built of cottonwood logs, in the form of a crude fort, and it had a cannon mounted upon one side of its wall. It was called Mission, or, the Mission, merely by reason of the fact that in those days and earlier most of the Indian agencies were set up where a Christian missionary enterprise had already been in operation. This was not the case here.

Major Camp, a regular-army officer, sent out from Fort Ellis, was the first agent for this Indian tribe. Within a few months a fire broke out and destroyed the entire agency structure. I remember the great excitement prevailing on account of the fact that the cannon was loaded. The fire was allowed to take its course, everybody trying to get away from near to the cannon. In due time it exploded. Nobody was harmed, but we hadn't any agency left.

New agency buildings were constructed near the former site. The new construction was all of adobe. The former place was then spoken of as "the old Mission," while this new place became "the 'dobe

Mission," and, finally, "Mission." The Indian bureau sought for some "Indian man"—that is, some white man married to an Indian woman—to serve as agent. A man named Pease, one who fitted this requirement, had been for several years a trader with the Crows. He made a journey to Washington and presented himself as suitable material for the appointment as agent. Although his wife was of some other Indian tribe, he was put in as supervisor of Crow affairs. Thenceforth he became known as "Major" Pease, in accordance with the old custom of using this military title in designation of an Indian agent.

Major Pease had known my family in Bozeman. Soon after he assumed charge of the agency he employed me and put me upon the pay-roll as a blacksmith. He already had a blacksmith, but my position as a helper was created for the main purpose of using me as a despatch-rider, a night-watchman, and an occasional interpreter, and was in pursuance of the government policy of employing, wherever possible, trustworthy white men who were intimate with the Indians and might use their influence toward maintaining friendly relations.

Before all this I had become well able to speak the Crow language. It appeared I was on good terms with all of them. I know I liked them, and this liking was accentuated in the case of the girls. I had many flitting sweethearts among them. It seemed to me then that these associations were only temporary, that after a while I should go again to my own people. Nevertheless, I was content just then.

Cherry, a tall and attractive Crow girl, became to me unusually interesting. She had brown hair, hazel eyes, evidently was of mixed race, although I never did learn the source of her white blood. I conceived a special liking—or perhaps it was a deliberate cultivation of liking—for her brother, whose name was Head-and-Tail Robe. I visited often with him at their tepee lodge. During these visits I never spoke directly to the girl. Yet, by means of the mysterious telepathy that flashes between congenial spirits, I came to know that she preferred me above all other young men. Her mother, a widow, evidently got an intuitive knowledge of the situation, and one day, in their lodge, she began berating me on account of my unkempt personal appearance.

"Oh, your ragged moccasins!" she derided. "You ought to have a wife, some one who would keep you supplied with good clothing and who would keep your long and curly hair well oiled and well combed." Pretty soon she continued: "Cherry can make good clothing. I'll have her make you a coat and some good moccasins."

"But he ought to have a white wife to make his clothing," the girl protested. "He would not want an Indian woman."

They went on in further dispute, or in affectation of dispute, on this question. I did not commit myself. But the talk fixed my mind upon the matter. I was twenty years old and was growing a budding mustache. Cherry was eighteen. I was sure I loved her—no doubt about it then or ever afterward. I determined then and there to defy convention, to turn my back upon the deprecating white people, to have an Indian wife, to be altogether an Indian in mode of life.

I took some canned goods the next day and set them inside the entrance to their tepee. On succeeding days, and in the same Indian fashion followed in making presents, I gave them some blankets, calico, sugar, coffee, bacon, beads—lots of beads. Each time I merely opened the tepee flap, set in the presents, and went away.

Mitch Buoyer's wife took an interest in the affair. "Cherry is a good girl, one of the best in the tribe," she assured me over and over. One day I authorized her to tell my adored one I wanted her for my wife.

Cherry came the next day to the doorway of my blacksmith shop. She stood there a few moments, smiling, then she sat down on her blanket spread upon the ground outside. How agitated I was! What calm self-control she exhibited! I went out pretty soon and struck up a conversation with her. Although I was not bashful,—in fact, quite the contrary,—I was embarrassed and shaky just then. I stammered out an inquiry if she had a good awl for sewing. No, she hadn't any such tool. I jumped to the work and made her two good ones. After a while she went away.

Late that afternoon I saw Cherry and her sister-in-law pass along the road, each of them carrying on her back a bundle. They went to Mitch Buoyer's house. As I was about to close shop for the day Mitch's wife called to me:

"Somebody at our house wants to see you, Tom."

I found a big room that had not been in use transformed into a homelike place. My little personal effects were combined there with those of Cherry's lodge. She had made up my bed in the best form it had presented for many months. That was her token of marital intent. From that hour we were husband and wife, by virtue of mutual consent. We remained so throughout many years, until we were parted by death.

No charivari custom, such as prevails among many white communities, was in vogue with the Indians. There simply was present-giving. I gave presents to her full brother and two adopted brothers, and they in turn gave presents to me. Cherry received many presents from her relatives and friends, such as food and clothing, a fine beaded belt, and other articles that the Indian women coveted. Her people were of the Burnt Mouth clan of Mountain Crows. Her father, who had been killed, was named Rabbit.

Cherry's mother took up her abode with us in the one big room. While among the old-time Indians, and to a great extent yet, the man does not speak to nor in any way notice his mother-in-law, mine served as our "old woman." She chopped the wood, built the fires, did all of the menial work. An old woman was, in past times, one of the essential elements of a full-fledged Crow Indian household. She relieved the young child-bearing woman of all heavy work. She served also as policeman, sentinel, sergeant-at-arms. She located and made up daily all beds in her lodge, or saw that they were made up by the girls, and it was her business to see that each occupant of the lodge used only that bed which was his or her proper one. She was the chaperone of whatever girls might be of her household.

Her regular sleeping station was just inside the lodge entrance. Her emblem of office was a stout club, this lying by her side as she slept. She had a recognized right to use this club as an aid to the discharge of her duties. Since everybody understood this, it actually occurred that her usage of the weapon was mainly upon dogs. It sometimes happened that during the night came a disturbing: Whack! Thump! "Ouw-w-w-w!" Some dog had failed in its effort to slip past the old woman on guard.

My wife set herself at making fine clothing for me. She soon prepared for my adornment a creamy buckskin suit, all beaded, and she built up for me a gorgeous war-bonnet. Her mother tanned all of the skins, which in those days were easily obtainable. I became the best-dressed man at the dances and at the missionary's church. Cherry was proud of me. The Indian women prided themselves upon the personal appearance of their husbands.

A good and sincere man named Byrd served for a while as school-teacher and preacher combined. As a teacher he was succeeded by an old man who had been living in Bozeman. Most of the few white people about the agency attended regularly the religious services. Cherry and I joined the church and were sprinkled. She was prayerful at home, and often I helped her. During Dr. Wright's time as agent, his wife and daughter led the singing, the daughter also playing the little organ somebody had given to us. Many Indians came to church for the apparent purpose of hearing the music. Little ones, wearing only a breech-cloth, would sit with chins in hands and listen rapturously to the unpolished harmonies. The Indian women liked the church marriage ceremony, especially the clause, "until death do you part." Various ones dragged reluctant Crow husbands to the missionary for him to pronounce these binding words.

A full-blood Indian preacher came to us from somewhere in the East. He used English well, and I interpreted to the Crows. At his first address he told of his capture by the whites when he was a small boy, detailed his feelings at the time, related how he had supposed he would be put into prison, perhaps tortured, chopped into pieces. Instead, he was treated kindly. An army captain had adopted him and sent him to school. Now he was out trying to show to all Indians the wisdom of adapting themselves to the ways of the white race. Over and over he impressed upon his Crow hearers, "Never let the white man go away and leave you." This Indian was a good singer as well as a good talker, and he wielded a strong influence in creating friendliness among the Crows toward the whites.

The school was not so popular as the church. One parental objection was to the teacher's urging that the children have their hair cut off, for sanitary rather than for educational reasons. The Indian custom was to cut off the hair only as a sign of mourning, and one who had this disfigurement was known as "a ghost person." The children were attracted, though, by the daily issue of a stick of candy to each pupil. Of course, the teaching was of a kindergarten sort, or even less than that. There was but one white child in the school. This was a son of "Fritzie" Meyers, a government employee. This father, mother, and son all learned to talk the Crow language.

The agent ordered all white men about the agency to donate at least five dollars to the church and the school funds. All complied promptly, and some exceeded the requirement. Another order obeyed at once was that commanding the white men having Indian wives to be married in due form by Rev. Mr. Byrd. The ring ceremony was used. Cheap brass rings served the purpose. Cherry wore hers as long as she lived. She marked it so that it might be identified and distinguished from others like it. Barney

Bravo interpreted for my wife at my marriage. In turn, I interpreted for his wife.

Dancing also was fostered by the agent. Jim Hale, the violinist, was carried on the pay-roll as a mason, but his genuine service was that of promoting the dances. Barney Bravo beat the snare-drum, and a man named Ike Allen sometimes joined him with a tin pan used as a drum. The dances occurred once or twice a week, maybe three times. Mostly the program was of quadrilles, with occasionally a waltz or a polka. White men and their Indian wives were the dancers. There were enough of them for three or four quadrille sets. White women came to look on, and sometimes they helped the Indian women in learning the dances. Indian men and women came as visitors. Only one Indian man danced. He was deaf and dumb. He was ambitious to learn white-man ways, and he always wore a white shirt to the dances. At the supper feasts we always hooked arms with our partners to escort them, according to the fashion of white people. We were teaching the Indians how to behave well in society. We were civilizing them. At home, too, I often had to give Cherry lessons in dancing and in ball-room etiquette as it prevailed in the West.

We went occasionally to dances at Benson's Landing, twelve miles up the river and on the north side, off the reservation, right where Livingston now is. Benson and Dan Nailey had a store there. They sought the Indian trade, the same as other frontier traders. Of course, they kept liquor. A few of the River Crows drank, but the Mountain Crows regularly kept away from whisky. They were afraid of it. The traders gave dances and feasts to attract the Indians, so that they would bring them the buffalo skins for bartering.

Bravo, Parker, Mitch Buoyer, and myself took our wives and went one night to a dance at Benson's Landing. Parker and Mitch showed the effects of booze as we started home very late. As we were fording the Yellowstone in our wagon some one shouted:

"Piegans!"

The Piegans shot at us and ran away. When we got home, a band of Crows set off to hunt for the Piegans. Late that day the Crows returned with one horse, one hair lariat-rope, and one Piegan scalp.

Some Piegans appeared once at one of our dances at the agency. Just as we were about to hook arms for escorting our partners to supper, one of our women called out:

"There's a strange face at the window!"

A moment afterward a bullet crashed through

the glass and hit the opposite wall. We all dived for shelter. As soon as we safely could do so we got outside and shot at random into the darkness, but there was no sign of our having hit any one. The next morning we found some telltale footprints.

A mode of distinguishing between Sioux and Blackfeet or Piegan war-parties was the fact that in those times the Sioux made their attacks on horseback, while the northern Indians preferred to be afoot when starting a fight. The Crows looked upon the Piegans as being very daring, slick, cunning, but not courageous fighters. They regarded the Sioux and their allied Cheyennes as bold and worthy foemen. Hence, while a Piegan coup or scalp was considered deserving of notice, a coup counted upon, or a scalp taken from, a Sioux or a Cheyenne conferred the highest credit upon the victorious warrior.

My costume was the same for church or for dance. The beaded buckskin suit and beaded moccasins were worn. My leggings were fringed, tasseled, and beaded down the outside. My beaded buckskin pouch for pipe and tobacco was suspended from a shoulder. The six-shot cap-and-ball revolver rested in a scabbard on one side of the belt, while a hunting-knife hung from the other side. The arms were not merely a decoration, but they were worn for defensive purposes, as hostile Indians were ever threatening our agency. For everyday wear I had the "annuity" clothing—that is, the shirts, shoes, and trousers issued to Indians. The Indians themselves made but little or no use of this apparel, so the articles could be bought for trivial payments or might be obtained as gifts.

Some of the white men married to Crow women were ambitious, were good workers, and a few of them prospered. But others were absolute vagabonds, existing as male consorts only. To this latter form of human parasite originally was applied the term "squaw-man," but the words gradually came into use as designating any white man married to an Indian woman. Sometimes it was difficult to draw the line between the worthy and the unworthy. The Crows of that time did not enter into farming nor into any other industrial undertaking. They hunted and trapped, their living being derived mainly from the killing of buffalo. They bought corn and pumpkins from men who farmed. They were especially fond of pumpkins, so the producer of this vegetable got a good buffalo-robe price for his yield. One certain Indian family was an exception to the rule that the Crows did no farming. This was the Suce family.

The Suce household, although listed as of the Crow tribe, was headed by a Mexican father. The mother was born a Piegan, but she had been captured during her childhood and had been raised as a member of a Crow family. There were two sons, Johnny and Chick Suce. A daughter married Dr. Frost, who served for a time as our agency physician, but who later engaged in farming and stock-raising. He was a kindly man, often doctoring the Indians without asking any fee. He and Chick Suce's wife and her baby were killed one day on their way home from the agency. Some Crows on a hill saw a band of Sioux kill them, and hurried to report the tragedy. Some of us armed ourselves and hastened out. But, as usual, the assailants were gone. Dr. Frost has descendants now among the Crows, a son of his being at the present time a missionary preacher.

Dr. Hunter, founder of Hunter's Hot Springs, served for a time as our physician at the old Mission agency. He was altogether a man of the South as it had been before the Civil War. He was portly and dignified, was incessantly chewing tobacco, wore full whiskers, kept his iron-gray hair bobbed at the neck, and his head always was topped by a silk stovepipe hat. His manner of speech was pompous, mingled with gentleness. His children had been christened Elizabeth Longstreet, Mary Lee, Davis Beauregard, and Stonewall Jackson. The Hunter household at the hot springs location was once raided by hostile Indians. The family fled and the home was looted.

Lieutenant Doane, then located at Fort Ellis, approached Dr. Hunter one day in Bozeman.

"Doctor Hunter," the young army officer began, "I want to ask you for the hand of that beautiful daughter of yours."

"My daughters all are beautiful, sir," the doctor blurted out. "To which one do you refer?"

The special one he had in mind was mentioned. She was Mary Lee Hunter.

"Yes, I'll give her to you, and you'll have a wife as pure as the dripping snow on yonder mountains."

I served as a scout several years afterward under Lieutenant Doane at Fort Custer. He was big and awkward looking, had an unusually large nose, wore long dark hair, talked always in a loud voice. He appeared not to know any feeling of fear under any circumstances, so the soldiers adored him. He died at old Fort Ellis, long ago, after having attained the rank of captain. His widow still lives at Bozeman.

Fort Ellis soldiers often came in details to guard our agency. On one occasion Sergeant Fry and seven of these soldiers were drowned when the boat of the ferry over the Yellowstone at Benson's Landing capsized. Dr. Hunter's son, Stonewall Jackson

Hunter, or "Stony" Hunter, also went to his death on this same occasion. Of the people on the boat, only an Indian man and woman swam to safety, the woman getting to shore with her baby strapped to her back.

Intermarriages between Crows and Piegans created a situation regarded as helpful to raiders. Among such pairings was that of a half-Piegan named Bob Jackson who married the widow of Dr. Frost after she had been widowed a second time by the death of old man Fox, her second husband. Jackson's Piegan friends came for prolonged and frequent visits with him. As guests they were held inviolable, but it was thought they used this immunity for horse-stealing activities. However, perhaps this same sort of complication existed among the people of the other tribes.

Jim Beckworth, the part negro who had been living for many years among the Crows before any white men settled among them, died a year or so after I first became acquainted with him. He was a light mulatto. The Crows regarded him as a very capable man. While out on a hunting expedition he died of erysipelas. He was buried at first in a five-foot-deep grave out northward from the present town of Columbus, the grave being covered then with a large flat rock and with other stones. In later years his body was removed to California. His last wife, "Strike Three Times," married Chick Suce after Beckworth died. She it was who was killed with Dr. Frost. The Crow Indians knew Beckworth as "Antelope."

I learned the sign-talk mostly from the deaf-and-dumb Crow who worked at odd jobs about the agency. My opportunity as interpreter for the agent came on an occasion when Vilas, Colonel Bruno, and another man arrived from Washington as commissioners to deal with the Crows about some matter. Pierre Chien, official interpreter for this agency, was sick. From time to time thereafter I was called in to interpret, in the absence of Chien, and after his death this sort of employment became common with me.

Pierre Chien had been a trader among the Blackfeet. He was a Canadian Frenchman, and he was fluent in French, English, Blackfoot, and Crow. His wife was a Blackfoot woman. His son married a Crow, so he now has descendants among the Crows.

The Flatheads, the Bannacks, and the Nez Percés Indians came often to visit the Crows and to hunt buffalo. They had good horses—better than had the Crows. The Bannacks usually had the fastest running horses. We were on peaceable terms with these tribes, but occasionally there was some horse-stealing from one another. We almost had a war with the Flatheads in 1872. The strained relations arose from a warlike incident at the end of a visit on the Yellowstone.

As the band of Flatheads was going away after a pleasant sojourn among the Crows, some of the departing young men could not resist the temptation to round up and take along a few Crow horses. Our first notice of this violation of the amenities came when Flathead Charley, a half-breed, and some of his older tribesmen brought back the stolen stock and offered apologies and mollifying gifts of blankets and robes. All was going well until a certain Crow, Little Iron, discovered one of his horses was among the returned animals. He was big, tall, surly, quarrelsome, a bully in his own tribe. He declared himself as having been mortally offended, and he wanted some sort of blood atonement. He fired his rifle flush into Flathead Charley's breast and instantly killed him. The other peacemaking Flatheads dashed away on their horses. We took the dead body and pitched it into the abandoned well at the first old agency site. The affair was kept secret as one between the tribes. There were rumblings of war, but no open warfare ensued. The Crows were displeased at the conduct of Little Iron. He always was held thereafter in disrepute, was almost boycotted.

I tried farming for a few months while Dr. Wright was agent. He persuaded Barney Bravo, Tom Stewart, and myself to locate on land. He gave us oxen, cows, implements, seed, and rations. Marlow Collins, an Iroquois Indian from New York, was making a success up the Yellowstone River at farming and stock-raising, and the agent wanted some more good examples for the Crows to emulate. Cherry and I and our boy, the junior Tom Leforge, found a cabin that had been built by a sawmill outfit at the mouth of Pine Creek, and we settled there. I put in a garden and some field crops. But the trapping and hunting were too good for me to be bothered with cultivating land. I got two otter. After two months of this rural life both Cherry and I were anxious to go back to the agency, where I went on duty again as blacksmith, watchman, interpreter, and despatch-carrier, with plenty of leisure for hunting, trapping, and cultivation of the social graces as they existed at this center of civilization on the Yellowstone in the earliest seventies.

Indian torture of a prisoner came once under my observation while I was on despatch duty out from the old Mission agency. This was the only time I ever saw such a sight. Mitch Buoyer and I had been sent out to find the River Crows and bring them in for some sort of business council. They were on the south side of the Missouri River and below the mouth of the Judith. Some northern Indians attacked a Crow camp where we had stopped. After a skirmish the assailants fled, and Mitch and myself joined some Crows in their pursuit. We followed almost twenty-five miles, when suddenly we found ourselves ambushed by a much larger body of enemies. Mitch and I jumped our horses into a deep washout, and we stayed there. One of our Crows was wounded and his horse was killed. The other Crows retreated, and we could hear them calling out songs and prayers to cheer the wounded one left on the field. Finally, we did not hear them any more. We saw the enemy Indians seize the wounded man and take him away a few hundred feet. We remained hidden, but we could peep out and see them. They proceeded deliberately to chop off separately and at intervals all of his fingers, his toes, his hands, his feet, thus gradually killing him. It was a horrifying sight, but we could do nothing to help our comrade. Notwithstanding we were close enough to hear the torturers in their conversation, we heard not a sound of complaint come from the victim. He stoically kept his self-control. Years afterward I learned from Indians of the capturing tribe the full story of his brave conduct. Mitch and I got away after dark, taking turns at riding my horse, which was wounded, Mitch's mount having been killed. I never shall forget the sickening scene we witnessed nor the distress we suffered that night on account of the prickly-pear penetrating the thin soles of our moccasins.

An appearance of hostile uprising by the Crows occurred once at the old Mission agency. It was just after Dr. Wright had succeeded Pease as agent. The River Crows were coming to the agency. At the outskirts a band of them paused, and the men were shooting at a certain white rock we all used as a target for practice of this kind. Somehow a Crow man was killed, probably by a glancing bullet from the stone target. But just at this time the agency butcher, Tom Kent, was in that vicinity killing some beeves. The Crows accused Kent of having killed their companion. They became very ugly and moved as if to attack the agency. We all went into the stockade. Some Mountain Crows who were there joined forces with us. We shut the gates and hid Tom Kent. Dr. Wright was greatly alarmed. But to the experienced white men, it appeared the Indians were only bluffing, were taking advantage of the situation to exact some presents. That used to be a regular Indian trick.

Barney Bravo and a Mountain Crow and myself finally went out as peace emissaries, with authority from Dr. Wright to promise conciliatory presents. We crossed a foot-log over a creek. Just as we got over, there stood Big Mule with his bow drawn and an arrow pointing toward us. He stormed at us and declared, "I'd like to kill both of you white men." The Mountain Crow intervened and defied them. He called them fools and told them if they should harm any one there, the white soldiers would come from Fort Ellis and kill many of their people. The dead Crow's wife and children wept and called out, "Accident! Accident! It was an accident!" Others took up the cry. Horse Guard, one of their chiefs, took his stand beside us and announced, "If you kill them, you'll have to kill me." He shook hands with me and called me "My son." Lean Elk, a River Crow dog-soldier chief, hurriedly assembled his dog soldiers, and they soon clubbed and pony-whipped the mob into quiet. Then a group of the malcontents invited us into a lodge to council with them. We were about to comply, when the victim's wife rushed to me and warmly shook hands with me. At the same time she whispered, "Do not go into the lodge; they will kill you there." We evaded going into it, returning to the agency instead, after having made promises of many presents.

Great jubilation soon was manifested because of the peaceable outcome. I asked one Indian, "What kind of present do you want?" "A saddle," he replied at once. He got it. Blankets, sugar, coffee, flour, bacon, clothing were given liberally to all relatives of the lamented deceased, so that lamentation might be converted into joy. A general distribution of presents was made to all of the Crows. Some refused to accept them, saying, "Give presents only to the relatives." River Crows and Mountain Crows danced and feasted together, the provisions all being supplied from the agency stores. We happened to have on hand plenty of dried apples. This was a favorite dessert among the old-time Crows. It may be that on this occasion dried apples did more than anything else to smother warlike thoughts and create good feeling.

Serious quarrels among the white men living with the Crows were uncommon. One grave incident of this kind happened, though, in our midst. Ed Williams was married to a woman known as Jennie. He had been a tailor, or a furrier, who made up fur overcoats and like clothing at Fort Benton. A man named Parker had Bad Woman for his wife.

Parker was the agency mechanic. The two women quarreled. The husbands, both drinking at the time, took up the dispute. Williams went to his home, got his gun, walked to Parker's open doorway, and shot him through the thigh. Williams was arrested and taken to Bozeman for trial, but the case finally was dismissed. The two men came to terms as friends and remained on an amicable basis. Several years afterward Parker was drowned while taking a despatch to General Miles. His wife, Jennie, gained notice as being the first Crow woman to dress like the white women.

Old maids and old bachelors were almost unknown among any of the Indian tribes of the West. I knew one Crow woman, though, who persistently avowed her intention never to marry. She was a medicine-woman and a prophet. She also was a good tanner, an excellent bead-worker, a very capable woman in every respect wherein one of her station in life might be capable. The people all held her in high regard, looking upon her as a chaste maiden. Her name was Two Moons. One day I jokingly asked her:

"Two Moons, when are you and I going to be married?"

She studied a moment, then looked about her.

She fixed her eyes upon a cluster of bushes of ever-
green laurel and pointed toward them. "Do you see
those leaves?" she inquired.

"Yes, I see them," I replied.

"Good. Now, keep watch of them every day.
When they turn yellow, come and ask me to marry
you."

This bright and much respected woman died soon
after she had passed the age of thirty. So it was not
yet time to conclude she was a confirmed old maid.

The cattle herd for agency and Indian use num-
bered twelve hundred or fifteen hundred head. They
were always kept ranging up near Yellowstone Park,
partly because of the good feeding there and partly
because Indians did not stay in that region, which
fact was supposed to diminish the number of thefts
and surreptitious butcherings. However, the Indians
in those times did not care much for beef except
when game was not obtainable. The first choice of
the Crows, as well as most of the other plains Indians, was buffalo meat. Beeves were brought in to
the agency from time to time and butchered for
issue to the Indians. Many a time I have seen them
throw away or feed to the dogs great chunks of
good beef that had been provided for them by a
kindly white-man government. In fact, during my
early life among them, I knew only four Crows

who would eat beef. The bacon that was provided for them in ample quantities was merely fried out for the purpose of rendering the lard from it. This was used for frying buffalo and other game meat, and it served a useful purpose in greasing the hides during the process of tanning.

Flour was freighted to the agency, at a considerable expense, part of it for the use of the agency employees but most of it to keep the supposedly wretched Indians from starvation. But the well-fed buffalo-hunting Crows ate only small quantities of this refined white-man nutriment. They accepted the issues, of course—took all that was offered to them, and asked for more. But what they wanted was the sacks, not the flour. They emptied out the contents or gave it to Yankee Jim or some other white man or sold it for almost nothing. A flour sack, with its decorative colored printing, was to an Indian woman a beautiful piece of material for working up into clothing or for hanging upon the interior wall of the lodge.

The "annuity" clothing which a benevolent Indian bureau at Washington sent out to the supposed naked and freezing savages on the Yellowstone was equivalent to seed sown upon bare ground. During the summer seasons, neither the Indian men nor their white-men companions in the hunting camps wore any clothing but the ever-present breech-cloth. When winter came they preferred the skin clothing, or merely wrapped themselves in buffalo-robes or blankets. As the wild animals began distinctly to decrease in numbers, the government apparel came gradually into use, with its ludicrous misfits. But in the earlier days, when Nature was bountiful, a pair of trousers or a pair of shoes could be bought from an Indian for twenty-five cents.

Any white man could live among the Crows without need for toil except such as would be incident to hunting and trapping, and even this could be reduced to extremely small effort. The life was simple, the necessities were easily obtainable, minor luxuries could be had from gratuitous sources. Every Indian had treaty claims for rations, for annuity money payments, for supplies of various kinds. Hence, the Indian wife of a white man could be the family "breadwinner" without being heavily burdened if the white husband was the sort of human being who was satisfied thus to live without ambition to do anything more. This temptation to utter idleness being present, even a naturally enterprising man was likely to deteriorate.

Myself and some other Indian white men were sent out from the agency one autumn to cut logs for additional buildings. Zed Daniels, a nephew of

Major Pease, was acting temporarily as substitute agent, Pease being in Bozeman, where he had a fine residence and where he stayed much of the time except when the Crows came in from their hunting expeditions. Daniels let us have a four-mule team, saddle-horses, and a big supply of provisions. We went to the upper part of Mission Creek. We took our wives and families, and some of their relatives also went with us. Both the agent and ourselves were glad enough to have these additional people with us, since they could help in resisting any hostile attack. It developed, though, that their only function had been that of helping us eat up the food. About every week we had to send somebody with the four-mule team to bring out more rations—coffee, sugar, beans, bacon, etc. However, Daniels did not grumble. He sent all we asked for, and more. When the earliest hints of oncoming spring began to manifest themselves, we broke camp and moved back down to the agency. We went to the office to draw our pay, this ranging from sixty to seventy-five dollars each per month.

"Where have you been all winter?" asked the Major, who then was on duty at the office.

We told him of our operations under the direction of Daniels. We all got our money. An inspector came soon afterward, and one day he and

Pease went up Mission Creek to compute the amount of building material available there. We who had been there knew what they would discover. We had spent the whole winter in loafing, dancing, singing, drumming, and feasting. Not a log had been cut!

Pease raised a storm with us when he came back. But we retaliated in assertions that our winter efforts had been about as valuable to the Indians as his had been. The matter finally was ignored, or was dismissed as being but an amusing incident. None of us were punished or blacklisted.

Such loose and help-yourself business ways permeated the whole system of Indian management in those times. Competing traders kept white men under pay to go or to stay among the Indians and induce them to do their bartering of buffalo-robes and other skins at this or that trader's store. Many times I received pay for this sort of commercial salesmanship. The biggest fee I got in any one instance of this kind was $250, half cash and half in trade goods. This deal was made with Nelson Story. He owned the sutler store at the agency, with John Waddell in charge of it. The River Crows had been drawn to do some trading with Tom Bowyer, known to them as "Blackbeard," who had a store at Fort Browning, where the Judith flows into the

Missouri. Story hired me to persuade them to bring
their robes and do their trading at his agency establishment. He was a "licensed" trader—that is,
his store was on the reservation, and therefore it
was to some extent under government supervision,
particularly in the matter of selling liquor, which
was not permitted to these licensed mercantile in-
stitutions. The robe-buyers and exchangers of merchandise who traveled with the hunting Indians or
who located themselves on non-reservation lands—
ordinarily just off the borders of, or conveniently
accessible from, the reservations—were known as
"free traders," or as "whisky traders." They could
sell liquor lawfully to white people, and they often
sold it to Indians through intervening purchasers.
In the old times this intervening purchaser, or any
unlawful peddler of whisky to the Indians, was
known as a "bootlegger," it being presumed that
while he kept in general a law-abiding or pious as-
pect he always had a bottle or two of whisky concealed in his bootlegs. My sympathies naturally were
with the licensed traders on the reservations. Hence,
my conscience was easy in accepting from them a
commission to bring the Indians to these places for
their commercial transactions.

This commission business was workable both
ways. The Indians liked to have some trustworthy

white-man friend to guide and advise them in their business dealings. So I had lots of good-will gifts from the Crows. When they gave me robes I sold them to the trader, getting from him a slight advance in price over what he would pay the Indians. While I knew that the traders reaped an enormous profit, I always saw to it that my Crow clients were not cheated beyond the bounds of the regular robberies established by custom and so well entrenched that my own weak protest would avail nothing except to bring discredit and disfavor upon me. My duty as a drummer for trade took me into the store and behind the counter, where I examined and passed judgment upon the offered robes and afterward passed out goods in payment for them.

One trick of the trade, in the matter of influencing Indians to deal at certain places, was the affectation or appearance of a compromise. It would be agreed that some of the trading should be done at one place and some at another place. In this case my business was to get the Indians to take their inferior robes to the competitor. They were to take to him only these, as though they had no others. When these all were disposed of, I would move away with my Indians and take them to the agency. The best robes came thus to my employer. A head-and-tail buffalo-robe—that is, an entire robe of one piece and in good order—had the standard price of five dollars in goods. An extra-good article would be higher. The used or second-hand camp robes came below the standard valuation. A split robe—one made up by the sewing together of segments—was salable at a valuation lower than that of the full head-and-tail robe.

Gifts to the prospective customers always inaugurated the procedure of trading. The children got candy, the women got handkerchiefs or beads, the men got knives or other suitable articles. These gifts were varied—calico, ammunition, sashes, skeins of thread (we had it in skeins, not spools), and all sorts of trivial things that the old-time Indians used to prize so highly. Good feeling having been established by this initial show of generosity, the robes having been counted and their total value agreed upon, the exchange selling of goods began.

The women traded first, then the children, and then the men took up what was left in the robe credit after the women and children had been satisfied. The goods were passed out through rectangular openings in the ceiling-high board walls that separated the shelves from the central interior assembling-place. Through this opening went saddles, bridles, ropes, blankets, calico, sugar, coffee, knives, guns, ammunition, tweezers for pulling stray beard

hairs, canned foods, beads in large and small quantities, pins and needles, cheap jewelry made of glass
and brass, beans, rice, dried apples, a large variety
of merchandise. Coffee, sugar, and other provisions
so measurable were sold by the pint, not by the
pound. A pint cup was used as the dispensing vehicle, and the actual quantity dispensed depended
upon how deeply into each cupful the thumb might
be thrust during the hurried process of dipping and
pouring. Sometimes the balance due for robes delivered was pretty low after the women and children got what they wanted, so the man had left
but little margin for buying. In such case his credit
was good, to a reasonable extent. Particularly, if a
man needed a gun or some ammunition, he could buy
it before going out on the hunt and pay for it from
his first robes delivered after his return. I never
knew of any failure to collect bills of this kind. In
fact, the Indian's dependent situation dictated payment.

The agent got robe gifts when the Crows came
in from the big hunts. In the return giving—which
reciprocity an Indian always has in view—the high
local official had the advantage of the rest of us,
since he had the disposition of the rations and
other government property. He made diplomatic
use of these. I have seen our agent receive as many

as three or four hundred robes after one hunt-return of the Crows. According to the Indian rule of etiquette in the giving of presents, the recipient is supposed to call a halt when he thinks he has all he ought to have. It appeared this agent never knew of the existence of this rule. I never heard him say, "Enough." He would not sell his robes to the trader. His practice was to bale them and send them to Salt Lake, where they brought ten dollars each.

A stranger came to the agency and arranged with me to guide and care for him on a hunting expedition. Cherry and I took a tepee lodge and went with him into the mountains. He killed some game animals, but devoted most of his time to mere rambling over the heights and the valleys. He often complimented Cherry on her cooking, congratulated me on her excellence as a housewife and as a mother to baby Tom. Our conversation centered much upon the ways of trade among the Indians. He asked many questions about the peculiarities of Indian etiquette, especially as to gifts.

"But why do they give the agent so many robes?" he pressed upon me.

"Oh, well, he is kind and generous to them," I explained.

After our return to the agency he lingered there a few days, talked to some others about the ways of the Crows, but spent most of this time in closeted conference with the agent. Then he disappeared permanently from our life.

A few weeks afterward I was ordered one day to take our ambulance and go to Benson's Landing, to meet there a party of visitors and bring them to the agency. There were two people in this party, a man and his wife. The man was Dr. Wright, who brought with him an official document setting forth that he now was appointed agent for the Crow Indians.

ON THE YELLOWSTONE IN THE EARLIEST SEVENTIES

HOSTILE Indian attacks upon the old Mission agency or upon some one traveling in the region were a common occurrence after its establishment and until the military campaign of 1876 and the ensuing advent of the soldiers of General Miles and other commanders. Perhaps an average of once a week would be a fair estimate of the assaults upon or threatening of the agency itself. The marauding Indians were Piegan Blackfeet from the northward and Sioux from the eastward. The Northern Cheyennes were allied with the Sioux, although the Cheyenne tribe was much the less in numbers of the two allies. A few Northern Arapahoes also cast their fortunes with these fighting protestants against white-man invasion of what they deemed to be their country. The old feud between the Crows and the Sioux on account of the intrusions into the Yellowstone region by the Dakota tribe was accentuated by the fact that the Crows kept on a peace basis with the white people while the Sioux usually were in open warfare against them. The Sioux fought not only the whites, but every adjacent tribe who were friendly to the whites. As they looked at it, what we knew as friendly Indians were traitorous Indians.

Three or four lodges of Bannacks came one time and camped on Shields River, ten or more miles from Mission agency. There were at that time only a few stray buffalo there, but the Bannacks were afraid to go further down the river into the buffalo country, so they remained there and hunted deer and elk. A band of Sioux came up the east side of Shields River and attacked the camp. They were repulsed, but one of the Bannack men was killed. Two of his friends came hurrying in to tell the Crows. I went with the band of Crows who responded to the call for help. The Indian preacher also went with us, armed to fight the Sioux. When we arrived, the attacking party was gone, of course. We scouted and trailed, but they evidently were too far away for pursuit. The Bannacks had hidden the body of their dead comrade to keep the Sioux from getting it or the scalp. They wanted to bring the corpse with them to the agency, but we buried it out in the hills in a deep grave.

Sioux Indians shot into my living quarters on three different occasions while I was at the Mission agency. One night Cherry and I and baby Tom went to bed at dark. Above our bed, I had two port-holes, for observation and defense. We were startled by *"Bang-bang!"* Hostiles were shooting into the agency and into the quarters of various people. Pretty soon a gun sent its bullet through one of my port-holes. The missile shattered Cherry's fancy soup-dish.

"Oh, they broke my soup-dish!" she raged. "Kill them!" And she grabbed a rifle and snapped it toward the port-hole, but it had no load in it. I shot my revolver at random, at first inside and then outside of the building. Others about the agency replied to the attack. It was a lively time for a few minutes that night, but nobody that I know of was hurt. We had in the agency stock an ample supply of 50-caliber needle-guns. They were from the Montana militia armory and had been issued to us. Of course, every man had also his personal gun, and often this was better than the firearm provided.

Cherry was utterly cool and nervy under fire. She was as brave as the bravest. She liked to sing and pray, she was jolly and amiable, but on proper occasion she would stand her ground and fight bravely if that were necessary. One time, Yankee Jim, who had been trapping on upper Mission Creek, came in and reported plenty of beaver and some otter.

The price of otter skins was particularly high, so Cherry and I decided to go out and try for some of them. The first night we camped two or three miles from the mouth of the creek and turned out our horses. I set my traps and caught four beaver. The next day we moved on up the creek. We camped that night near a big beaver dam and again set the traps. On the following morning at daybreak Cherry went to a hill as lookout while I started for the traps. Pretty soon she coyote-howled, and when I looked toward her she signed me to return quickly, that Sioux were in sight. We fortified ourselves in a washout gulch. Six Sioux on horseback began shooting at us from various positions. I responded to their fire, but my cartridges had become damp and there was trouble in ejecting the empties from the gun. Cherry sat there, cool as a cucumber, and wiped cartridges for me. She sang war-songs to cheer me, prayed her Indian prayers, and kept saying we'd get out in safety. She certainly put courage into my heart on that day. After a while a Sioux tumbled dead from his horse,—or one could not be sure whether this indicated death or was only a trick. Anyhow, before I could realize what she was doing, my wife was far out on her way to the dead warrior, a hundred yards from our sheltering gulch. She seized the fallen foe's gun and ammunition and dashed safely back into our impromptu fort. It was a rifle having a sawed-off stock, as the Indians used to modify them for hunting buffalo. It kicked, so I used it, while she then used my gun. The remaining Sioux retreated, leaving their dead companion. Cherry was entitled, according to the Indian custom, to count a coup because of her capture of an enemy's gun. "Skookum Joe" afterward saw the body of the Sioux we had killed.

Some Sioux shot into the agency stable on a certain occasion. One of our horses was picketed out a little distance west of it. A warrior came charging past this horse. It seemed he paused not an instant. Nevertheless, as his mount galloped along, he leaned down, cut the rope of the picketed animal, and went on, leading it after him. All the women and children ran into the agency stockade, as they usually did, when the alarming cry reached them. Tom Shane had his rifle at hand, and he shot several times at the bold raider, whose horse he killed. A companion dashed up and took the dehorsed warrior on behind him. The two got away on the one mount, leading the stolen animal. Some others of our agency people joined in shooting at them. Bullets flew all about them, but none appeared to have touched them.

The agency stockade was two hundred feet

square. It consisted of buildings set beside each other, facing inward and having their backs toward the outside. These buildings were of adobe material, except two of them. The living quarters mainly were outside of and immediately adjacent to the stockade. All agency and residence structures had port-holes for shooting from the interior.

We always kept a few saddle-horses picketed out near at hand for emergency use. We had breast-work pits wherein a guard might hide at any time we actually expected thieving operations. But we did not always know when to expect the visitors. One time we set out a bait. Cherry had a gentle old horse that would graze quietly under exciting conditions, so we picketed out this one, while Sam Shively and another man and myself went into an ambush pit. We stayed there all night, one or the other of us on guard—or supposed to be on guard. Notwithstanding it was a moonlight night, at daylight the next morning we discovered our bait horse was gone. A Sioux had cut the rope and got away with it.

Jim Hughes, the agency freighter from Bozeman, was killed on the divide between the Gallatin and the Yellowstone. The Indians cut up his harness and took the horses and whatever wagon plunder they wanted. A man named Countryman and his son

Dan were on horseback in company with Hughes. They got away without injury. Some of our people charged them with cowardice for their conduct.

Charley Norris and Max Hosea were caught out and attacked. We could see them racing toward the agency, with the Sioux after them. All were on horseback. The Sioux were striking at the fleeing men, using whips or clubs or other weapons. When we recovered the bodies of our friends we found their faces and heads horribly hacked. Since the small band of hostiles was so bold in thus chasing our people into the agency during broad daylight, we assumed that a large band was hidden away somewhere in the near background. It was apparent they were trying to lure us out, but in this instance we did not go.

Cherry and Bravo's wife went one day to gather currants or wild cherries. After a while they came running and shouting: "Lots of Indians!" All of the people hurried into the stockade. We could see the brush moving at times, and it appeared we located the position of skulking raiders. Bravo trained our cannon upon this patch of brush and fired its charge of shrapnel. The brush moved in a more lively manner, and we heard, *"Woof, woof!"* Investigation proved our defensive measure had killed three of our herd of agency hogs.

Our harassments were mainly during the summer season. This was due partly to the indisposition of all Indians to go on extended war expeditions during cold or inclement weather. But in our case a determining feature was the fact that our Crows collected in large numbers about the agency during the middle and latter part of the winter and went away when spring came, to hunt the buffalo for lodge and clothing purposes and to gather the summer roots and berries. So, while war-parties of either Sioux or Crows might be out in cold weather, the warm part of the year was much the most active time.

I found an Indian "sign" one time on my way back from Bozeman, where I had been sent to get our mail. Half-way down Fleischman Creek my attention was attracted by a whole blanket spread out on the grass beside the trail. It was a good red blanket, with a black stripe across each end. On its middle was lying a bunch of wild rye, this neatly tied together by twisted long blades of green grass. One corner of the blanket was folded over and weighted thus. My interpretation was that the bundle of wild rye meant, "We are all together," and the folded corner of the blanket indicated the direction of travel. I decided these were Sioux, and that other Sioux, for whom the sign was meant, were not far behind. So I got away from that vicinity as rapidly as circumstances would permit. A few days afterward we heard that Sioux had stolen the horses of a party of white-men trappers on Brackett Creek.

A battle between Bannacks and Nez Percés took place on Fleischman Creek, about twenty miles from our agency, during the winter of 1872-73, I believe. Eight or ten lodges of Bannacks were camped here. Although there was almost daily traveling back and forth over the mountain, the snow along the little valley was very deep. A dozen or so lodges of Nez Percés were camped in lower Yellowstone cañon, a few miles above the present Livingston. The Nez Percés and Bannacks already were at war, so the Nez Percés determined to make an attack upon the Fleischman Creek camp of the enemy. Some white men who were in a camp near the Bannacks learned of the prospective attack and warned the Bannacks. The white men also lent their neighbors some good guns and a supply of ammunition. The Bannacks hid their women and children in snowbank tunnels and waited for the expected onset.

The Nez Percés warriors came afoot. They sneaked cautiously up to the enemy lodges and opened fire. But the intended surprise was reversed. The Bannacks were behind snowbanks instead of in the lodges, and their prompt and spirited responsive fire disconcerted the assailing party. The Nez Percés retreated, tunneled into the snow, stayed there until darkness came, then went away. They left behind them one dead tribesman and took along one who had been wounded in the thigh and in the back. One Bannack was wounded. The Nez Percés wounded man was taken to a camp of whites on Shields River and there he was given the surgical treatment known to pioneer white-men trappers. The entire band of Nez Percés then left the Yellowstone and returned to their own country west of the Rocky Mountains.

I was sent out many times on long journeys to find the Crows and tell them to come in to the agency for receiving issues of goods, rations, gifts of various kinds, or for some council about their reservation affairs. I never went out alone. Always two of us went together. We took turns at spying ahead of us from hilltops. This was one of the first principles of safe travel in those times. The River Crows were most difficult to locate, since they ranged over a wide hilly country north of the Yellowstone and far away from the agency.

On one journey after the River Crows, Mitch Buoyer was with me. We traveled at night, as was our regular way of doing. We did not find the Crows in Judith Basin, where we had expected to come upon them. One morning as we scanned the country from the top of Black Butte we saw something that puzzled us. Apparently, a bear and her cub were lolling on a hillside a quarter of a mile or so across from us. Yet, bears did not inhabit this hill-and-prairie country. I got out my medicine-pipe and we sat down for a smoke and a council. We decided that probably the bear theory was the correct one, since occasionally one of these animals would attach itself to a buffalo herd, and perhaps this one and the cub were only a short distance away from their bulky and shaggy companions. Anyway, we cautiously approached the point under observation. We found there a two-year-old Indian girl wallowing over the dead and decaying body of an Indian woman. The child was as wild as a wolf. It ran, but we caught it. It bit, scratched, fought like a young tiger. It was starved to a pitiful, skeleton-like leanness. Its hands were like claws, its shrunken face resembled that of a sick monkey. The woman evidently was a Sioux, as indicated by the character of her ear decorations and by the kind of beadwork on her apparel. Moreover, the child kept screeching "Mother" in Sioux, which the half-Sioux Mitch Buoyer understood. We considered what to do, a hundred miles away from our agency, with this sort of captive.

"By jolly, Tom, I'm not going to leave this baby here," Mitch finally declared.

He petted the little one, and finally got her quieted. Then we made some weak tea, soaked a cracker, and fed the starving midget.

"Mitch, my medicine tells me we'd better leave this country and go back to the agency," I announced. He agreed with me.

On the way back we encountered some white emigrants on the Yellowstone. A childless elderly couple begged us to give to them this Sioux orphan. Mitch had made up his mind to keep it, but I persuaded him to give it to these white people. Several years afterward I heard something of the outcome of this affair. The foster parents were respectable and prosperous people of Fort Benton. The girl grew up to be very bright, and was being sent to school and provided for in every way as if she were their own blood offspring. How glad it made my heart to hear that!

We same two were out bringing in the Mountain Crows at another time. A few lodges of people were with us in the advance section of the returning tribe. We camped on Pryor Creek, just below the cave. We were having a glorious time, with plenty of buffalo ribs for roasting—the most delectable meat the Almighty ever made for mankind. We built a big sweat-lodge beside the creek, and all of the men went into it for a sweat. We jumped into the warm summer waters of Pryor Creek and played there. We gathered in a semicircle and smoked, talked, recounted coups, sang songs. Our women were roasting buffalo-meat.

Behind the sweat-lodge was a ravine full of plum-trees and other small shrubbery. Suddenly, a big bear came crashing through the thicket, knocked down our sweat-lodge, and frightened all of us into precipitate flight into the timber and into the creek. It kept possession of the ground for a few minutes. Then Mitch Buoyer got after it with a club and drove it away. Nobody would shoot the animal. Such an act would have been in violation of Indian tradition. In a case of this sort it is supposed the invader is crazy or has been sent by the Great Spirit, and it is held in respectful regard.

Quivey, a white man, went with me one time to find the River Crows. We came to them in Judith Basin, where they were trading with a man named Dawes. When we were ready to start back the trader gave us some cooked ham. We were very hungry when we went into camp the first night. In addition to the ham, we had with us some cold and hard biscuits and some canned fruit. We had no dishes except a frying-pan. We located ourselves under the heavy boughs of a cottonwood-tree, built a fire there, and started to prepare our supper. I warmed the cooked ham in the frying-pan. Then I put the biscuits into the grease and warmed them too. Quivey had begun to eat first, and he was pretty well along toward completion of his meal when I began. It was raining, and drops of water kept falling into my frying-pan. Notwithstanding the annoyance, I kept on at the work, and we exchanged felicitations on the toothsomeness of the ham and biscuit. Suddenly, plunk! An Indian hair braid fell into the frying-pan. Investigation proved that we had built our fire exactly under a tree-burial corpse. Quivey cursed and began vomiting. I became nauseated, but my food stayed down even though it had been wet with dead-Indian drippings. The sensitive Quivey continued sick the next day, and he cursed me because I felt all right. I promised not to tell, but it was too good to keep a secret. The Indians teased him, "Want some dead Indian?" until he complained to the agent and gained his intervention. Quivey was the most profusely profane man I ever met. He was excitable, looked upon as crazy at times. If thunder and lightning came he flooded the air with his profanity, tore up his hat, slashed his clothing, acted generally like an insane man.

A great prophet and healer among the Mountain

Crows was Father of All Buffalo. He was the most noted medicine-man of his time, and old Crows of the present look back to him as one having the highest possible attainments in divination and the curative art. At one time when I was out with the Crows after buffalo we were camped on Sage Creek, a stream that flows into Stinking Water River, west of the Bighorn Mountains. Some young men in the camp were practising at tossing the lariat rope. They accidentally knocked down his medicine tripod, from which he kept suspended three rawhide bags that held his charms. Since these bags ordinarily were never allowed to touch the ground, the "medicine" influence was then supposed to have been greatly impaired if not wholly lost. Father of All Buffalo at once absolved the youths from blame, but he was in great mental distress. The people all sympathized with him, and to propitiate him, and perhaps, also, his helpful unseen spirits, they brought him many blankets and other presents.

Father of All Buffalo gathered up his medicine, mounted a horse, and rode away from the place where the evil spirit had caused the young men's lariats to discommode him. He stopped about a mile from the camp, dismounted, and began to overhaul the contents of the rawhide bags. I rode past him as he was at this work. He got some buffalo chips and made a fire. In this magic fire he burnt sweet-grass, so that its fumes might remove the baneful effect of the contact with the earth. He appeared worried, extremely crestfallen, said he expected soon to die. Other Indians passed him, they going on out over the hills to hunt.

The women moved camp that afternoon. As we hunters were assembling at the new location, a Crow dashed on horseback into our midst. As he came pell-mell toward us he was shouting:

"Father of All Buffalo is dead! The Sioux killed him!"

A big band of us hastened out to where we last had seen him. There he was—dead, scalped, all of his medicine and some of his clothing gone. He was of immense bodily size, but we brought him in for the people to see his condition and vow vengeance before his burial.

All of the people wept. The whole camp set out the next day for the agency. It was a sad procession over the entire distance. Father of All Buffalo's wife and other relatives dragged along in the rear or far off to one side, as was the custom for mourners. Lots of friends joined them, so we moved very slowly. In the mornings and in the evenings some people went to adjacent hilltops and wailed out their feelings of sadness. One man said, "The fire of this village has gone out." This dejection of spirit lingered long with the Crows. For many years thereafter, occasionally somebody would go out upon a hill and mourn because of the loss of Father of All Buffalo.

When Colonel Baker and his soldiers came from Fort Ellis to the Yellowstone, in 1873, I got into the battle they had with the Sioux on the north side of the river and opposite the mouth of Pryor Creek. George Ray, Mitch Buoyer, a man named Peeples, myself, and some others were on a hunting trip when the military force came. We decided to tag along as camp-followers. Colonel Baker had us called to his tent, there to smoke with him and to tell him what we knew of the hostiles. The day before, as we had been hunting, we had seen some of them and lots of signs of others. Early the next morning the Sioux attacked the camp of the soldiers, the first act being the killing of a picket-guard. Mitch, Peeples, and I kept together during the most of the fight that followed. I had a Spencer carbine, seven-shot, 50-caliber. I did some shooting, but I saw no certain effect of my efforts. As the conflict warmed up, Peeples left us and ran for shelter behind a tree. On the way a Sioux bullet laid him out dead. I can not remember now the casualties of the soldiers, but from the vocal sounds made by the

Sioux I learned that some of their men were killed. They retreated, and a few dead bodies of their warriors were found afterward.

The biggest battle of those times between the Crows and the Sioux was fought at the mouth of Pryor Creek, on the south side of the Yellowstone and opposite the site of the Baker battle. The agent had sent Mitch Buoyer and me out after the Mountain Crows. We took the "mountain trail"—that is, the trail along the high regions far back southward from the Yellowstone. We chose this route because there was timber along it practically all the way. The timber was our protection, since the Sioux liked best the open country for fighting and rarely made an attack in forest areas. We set out up Mission Creek, thence we crossed over into the Stillwater basin. It was early July, and the horse-flies drove our horses crazy.

I went up a hill to look over the country while Mitch stopped to wash. I discovered a dark bay horse dragging a lariat. I got hold of the rope, but the horse plunged and snorted so that my hand was burnt and I let loose. This indicated it was an Indian horse, as they are afraid of white men— likely the odor is different. Mitch came up and said: "We'd better kill him." But we did not, since our gunshot noise might have been heard by enemies.

We forded the Stillwater and kept on following the Bozeman road along the foot of the mountains.

We camped that night on Red Lodge Creek, a tributary to the Little Rosebud. Mosquitoes swarmed upon us. We were up early the next morning and moved on down to Clark's Fork. Lots of rattlesnakes along the way. We stripped off our clothing and swam Clark's Fork River. We wrapped our packs into a bull-boat bundle, tied a rope to it, and dragged it floating after us as we crossed. We swam beside our horses, on the downstream side, of course, as a man ought always to do when swimming beside his horse. We had a good pinto pack-pony that would follow without leading.

We hurried on toward Pryor Mountain the next day. We wanted to get up there and look over the country for any appearance of Sioux. Lots of buffalo were along our route, and we killed a young bull. We ate the raw liver, drank a little of the gall, stripped off the lining of the second stomach to keep and eat later in its raw state, and we cut off some other choice pieces of meat. When we got to the top of Pryor Mountain we stayed there all night and until after noon the next day. Our main object was to watch the buffalo, to see if they were in any agitation. That is the best way to discover the presence of human beings in any wild country—

watch the animals. If they continue quiet, it is evidence that no humans are in their vicinity. In those times, if the buffalo went galloping here and there, it indicated that mankind was the disturbing element. These animals never ran away from any other animals. In fact, this same rule is applicable in the case of wild creatures in general—they are wild only when man is present.

We saw a big smoke far down Pryor Creek as we made our observations from the top of the mountain. This was seen after noon, so it evidently was from a large camp. A small camp-fire smoke ordinarily is not noticeable very far away as the day progresses. Early morning is the best time to look for camp-fire smokes, since a freshly kindled fire makes more smoke and also the morning atmosphere is more clear. After we left the mountain we stopped on Pryor Creek and had a smoke and a council. While we were talking my horse whinnied.

"We're not far from somebody," Mitch said.

We kept quiet and listened intently. Then we mounted and set off farther down the creek. It was just coming dusk. By and by we heard a horse-bell. Soon afterward our lagging pack-pony whinnied. We stopped again to listen. We heard an Indian drum: *"Tum-tum-tum-tum-tum!"* Voices in song were clearly audible. They were voices of Sioux, and Mitch could understand the words. The purport of the song was, "We'll see you in the morning, Crows."

We hastened away from that vicinity. After an hour we dismounted for another smoke from my little medicine-pipe, hiding ourselves under a blanket so that the fire of it could not be seen. Excited buffalo were hurrying past us. We decided to keep on going all night. At gray dawn we went up a coulée to the top of a hill where the town of Toluca now stands. Mitch climbed a tree and used his field-glasses in an examination of the country. He saw Indians, but all he could make of them for certain was they were not Crows. We moved away from them and over to Cachewood Creek, where we stopped to wash and to have a little breakfast.

"Bang-bang-bang!" A body of Indians appeared on a hill near us. But they were the friendly Nez Percés, whom we already knew were hunting with the Crows during this summer. They had seen us, had recognized us, had followed us, and now they were signaling a friendly greeting by shooting into the air. They had on war-bonnets and were ready for a fight, as they had seen the Sioux. These Nez Percés were the Indians Mitch had seen with his field-glasses when he had climbed the tree at dawn.

The Crows were near at hand, on the Yellowstone at Pompey's Pillar. As we approached their camp a great body of them came out afoot and on horseback to meet us. Their scouts had discovered the Sioux, had found an especially large aggregation of them on the Little Bighorn River. Game had been observed running all about the country. All signs pointed to much Indian movement in this entire region. The Crows were convinced they would be compelled to fight a pitched battle with the Sioux. The old men went into council to discuss the situation.

An old medicine-man invited Mitch and me to have a sweat-bath, which invitation we accepted. He asked us, "Did you go to the Spirit Cave?" having reference to a certain cave far up Pryor Creek which the Crows regarded as a sacred place where dwelt mysterious and powerful spiritual forces. Mitch replied, "Yes," to comfort the old man, although in fact we had not been there. We were commended upon this devout conduct. When we had ended our sweat, thus purifying our minds as well as our bodies, the medicine-man led us into the council-lodge.

We had to tell first about our journey out from the agency. Questions were asked us about the health and general condition of this or that person dwelling at the Mission. We told where we had camped each night, and all sorts of trivial incidents of the trip were related and listened to seriously and attentively, as if they were matters of great significance—and occasionally this might turn out to be the case, which possibility may have given rise to the tedium of Indian procedure in entering upon any kind of business. With them, stories must be always in orderly succession of incidents, must begin always at the far-back beginning. So after we had brought our narrative on to the right point we informed them what we had seen and heard of the Sioux. Mitch gave an account of the drumming and the singing, "We'll see you in the morning, Crows."

Heralds were sent to ride among the camps. They called out that the women and children must stay close in, that the young men must be up late and early to watch vigilantly for the enemy. Nez Percés heralds also rode about their camps and proclaimed the situation and issued the commands of their chiefs. Before night came, an order was being promulgated: "To-morrow morning we move to the mouth of Shooting-at-the-Bank Creek (Pryor Creek). It is a better place for us to fight."

About two thousand Crows and two hundred or more Nez Percés set up their lodges in the same half-circle at the mouth of Pryor Creek, most of them on the west side of the creek, the opening of the horseshoe being on the south bank of the Yellowstone. Here they prepared themselves for the expected onslaught of the Sioux. Women dug rifle-pits, most of them outside the lodge circle, but some of them inside. Men put their guns and ammunition into good order, overhauled their war-bonnets and other paraphernalia of mortal conflict, arranged their paints for ready use, "made their medicine." Horses all were brought in, many of them were put upon an island in the Yellowstone and guarded there. No fighting this day, but there was a continual uproar of heralding and haranguing. Nobody slept much during the succeeding night. I was wakeful, but I believe I was not afraid. We had a good supply of rifles, needle-guns, and ammunition. Our warriors appeared anxious to fight. We had chosen our position. Still, the number of oncoming Sioux exceeded ours, by how much we did not know. We could find out only by waiting.

The Sioux appeared the next morning on the distant bluffs and on the valley below them. Criers were going among them, warriors were galloping here and there, they were organizing for the attack upon us. To me it looked like an immense throng of them. Our Chief Blackfoot put his soldiers—his regular-army policemen, or dog-soldiers—out upon a side bench, there to be held in reserve as a home-guard.

He ordered me to go with them, and I went. Many old men were there too, all just remaining there and awaiting orders.

Our Crow warriors were doing their medicine, each according to his own way of imitating the vocal noises and the actions of his own special animal-friend which he believed protected him in time of danger. There was a tumultuous mingling of whoofing like a bear, talking like a magpie, howling like a wolf, screaming like a curlew, hooting like an owl, mimickings of the sounds and movements of a crane, a badger, an eagle, an elk, of many varieties of lower animal life. I was wearing dangling from my long back hair my red plume that had been given to me by a medicine-man. Yes, I believed in it as a helpful charm. My clothing was but the trousers and moccasins. My body and face were painted in true warrior fashion. I was mounted bareback on a white horse having red ears.

Alternate charging by Crows and by Sioux occupied the first hour of combat, with but little damage to either side. They were "sparring," the Sioux evidently trying to draw our warriors out further from the camp and its entrenchments. Buckskin Williams and Crow Davis, two other white men, were with the Crows. I saw Williams in the battle. During the entire day of turmoil I did not see Crow Davis in any position of danger, although he afterward set up strong claims to special valor on the occasion.

When the Crow warriors began riding the daring-line I left the regular dog-soldiers and joined the fighting front. Pretty Eagle, a dog-soldier chief and a great fighter, ordered me back. I returned, but soon I was again with the active warriors. Man after man would gallop his horse along in front of the array of Sioux, shielding himself as best he could by riding on the animal's side while the enemy sent bullets and arrows toward him. Then the Sioux in their turn would give us a return game of the same kind. I rode the daring-line, although I admit having been prudent enough not to pause or to get too close to the other side. But how it thrilled me and put courage into me! To be on horseback and in danger is a choice situation in life if one can measure exactly his limitations.

The dares on foot began to be put into operation. An Indian of first one side and then the other would walk out toward the enemy, would take his position on some little eminence, and there he would announce his name and utter defiant or tantalizing remarks. This feature of the game also aroused in me a desire for emulation. I moved out—thoughtfully restraining myself from too intimate an approach—and called out the warrior challenge:

"I am Horse Rider, a white man. My home is at the agency on upper Elk River."

"Yes, we know you," somebody answered back in English from the Sioux assemblage, and an instant afterward a bullet sang its mournful tune somewhere over my head.

I wanted to run right then, but pride and my knowledge of the inaccuracy of marksmanship and the feebleness of the bullets at that distance prevented me from committing this sort of mistake.

Various Crows could talk Sioux and doubtless there were Sioux who understood Crow. I had learned from Mitch Buoyer a little of the language of our foes.

"We had two white men with us, but they went back," some one called over to us. Then they joked at me: "Maybe you want a Sioux woman. We have some fine young women for you if you will come and get one of them. They are better than your Crow woman."

This sort of jolly bantering occurred at various intervals between the active warring demonstrations. One old Sioux man called to me, "My son, I want to talk to you." I referred him to Mitch. He asked Mitch to what branch of the Sioux he belonged, and Mitch told him, and he told also of his residence at the agency and of his having a

Crow wife there. They shouted to each other an exchange of talk about mutual acquaintances, speaking of McKnight, Jim Bridger, and others. They had a pleasant visit, while the rest of us awaited its termination.

One special Sioux, wearing a war-bonnet, sat on his horse and shook his coupstick at us for a long time. Many shots were fired at him, and although he was within shooting distance, there was no appearance of any bullet finding the mark.

The women of both sides were in the near background of their respective fighting men. They joined in the scornful defiances. Our women cheered us when we did something worthy of notice, and they sang their strong-heart songs to keep up our courage at all times. At one time I felt a full glow of personal pride when our women sang, "The Horse Rider is with us and we shall get the scalps of all the Sioux." Nevertheless, I sang the death-song when I went out to stand and challenge while being shot at.

The alternations of charging, of defensive resisting, of cessations for mutual banter, of firing at long range with occasional result, continued until late in the afternoon. We got distinctly the best of the encounter, this perhaps due to our better position and our superior arms, if in this latter respect there was any difference. An hour or so before sundown we heard among them an unusual shouting of orders. We expected a charge more desperate than ever, and we set ourselves to receive it. But their women went away out of sight while their warriors opened an extraordinary fusillade of gun-fire upon us. This made it apparent they were about to abandon the field. As their men went back over the hill, ours followed after them. Pretty soon the Sioux retreat became a flight. They discarded weapons and some of them lost their horses. I believe their women all got away, but not all of their men did. I saw some who did not.

I went four or five miles in the pursuit. I saw some conduct that I did not like and that I never shall reveal. Crows were taking scalps, counting coups, grabbing guns from each other for a "second-coup" count. I counted some coups, merely to adapt myself to the situation. Our Crow women were following the men, cheering them, and—well, they were helping in ways that the old-time Indian women were taught to help in exterminating enemies. I saw one Sioux who evidently was in great agony. His scalp was gone, and he was groaning as he groped about on hands and knees. He crept into a ditch. I mentally prayed that he might die there without further molestation.

The pursuing Crows came straggling back that evening, that night, the next day. A few of them followed the Sioux all the way to the Bighorn River. The returning ones all had horses or other plunder. This had been the most extensive battle between Crows and Sioux since the advent of guns among them. Forty years or so before this time they had met in a terrible conflict near Pryor Gap, twenty-five miles up the creek. In this earlier encounter the weapons had been bows and arrows, spears and knives, clubs and stones, with only a few, if any, inefficient guns.

Eight Crows were killed in this battle at the mouth of Pryor Creek. I do not know the number of wounded. Goose Head, lying in a lodge next to mine, was shot through the body. I went in to see him as the medicine-men were doctoring him. At daylight the next morning I heard the wailing begin about his lodge, so I knew that he had breathed his last. The women were jabbing themselves in their faces and their foreheads, were slashing their legs, were cutting off finger-joints—all this as a sign of grief to the point of desperation.

Our orders had been to bring in the Crows as soon as we could find them, as a delegation of them were to be sent to Washington. But they were not yet done hunting, so we had to move along with them and do the best we could to keep them going toward the agency. We went up toward Pryor Mountain and got some more buffalo and other game, to obtain the robes and skins for new lodges and clothing. Next, on the west bank of Clark's Fork, we camped a few days beside some big springs at the foot of a mountain. While the men were hunting, the women were gathering roots and berries for immediate use and for winter storage. We progressed slowly, but the progress was toward the agency.

The Nez Percés traveled with us all along the way. They were headed by Chief Looking-Glass. Ah, but there was a grand man! He naturally was as gentle as a man ever can be, but during our battle his voice could be heard urging us to the fray. The Crows accorded great credit to Looking-Glass and his followers for their aid in repulsing the Sioux. They remembered this, too, when Looking-Glass and his people came through here with Chief Joseph in 1877.

Friendships were firmly cemented between Crows and Nez Percés during these days of joint journeying. Sweetheart associations between young people of the two tribes were numerous. Some intertribal weddings took place, Crow women going with the western neighbors, their women remaining with us.

It needed now an actual personal acquaintance always to distinguish between members of these differing Indian stocks, so closely united in interest and in purpose had they become.

I got a big name among the Crows for my part in the battle and in the incidents precedent and subsequent to it. At the "Diving Water" River—the Boulder River, where Big Timber now is situated—we stopped and camped for a council. Chief Blackfoot sent for me to come into the conclave lodge. He said, "To-morrow you shall go with the first warriors into the agency." Some young men already had gone on ahead as couriers, according to custom, but Blackfoot had reference to the formal return of victorious warriors into the home camp.

We chosen ones blackened our faces, this in token of revenge accomplished and that the war spirit was now dead, like burned-out coals. We rode at the head of the straggling procession of more than two thousand red people, their travois, their horseherds, their dogs. The mourners stayed far behind or aside, as was the fashion. We leading ones rode abreast into the agency village. We sang songs of victory and we fired our guns into the air. I believe that General Grant, parading at the head of his army after the Civil War, did not feel any more important than I did in the vanguard of this Indian home-coming.

Shot in the Jaw led my horse, with me mounted upon it, about the agency and the lodges of the Indians. He heralded my great merits and sang songs in praise of me as he walked along and stopped at various places. I received many gifts. And, of course, my Indian relatives had to give away lots of presents, to show how good they felt because of my high standing among the people.

Some of the Crows proposed to send me as one of their delegates to Washington, but there were so many who wanted to go that I felt impelled to refuse. Besides, I had on hand other matters that fully engaged my energies just then. Barney Bravo went. About two dozen Crow men were in this delegation to the national capital. I recall just now the names of four of them—Thin Belly, Iron Bull, Eagle, and Long Horse. If my knowledge be not faulty, this was the first journeying of Crow Indians to the national capital.

Friendly visiting between Crows and Sioux was an occasional event, notwithstanding their continual war status. The visiting always was done out in the open country, never at the agency. Women and children of each tribe were captives in the other tribe. Prisoners sometimes were exchanged at peaceable meetings. Usually, though, all Indian prisoners brought from one people to another soon became satisfied to live with their captors and voluntarily remained there.

An open and announced approach in broad daylight and without the least appearance of stealth gave rise to a presumption of amicable intent. Whoever at any time might enter an Indian camp in such manner was considered exempt from harm. Even the bitterest enemy might go into the midst of his foes if he went openly and direct, with all indications of peaceful intention and with all evidence of trust in their favorable reception of him. It would be too easy to kill him, therefore it would be no honor to do so. Another idea influencing this conduct was that the visitor either was crazy or was sent by the Great Spirit. Anyhow, the rule that hospitality should be extended to every peaceable visitor, be he friend or enemy, rarely was violated among the aboriginal tribes in the West. In two instances I happened to be in Crow camps when Sioux came for a social call. In one case there were a dozen or more of them, all men. Our scouts saw them coming and reported to the camp. They rode in a straggling group across the open country. Except for the pausing to fire their guns into the air a short distance from our camp-circle boundary, one might have thought they belonged there and were coming quietly home from some unimportant excursion into the adjacent hills. We gave them a smoke, some minor gifts, and a feast. I know of no business they had with us other than the pleasant sign-talk conversation. I went one time with some Crows into a Sioux camp. It was a small camp, but I was somewhat nervous while there. We took a peace-pipe with us, and we all smoked together. All appearances indicated we were a group of lifetime acquaintances and friends. We did a little trading with the enemy Sioux. They had mules, and our people liked to get these animals for dragging the lodge-poles. Of course, we stole some when the rare chance came, but we could not get enough of them in this way. It always was presumable that the Sioux did not have honest claim to ownership of their mules. Many of them had the U. S. brand.

I helped to make a treaty between the Crows and the Shoshones. Forty or fifty lodges of Crows, with Chief Blackfoot at their head, went over the mountains to the Stinking Water River, into the borderlands of the Shoshones, or Snake Indians. I was sent as an emissary to Chief Washakie of the Shoshones. At his camp I learned they had just had a fight with the Cheyennes. They had two scalps and were in high glee—singing, dancing, generally celebrating. "Piute Jack," a white man among the Shoshones, was there, and he helped me in getting a hearing. I said to them: "You are at peace with the whites, and so are the Crows and the Flatheads and the Bannacks. Let us all get together and help the whites drive the Sioux and Cheyennes back into their own country."

This proposition was received with favor. The Crows were sent for and they came and camped near the Shoshones. Several days of visiting occurred before the formal peace-council was held. Yellow Leggings, my adopted father, was the Crow orator-spokesman. He named the proceeding "the prairie treaty." I proposed to put it in writing, and they at once commended me for the idea. I got a piece of brown wrapping-paper and pounded out a bullet until it had a point suitable for a pencil. With a tobacco-board (a board used by the Indians in cutting up their plug tobacco for smoking purposes) for a desk, I wrote:

"We meet to-day to shake hands forever. If any horses of Crows or Snakes be stolen by the other, they shall be returned peaceably. We never will make war upon each other."

The two head chiefs put their marks at the bottom, and I kept this paper for a long time before misplacing and losing it. I afterward bethought myself that its legality might be questioned by reason of the fact that it did not have written into it the date nor the place of the agreement, but it served well as a good document. It served so well that up to this day the treaty has not been broken.

We danced and feasted and exchanged presents for another day or two after the agreement was concluded, and then the Crows set out for their own side of the mountains. While on the way to and from the Shoshones I was entertained in the lodge of a Crow named Gros Ventre. I remember that he was a great sun-worshiper. Two ten-year-old girls, Plain Painter and Stoops to Charge, were appointed to be my bed-makers and general caretakers while in this lodge. When Plain Painter grew up she became the wife of Flathead Woman, a Crow, and she still lives here on the reservation. A few other old Crows who were there are yet alive.

Two enterprising young Shoshones followed us on our first day out and stole some of our horses. Shot in the Jaw and I were sent back to get the lost animals. We reported the case to Chief Washakie, and he had the two offenders brought to his lodge.

"You have no ears," he reprimanded. Then he declared to us, "I'll have them whipped and made ashamed."

He compelled the young men to restore to us the horses they had taken and to give us presents of blankets and robes. Then he had a group of his dog-soldiers get pony-whips and lash them on the bare skin of their backs. The youths appeared utterly shamed, but they bravely took their medicine without protest or groan.

Some Bannack Indians—known to themselves and to other Western red people as "Bad Lodge" Indians—were camped on the Stillwater River. Their chief, whose name was Kind Man, had just died as we came to their cluster of lodges. We stayed to sympathize with them and see the burial. His two wives had hacked off in ugly fashion their hair, many of the people were mourning and gashing themselves with knives. They smeared red paint over his face and dressed him in his richest costume. Then they wrapped him in a blanket, including with the body a bow and arrows, a muzzle-loading gun, a knife, a battle-ax, his pipe, and some kinnikinick tobacco. Outside of the blanket they wrapped a buffalo-robe, the smooth side decorated with religious paintings and rolled inward, the woolly side exposed. Thongs of rawhide were used to tie the bundle. Poles were cut, peeled, painted with red stripes, and a scaffold eight or ten feet high was constructed. Upon this structure was placed the remains of Kind Man, there to be left until Nature was satisfied. Eight or ten of his horses were brought around the scaffold, then killed and left lying there. The whole procedure was like that followed among all of the Indians in that region during those times. In the present day they are learning to cover up the dead and keep all of the property, as we white people do. Dear me! there aren't any genuine Indians nowadays.

Hiram Lee and I left the Crow camp on the Stillwater, to hasten on to the agency. Fifteen miles a day was pretty good traveling for the entire camp, while we two on horseback could double or treble that distance without effort. A few miles out we were overtaken by seven or eight of Chief Blackfoot's dog-soldiers. They informed us he had sent them for us, and we were compelled to go back. Blackfoot reprimanded us for having exposed ourselves thus to possibilities of hostile attack.

"Your mother told you not to go," he reproved me, making reference to one of his wives, a Sioux woman, who during this expedition had adopted me as her son. "I am responsible for you as well as the other Crows while we are out together. You must stay with us until we are near to the agency."

But the next day we grew impatient and stole away again. This time Blackfoot himself came with a band of his dog-soldiers. After some parleying he finally said:

"You have no ears. But since you are bound to go, give me a piece of paper to show that I am not any longer responsible for your safety."

I tore a corner off the treaty paper and handed to him the detached fragment. He accepted it, then he held up a hand and solemnly admonished me:

"To me you now are lost. But the sun sees you. All I can say is, Be sharp, be like a wolf, always awake and looking."

General Clapp came to the Mission as agent, succeeding Dr. Wright, who had resigned and returned to the East. General Clapp had earned his military title in army service, and before he came to the Crow reservation he had been minister to Honduras. He proved to be an honest and capable agent, as had Dr. Wright.

A new location for the agency was decided upon. It was to be on the Stillwater River, just above the mouth of its Rosebud Creek branch. The boundaries of the reservation had been diminished by treaty agreement, and the old agency location now would be in white-man land. Preliminary surveys for the Northern Pacific Railroad had been made along the Yellowstone during the previous summer—the summer of 1873—under the military escort of Generals

Stanley and Custer. Cherry and I and our son Tom would live at the new agency. Tom? That was the name I had given him, but he had another name, conferred upon him by the Indians and altogether used by them. According to his mother and all of his Indian relatives and acquaintances, he was "Takes the Pony-Whip."

During this spring of 1874, myself and Johnny Suce, the half-Mexican-half-Piegan Crow Indian, were sent out to inform the Crows of the change in the agency's location. The most noteworthy incident of our trip was our discovery of the steamboat *Josephine* coming up the Yellowstone. We had lost our packs, and our horses had escaped from us as we were crossing the flooded Yellowstone River. We hailed the steamboat, and it was steered to the bank for us to get aboard. It was the first time I ever had been aboard a steamer craft, and this was the first one Johnny ever had seen. We ranged over the vessel and gazed wonderingly at its mechanisms. We were invited to eat, which invitation was a most pleasing one. A negro served us. I do not remember now what was brought to us as food, except one article—corn-bread! Oh, but it was good! It was the first corn-bread I had seen since I left Kansas ten years before, and it was an article of diet entirely new to Johnny.

A chubby man wearing full whiskers and a military uniform sat on the deck and looked out over the country. After a while I learned this was Colonel Fred Grant. His appearance stuck in my memory, so the next time I saw him I at once recognized him. This second glimpse of him was four years afterward, in 1878. I rode out from Fort Custer one day that spring while on duty there as a scout. Rain had made the whole region soggy. Along the road I met an ambulance mired in the mud. While the driver was lashing the mules, Colonel Fred Grant was "bringing up the rear" by manual effort exerted upon a hind wheel.

THE AGENCY AT ABSAROKA

THE Crow Indian word, or sequence of syllables, *ab-sar-o-ka,* was wrongly interpreted by the earliest white-men students of this language. It is possible, or even highly probable, that when, in their first contacts, some Indian of this tribe tried to explain to a white man the meaning of the tribal name for themselves he pointed toward a bird, and this bird happened to be a crow. So the white man spoke the English word "crow," or its equivalent in some other white-man tongue, and the Indian unwittingly nodded assent. Hence, the white man told others of his race that these people called themselves "Crow" Indians. As often occurs, error thus got the start of truth, and truth never has been able yet to catch up with it.

Ab-sar-o-ka means "forked-tail bird,"—not "crow." Among these people is a tradition that in past times when they lived in the region where eastern Nebraska and Kansas now appear on our maps a peculiar kind of forked-tail bird resembling the blue-jay or magpie inhabited that country. From this bird they took, or had put upon them, their tribal name. Thenceforth they were the *Ab-sar-o-ka* Indians—the Forked-tail-bird Indians. But the dominating white man persisted in calling them Crows. As ever has been the case under like circumstances, the white man won the endurance contest. Since his advent among them, they have become the Crow Indians.

Our new agency was named Absaroka. It was located a mile or so up the Rosebud Creek from the present white-man town of Absaroka and about two miles from where the little creek flows into the Still-water River—or, the Buffalo-Jumps-Over-the-Bank River, according to the proper rendition of the old Indian designation for this stream. Mitch Buoyer and I chose the exact site after it had been determined to set up the reservation headquarters somewhere in this vicinity. Since in the course of our duties as despatch-carriers and our travels as hunters we had become well acquainted with the local geography, the agent detailed us to this special duty of finding the best position for his official home.

A stockade was the first important construction, because trespassing and hostile Sioux Indians were more numerous there than they had been around the Mission agency. The stockade was of adobe, in general character like the structure we were abandoning sixty or seventy miles to the westward. Inside this stockade were the offices and stores. Log cabins as places of residence were built outside in the vicinity of the adobe stockade. The agent had a two-story log house. All of the others were of a single story.

Eighty thousand dollars, if I recollect clearly, was the amount appropriated for expense incurred in moving the agency from the old site to this new one. General Clapp, the agent at this time, employed the Nelson Story freight outfit to do most of the transportation work. In his entire management of the removal, the efficient agent did so well that only a little more than half of the appropriation was used. He reported the situation and was told to devote the balance to current expenses. Not many months afterward he resigned. He went down the Stillwater, the Yellowstone, and the Missouri in a Mackinaw boat, to Omaha, I believe. He was succeeded by Keller, and later this one yielded his position to Armstrong.

Armstrong's sister came with him to Absaroka. She was an elderly unmarried woman, well liked, highly respected. During her sojourn there she served as our school-teacher. White and Indian children attended the same school. One day Miss Armstrong had occasion to discipline one of the larger Indian girls. The offending pupil was being given a thorough shaking when, either accidentally or as a defensive measure, she grabbed the teacher's superb coiffure of dark-brown hair. The seizure and consequent jerk detached from the head the entire mass of voluminous coils and beau-catcher curls. Bewildered, horrified, crazed by terror, the girl fled from the room as she shouted:

"Oh, I scalped the teacher!"

She plunged through the waters of Rosebud Creek and ran all the way to her home lodge. No inducements could lead her to return to the school until after the permanent departure of this local supervisor of educational affairs, which occurred soon afterward. Embarrassed by the exposure of her natural baldness, Miss Armstrong left in a few days for some other field of activity.

An epidemic of measles raged among the Crows for a time while I was at Absaroka. Of course, in its treatment they depended mainly upon the sweat-lodge. Their indiscriminate use of this often valuable mode of treatment—or, rather, their insufficient knowledge of the character of the ailment —resulted in many deaths. Old and young succumbed to the combined effects of the disease and the heroic measures adopted in the attempt at cure.

The affliction wiped out Crow Indians in a way comparable to the devastations of smallpox during a preceding generation of them.

An unmarried, middle-aged, but gay, doctor was on duty with us during the time of the measles invasion. He did very good service in cases where he was allowed to pursue his line of treatment, but he had not the full confidence of discriminating people. His flirtations were too numerous. After a while, though, he met his match. This was a Crow Indian widow having two small sons. She was known as the most accomplished coquette in the tribe. The doctor married her. After a few months she decided she was too young to tie up permanently to him, so she quit him and went far away to her people in camp. Notwithstanding her many love affairs, she was regarded as an unusually good-hearted woman. Her two sons were remarkably good boys, and they grew up to become remarkably good Crow men.

An old Frenchman doctor served for a long time as our agency physician. He had been an army doctor. He was a good man and was considered a good physician. I had him in attendance upon Cherry when our second child, a girl, was born. That is, he came and observed from a distance and made suggestions. Cherry, like other Crow women of that time, did not desire white attendance under circumstances of this kind.

I was doing odd jobs—sometimes on the pay-roll as a blacksmith or other employee, sometimes hunting and trapping on my own account—when we moved to Absaroka and during much of the time after we arrived there. General Clapp had me listed on the roll as "lookout." This status involved picket-guarding, scouting, despatch-carrying.

On one cross-country errand, during the time when we were in course of transferring the old agency to the new one, General Clapp sent by me a despatch to the old agency, together with some mail to be sent from there on to Bozeman. I put off the commencement of the journey until after dusk, to evade hostilities. Then I tied up my horse's tail and got ready to go. This tying up of the horse's tail was to enable it to run faster. I do not know to a certainty whether or not this arrangement effects that result, but the old Indians used to say it did, so it became my practice to do it. The despatch-paper was stuffed into the bosom of my shirt, so that if attacking Sioux should get after me, it would be safer there than in the bag attached to the saddle on my horse. If the man should become separated from his horse, the man might escape;

but the Indians never allowed a horse alone to get away. If it was not killed, it was captured with a lariat.

I knew well every mile of the trail. I set off, following up the Stillwater; but after allowing my horse a drink and giving my head and face a bath, I went aside and traveled at a distance from the regular trail along the river, so as not to frighten the elk and thus reveal my presence to whatever Indians might be in this vicinity. Late in the night I selected a place for a short sleep.

Buffalo bones were very common in those days and in those regions. Right where I stopped, under a big pine-tree, were lots of bones. By the starlight I gathered a quantity of these and made a bed fence, then I gathered grass and pine-needles to fill in the enclosure so as to have a cushion five or six inches in thickness. The despatch was hidden aside under a stone, the horse was picketed out. Everything was quiet, and I went readily to sleep. When I awakened the next morning the first sight that caught my vision was a skull grinning at me from a distance of four or five feet from my face. It became evident that my bedding-down place was under a tree wherein dead Indians of past years had been placed upon scaffoldings according to the old mode of tree burial. All of the bones I had used in making my bed frame were Indian bones. I think I was not actually frightened, but I remember that I got away from that vicinity as fast as I and my horse could move.

Ghosts of dead people and spirits of all kinds had a prominent place in the mental life of the Indians as they used to be—and of many of them as they are to-day. While I was serving as official interpreter at Absaroka, there were at a certain place along the Stillwater two dead squaws on scaffolds by the roadside. Many Indians were afraid to go along the trail by this wayside cemetery. One day I proposed to one of them that I, being in official governmental position, could give him a written pass that would get him safely through this dangerful area. I gave him the "pass," it warded off all harm. After that I wrote a good many other protective missives in which the ghosts were supposed to be commanded not to frighten or do any injury to the bearer. One government employee took up this safe-conduct idea as a business proposition. He charged each Indian a buffalo-robe for procuring this freedom from annoyance by the unseen agencies. He soon was found out and was relieved from all further duty there.

A hostile attack upon our loggers occurred six or seven miles downstream from Absaroka. Eight or ten of us were in a camp there, getting out timbers for additional agency buildings. John Renfro was our cook. White Calfee had horse and mule teams of his own, and he was hauling our output to the agency. We were using also several yoke of oxen belonging to the Government. Each night we turned out the stock for grazing. Horses or mules sometimes would be paired in the grazing, a rope looped about the neck of each, so that they must keep together only a few feet apart. Any two horses thus tied together a few times will become so habituated to each other that thereafter they will move about in close companionship without any rope connection. Such looping also made it a little more difficult for thieving Indians to chase them away. The oxen also were yoked in pairs during their range feeding times, to hinder the operations of raiders.

One morning our cattle could not be found near the camp. It appeared from what tracks could be discovered they had wandered up the valley toward the agency. Tom Stewart and Mexican Joe set out to look for them. After these searchers had been gone an hour or so, Hugh McMillan, Charlie Carr, and I started for the top of a hill to survey the country and try to locate them. Carr was a stutterer, and, as usual with such disabled people, he was keeping us amused with his remarks as we furtively crept from place to place on our way toward the crest of the elevation. Hugh McMillan had suspended by a leather string about his neck a bootleg, cut off and sewed together at one end to hold his cartridges, of which he had just then an ample and weighty supply. About fifty yards from the hilltop we caught sight of Stewart and Mexican Joe hurrying the lost cattle along the valley. Pursuing them and shooting at them were five or six Indians on horses. As we stood there a few moments watching the lively scene—

"Bang-bang-bang!" A band of Sioux opened fire upon us from another hill a hundred yards or so across from ours.

We fled, and dodged among the rocks, trees, and gulches toward the timbered valley. McMillan fell behind, because the weight of the bootleg ammunition-bag tightened the string about his neck so as to choke him. Carr and I separated. The whole camp of men scattered and located themselves here and there for individual sharpshooting. White Calfee's thumb was hit by a bullet as he was unhitching his mules to let them get away. McMillan and I came again together and the two of us crept up a draw where we knew there was a good position for concealment and deliberate shooting. We fired carefully, but I believe the only result achieved by us or any of our fellows was the killing of one Sioux horse.

The hostiles got among our log piles, and they used these as fortifications. The intermittent exchange of shots continued over a period of about two hours. None of us except White Calfee was injured, but Mexican Joe was missing when the fight was over and we collected ourselves together. Stewart had seen him fall from his horse, but we could not find him anywhere in the neighborhood of where this last view of him was had. A year afterward what appeared to be the remains of his body was found several miles down the river. The little tributary creek where he was killed became known and continued thereafter to be known as Mexican Joe Creek.

The Sioux killed some of our cattle. They took from them no meat except the tongues. But they carried away all of the ox-bows. These they wanted for making bows and arrows. Such fine material for this purpose was much in demand among the plains Indians. Nelson Story brought in a good many ox-bows for trading to the Crows. I used to have a bow and arrows made up from one of his importations.

Jim Hildebrand was a foreman, or subordinate manager, for Nelson Story in that phase of Story's enterprises wherein freighting or lumbering was concerned. During the spring of 1875, Hildebrand had charge of the Story outfit that was getting out pine logs for shingles. They were at work on Rosebud Creek above the agency. One morning after he had put the men at their work he walked a hundred yards or so up a hillside and sat down there upon a big rock. He was there but a few minutes when—

"Pop!" A Sioux got him. The bullet shattered an arm.

The workmen heard the shot and saw a lone Indian running away over the hill. They hurried to Hildebrand and carried him to the camp. Before any remedial measures could be used he bled to death. He had been regarded as a good man, very capable, an important factor in Nelson Story's business organization, and his loss was considered to be a disaster to the entire system of Western civilization.

A peculiar stranger appeared one day at the agency. He came afoot from the eastward. I was with some others at our slaughter-house when he trudged across the valley and approached us.

"How-de-doo?" he greeted us.

His manner of speech made it evident he was a foreigner of some nationality not at once identifiable to us. He had a full and high forehead, was good-looking in face and form; but there was an undefin-

able freakishness in his composite make-up. He was
bareheaded and carried no pack nor baggage of any
kind except a pair of moccasins tucked under his belt.
His feet were encased in a pair of shoes that appeared two or three sizes too large for him, and
they showed only a moderate extent of wear. He
evaded or declined answering all questions as to
whence he had come—the first question a Westerner
of that period ordinarily would put to a newcomer.
On this point his only reply, several times repeated,
was:

"God told me to come here."

The moccasins he had in his belt appeared to be
entirely new, with no indication of having been
worn. Somebody commented on this condition and
asked him where he got them.

"I found them," he replied promptly, with every
appearance of frank and honest statement of the
case. Then he added: "They are Sioux moccasins."

Notwithstanding our uncertainty as to the sort
of man we were dealing with, we asked him, of
course, if he was hungry and if he would come
with us and have something to eat. He replied that
he carried food with him, and he pulled from his
trousers' pocket a handful of roots and began to
munch at them. We urged him to go with us and get
some better food. After some manifestation of re-

luctance he accepted the invitation. We set before him some hot coffee, plenty of bread and meat, an ample quantity of stewed dried apples. He pitched into the victuals and ate like a hungry wolf. After he had ended his meal he was offered a pipe and tobacco. The offer was declined, but he drew from his own pocket a little stone Indian pipe and some kinnikinick, with which exclusively personal equipment he proceeded to have his own solitary smoke. The conversation lagged somewhat because of the visitor's seeming indisposition to converse much. Finally, a new angle to the situation was presented when he dug up from a pocket a small, single-shot, cast-iron pistol.

"Got any caps for this pistol?" he asked.

No, none of us had any ammunition of that kind. In fact, none of us ever had seen nor even had conceived of a firearm constructed on the plan of that one. Evidently he had brought it with him all the way from wherever he had come from.

He certainly was a puzzle to us. Aside and among ourselves we discussed and conjectured and argued about him all the rest of the day. Was he insane? Was he an escaping criminal? Was he a renegade Sioux white-man spying upon us? His status was not settled, and never afterward did it become settled. That night he slipped away.

When we missed him the next morning a search was inaugurated. We found only his discarded shoes. Some time afterward the Crows discovered the dead body of a white man forty miles to the southeastward, in the neighborhood of where the town of Gebo now stands. From their description of the remnant articles we became satisfied this was our mysterious visitor.

Incidentally, while we were out looking for our lost guest that morning we found a ghastly remnant not connected with him. This was a dried and withered human hand. A perforation showed where it had been hung on a string, doubtless to be carried about as a trophy of successful warfare. The yellow-and-black discoloration made it impossible to determine whether this had been the hand of a white man or an Indian.

A Crow war-party was being organized on a certain occasion while I was at Absaroka. Just then I was not in the government employment, so I decided to go on the war-path. The principal object of the expedition was, as regularly was the case in those times, the stealing of horses from the Sioux. This would be likely to involve some fighting, but actual conflict was not positively sought. If horses could be stolen and brought home without bloodshed, particularly without the enemy having discovered the presence of the forayers, this was an accomplishment looked upon as highly complimentary to the ability of the latter as cunning schemers. The killing of an enemy was much more commendable, but this acme of boldness was not necessary to constitute a successful enterprise. However, if inferior forces of the enemy could be encountered, particularly if a lone individual could be attacked by numerous assailants,—a situation much favored and sought after by war-parties of old-time Indians,—a joyful massacre became the main feature of the advent upon plundering activities.

We went down the Stillwater, on down the Yellowstone, and set up our operating camp below the present Huntley. There were about twenty of us, all Crows except myself. I was appointed to serve as a "wolf"—that is, a scout ahead of the party when in movement and a picket-guard when in camp or at rest. There were four of us acting in this kind of employment. Hostile Sioux and Cheyennes were all about us. They also had out their "wolf" observers.

One day on Tulloch's Fork a companion scout and myself set off for the top of a butte, to look over the country. It was an elevation well known as a favored point of observation, and on its crest was a stone "fort," such as one would find then, and might find now, on many such high places. Like other positions of its kind, it was used by whatever Indians or white men might wish to use it and might take possession of it. We two crept from rock to rock as we ascended the butte. As we got near the summit an object of the utmost interest attracted our notice. This was a lone Sioux Indian sitting there inside the stone rampart and cleaning his gun. Pretty soon another Sioux joined him. It was evident they were on guard duty.

When we had worked ourselves into a position exactly to our liking we both took a rest aim and fired simultaneously. We killed instantly both of the Sioux. We rushed to them, counted coups, seized their guns, and ran away. We did not pause to scalp them, since it was altogether probable they belonged to a party for whom they were scouting. Aside from the danger involved in lingering there, we already had in the dead enemies and the captured needle-gun and Sharp's carbine enough of glorious achievement to serve us for a long time as a foundation for boastful rehearsings.

As we returned to our main party we performed the regular ceremonies properly appertaining to the coming home of some one who has done something important or has some important news to communicate. We howled like a wolf and fired our guns into the air. We weaved or tacked from side to side in our approach. This all gave notice of our pretense to serious matters for consideration. A little heap of buffalo-chips was made. We boldly dashed up to it and kicked it over, by this act registering an oath that in the matter now about to be entered upon we should tell the truth, the whole truth, and nothing but the truth. When we had told our story it was decided that the whole party would live longer and enjoy greater prosperity in some other neighborhood. The decision was put promptly into effect. We got some horses, both before that incident and afterward, but those were the only ones of the enemy we met during that war-path expedition.

Wagons came first into use among the Crows after we had moved to the Absaroka agency. We had been using such vehicles as agency property, but now the Indians themselves were being supplied, as another of the government measures looking toward the making of farmers out of buffalo-hunters. Those issued to the Crows were light in weight, were of the narrow-track model, and were said to have cost fifty-five dollars each. The Indians were not anxious for them for their own use, but they accepted them. In many instances they were traded to white men for sugar, coffee, calico, or other articles of trivial value. But this sort of traffic was soon stopped. An order came to arrest any one having in his possession property bearing the I.D. (Indian Department) brand and not authoritatively issued to him by government agents.

Mowers, rakes, and other farm implements also were sent out to be distributed among the Crows. A few of them made use of these for cutting and gathering wild hay. The small quantities of hay were sold at a good price, usually to the agency authorities for use in feeding the government stock. Of course, there was not then any fenced-up land in that region, except for the small enclosures where garden-truck was raised. For their ordinary camping and hunting travels, the Crows still gave preference to the saddle-horses, the pack-horses, and the travois made of lodge-poles dragged by horses. I got the agent to issue to Cherry one of the wagons. But I had a hard time getting her to ride in it with me. She loved to ride on horseback, she could manage well the most spirited steed, but she was afraid she'd fall out of a wagon.

The Indian horses were small. The white men with whom the Indians came in contact had heavier draft-animals. It was easily seen that the heavier horses could pull bigger loads. In his peculiarly constructed mind the Indian pondered over this situation and determined upon a mode of overcoming his deficiencies in motive power. His solution was to put a heavy man upon the back of each pony hitched to a loaded wagon. Thus held firmly down to the ground, it was reasoned that little horses could pull as effectively as big horses.

When the Nez Percés under Chief Joseph left their Idaho reservation and fled across Montana toward Canada I was at Absaroka. This was during the summer of 1877, and I already had been in scout service under Generals Gibbon and Miles and at Fort Custer during the preceding year or more, but now I was again for a while at the agency. In past years I had done a good deal of trading or present-exchanging with the Nez Percés, had hunted with them, visited with them, had enjoyed the companionship of sweethearts among them. They always had been peaceable Indians, had not been in any prolonged trouble with the whites, had been especially friendly with the Crows, particularly had given us valuable aid in the fight with the Sioux at the mouth of Pryor Creek, just three years before this time. So, when I was asked to accompany the United States military forces as a scout in the interception of the Nez Percés, the order was evaded. In addition to my friendship for them, my sympathies were with them in the particular affair that led them into an attempt at departure from the dominion of the United States and settlement under the Canadian Government.

I met Looking-Glass, Chief Joseph's subordinate chief, and talked with him. The Crows knew him by the name Arrow Head, or Flint on the Neck, because of his habitual wearing of a flint arrow-head suspended from his throat. I had a great admiration for this Indian as being a man full of natural gentility. For this reason, even though there had been no other, he was assured of my sadness of heart because of their distress and was promised that whatever influence I might have among the Crows would be used toward dissuading them from giving their aid in intercepting him and his people in their movement through our reservation lands. Most of the Crows felt this same way. Many of them, though, affected to array themselves against the Nez Percés, but in reality their warlike operations were restricted to the capture of ponies. The action of the Crows in keeping themselves aloof from gun-fire has been branded by writers as indicative of cowardice. In fact, though, it was within my knowledge that they were keeping in grateful memory their past connections with the people now in a vexatious situation. Although I served long enough in the military department, before that time and afterward, to get the meaning of fealty to constituted authority impressed very deeply into my mind, I have not yet become old enough to experience any sense of shame because of my refusal to go to war against Joseph and Looking-Glass and their wronged Nez Percés.

The Bannack Indians made some trouble soon after the Nez Percés had gone through. I felt friendly toward the Bannacks, but the feeling had no basis sufficient to deter me from military activity against them. Buffalo Horn, a Bannack who had served with me as a scout under Major Brisbin, at Fort Keogh, was at Absaroka when his rebellious tribesmen came into our region. He invited me to go with him to visit a village of his people on the Stillwater. Of course, I could not go; but he went, and he stayed with them.

Troops from Fort Custer came out to head off the Bannacks, who were coming down the same Stillwater trail which the Nez Percés had followed. The Bannacks decided to surrender to the troops, and they moved in a peaceful manner to do so. Nevertheless, volleys of gun-fire were poured into them and several of them were killed. I remember that one woman had a thigh broken by a bullet. She hid out with her baby, but she was discovered, brought in to the agency, and cared for until her recovery. It seemed to me the killing of these Indians when it was plainly evident they were trying to surrender was a violation of the humanities. They did not respond to the fire. Before the surrender, there had been a little skirmish, in which Captain Bennett was killed. It is likely this fatality aroused in the soldiers some personal revengeful feelings which true military discipline could not restrain altogether.

"Frenchy" Bethune was serving as one of the scouts for the soldiers. The Indians knew him as "Little Rock," or sometimes as "Big Pipe." After the surrender of the Bannacks and during the process of their alignment as prisoners, this man Bethune rushed out and began grabbing horses and mules that had belonged to them. An officer stopped him and made him release his booty. Pretty soon, though, he was at it again, collecting for himself a goodly bunch of choice stock, since no other such forayers were at work just then. This time some soldier took a shot at him. He fell dead. I never heard who shot him, and probably there never was any official inquiry into the case. Both he and Captain Bennett were buried right there on the field. Maybe the captain's body was removed afterward; but I believe nobody disturbed the remains of Bethune.

The Indian custom of connecting fasting and prayer had appealed to my fancy long before we came to Absaroka. But it was here that I carried out for the benefit of my soul the most extensive undertaking of this sort. Barney Bravo and I agreed to do together the old-time Indian cleansing penance. We got a medicine-man to prepare us. He put us through the sweat-bath, then he pricked flesh from our arms and legs and gave it to the Sun. We journeyed out toward the Pryor Mountains and located ourselves there on a high cliff plateau. We stayed there four days and four nights without any food. During the days we conversed but little, devoting ourselves to prayer and meditation. At night we rolled ourselves into blankets and slept. About the third day I saw an eagle soaring over me. After that, when it was daylight, I could look up at any time and see this eagle. Right now, looking back more than fifty years to that time, I am not sure whether this was an actual eagle or the vision of an enraptured mind. Anyhow, the eagle became my medicine-animal. For many years thereafter I believed firmly in its protective influence over me. Bravo said he kept seeing a raven, but I did not observe any such bird, although we were there together all the time. The raven became his medicine-animal. To the white-man side of my mentality, this all seems foolish, but even in this part of my mind there is no certain conviction that the white man's notions about such mysteries are any better than the Indian's notions.

I am altogether convinced that the seeking of distant solitude and there working up a good cry, and a continuance of this weeping for a suitable length of time, is a procedure healthful for both the body and the mind. On various occasions during my past life it has helped me. As my children grew up— both my Crow Indian children and my two white daughters of later years—I urged upon them the practice of going out into some lonely place, if mental depression came, and there stirring up a spell of prolonged lamentation. This is the best cure for downheartedness. Fasting, prayer, wailing, were used with great satisfaction by the ancient peoples mentioned in the Bible. The procedure ought to be as good for us as it was for them.

I attended in full one sun-dance held in the neighborhood of Absaroka agency. The Crows used to have this supreme ceremony every year or two, or sometimes three years would elapse between the events; but never would it take place more than once in any year. The summer was the chosen season, the phases of the moon being considered in settling upon the exact time. A council decided upon and ap-

pointed the days, the council being advised and
guided by the opinions of weather-prophets. The
planting and harvesting of the small tribal tobacco-
patch had a connection with it. Tobacco was regarded as a gift of the Almighty—or First Maker,
as the Crows used the designation. But I never
understood fully the relationship of tobacco to the
sun-dance. In fact, many of the old rites were to me
then so commonplace that I made no special effort
to find out their significance. Whatever I learned
came to me merely by casual contact, not because
of any great interest felt. This was the usual way
with the white men among the Indians. Some of
them actually avoided the ceremonial occasions, re-
garding them with scornful feelings. Perhaps for
this reason, the Crows never liked to have white
people present as curious onlookers at their tribal
rites, especially the sun-dance. On this occasion,
when I was present, there was no other white person
at the gathering.

The object of the sun-dance was to worship and
to propitiate the First Maker, or Person Above. In
preparation for the central event, many devout people went to hilltops each morning and each evening,
there to pray for the success of any coming enterprises or to ask favorable notice for the tribe in
general. The prayers were addressed to the Sun, this

material object being looked upon as the substantial intermediary between the human being and the Person Above, who was too august to be addressed directly; or, by some people, the sun was supposed to be the dwelling-place of the Almighty One.

A "sacrifice" man for the sun-dance was chosen by the council, often after repeated deliberations. Always there were various volunteers or candidates for the distinction. It was an honor of the highest nature to be selected for this place, since the design was to choose the purest-hearted man obtainable. Such chosen one was regarded ever after as a wise and good man, and he had a great influence upon the course of tribal affairs.

Cottonwood poles about twenty feet long were cut for use in setting up the broad conical sun-dance lodge. The lodge had no covering except one green buffalo-skin wrapped about its peak. This skin had to be from a buffalo heifer, preferably one that never had borne a calf. All of the poles were erected in place except a final one. The "sacrifice" man was tied to the end of this final pole. The heifer skin was given to him, and he and the skin were lifted thus to the top of the structure. There he wrapped the skin about the upper ends of the poles, and then he carefully slid down to the ground.

A cluster of dried buffalo tongues was hung upon

one of the poles, five or six feet above the ground. No other kind of tongues would do, since the buffalo was regarded in the old times as the special animal created for and sacred to Indian use. When the heifer skin had been put into place and the chosen man had descended, he entered upon the ceremony of partaking of the buffalo tongues.

The people all assembled in two parallel bodies or lines extending straight out from the sun-dance lodge and leaving between them a long avenue a few feet in width. The "sacrifice" man walked slowly along the length of this pathway. As he moved along he called out for the favor of the Sun and admonished the people ever to keep in mind the Person Above, to deal with each other mercifully, to respect the old people, to keep their hearts pure in every respect. When he reached the buffalo tongues he cut off a slice, ate it, and returned along the way he had come. If no hindering influence deterred him during this crucial pilgrimage back and forth—which was regularly the case—the condition was regarded as creditable to him and as a good omen for the tribe.

The self-torture feature of the ceremony was incumbent especially upon the "sacrifice" man. Others might join him, but their conduct when undergoing the physical distress was purely a personal matter,

while his conduct was representative of the extent
of tribal hardihood. So his responsibility was very
great. When his flesh was cut and the thongs in-
serted by the medicine-men, he was to make no
sound other than to sing or to pray, as though he
felt no pain. When he was dancing about the pole
to which his attached thongs were tied, he must
exhibit no appearance of physical distress. His attitude of apparent indifference to bodily harassment
must be continued throughout the entire time necessary for him to tug himself loose from the thongs
tied into his muscles and sinews, this time extending
possibly to two or three days. According to the
degree of his stoical behavior under all of this in-
fliction, to this extent did he bring to the tribe the
favorable inclination of the Person Above. He was
under constant observation, he knew that constant
self-control was expected of him, that he was to be
an example for emulation, and he endeavored to
act accordingly.

Women took part in the sun-dance ceremonies,
but not in the physical-torture feature of the gathering. They were afforded an opportunity to assert
and to prove virtue, or chastity. Whatever woman
might engage upon this procedure took first some
elk droppings and scattered them all along the
gauntlet avenue between the two lines of people. To

the Crows, the elk was close to the buffalo in their reverence for it as an animal provided especially for the Indians. When the woman had prepared her way by this scattering of the bodily discharges of the elk, she put herself at the farther end of the lines and set off to walk between them to the buffalo tongues hanging on the lodge-pole. On such occasions she always was dressed in her best costume, was painted in a way that to her seemed most beautiful, was in every way appareled and groomed to her maximum capability. She approached the buffalo tongues, drew her knife from its sheath, deliberately cut off a slice. She held this aloft and spoke in general substance about like this:

"By the Sun to-day: My name is ———. I am the daughter of ——— (or the wife of ———). Open your ears, listen, give heed to me, my people. Not any man knows any wrong of me. If I speak not the truth, may I never get back over the trail I have come."

She ate the slice of buffalo tongue, thus sealing her statement as an oath. Then she walked slowly back along the people-lined avenue whereon she had come forward. If any man knew evil of her, it was his duty to the tribe as well as his privilege to toss out an arrow upon the ground in front of her. If that were done, the act was regarded as conclusive and incontrovertible evidence proving her unchastity as well as the falsity of her oath. The woman and all of her immediate relatives fell at once into disrepute and disgrace that nothing done thereafter could dissipate.

At this sun-dance where I was present a young woman presented to me a startling proposition:

"Tom, if I should go and eat of the buffalo tongue and return without challenge, would you marry me as your wife second to Cherry?"

The question amazed me. She was a cousin of Cherry, who at that moment was by my side. I was not sure at first whether she meant it or not. But it soon became evident that she was in dead earnest. She was a beautiful girl and of good repute. I had no doubt she could travel safely over the trial pathway. But whatever might have been my natural inclinations, it seemed there was nothing for me to do now but to give my assent.

She entered upon the test. All went well with her. The next day she moved into our lodge as my second wife. She and Cherry got along peaceably together, acting toward each other as sisters, and asserting themselves to be such. Notwithstanding this, I urged her to go away, my action being taken because of the governmental disfavor I might incur. She went without protest. Her status then, according to the

Crow custom, was that of a respectable young widow.

On this same great ceremonial occasion my adopted sister said to me:

"Tom, would you be proud of me if I should eat the tongue?"

"Yes, sister, I would."

As she came up through the throng of people her face was as radiant as if she were gazing upon a most lovely heavenly vision. Her stately and confident carriage was in itself proof of her purity of heart. How proud I was of this tall and handsome sister of mine! When her ordeal was ended Cherry and I sprang forward and hugged her. Her relatives all rushed to her and almost smothered her with their congratulatory demonstrations of love. The whole concourse of people joined us in the ovation. My emotions got loose and flooded my face with tears of joy. Oh, sister, long gone from this life! you always were that kind of girl and that kind of woman.

How I wish I could see now a genuine old-time sun-dance! To the businesslike white man, it was only an orgy of bloodthirsty savage paganism. To the spiritual-minded Indian, it was the supreme test of clean manhood and womanhood. It instilled into and stimulated in them the hardy and high qualities of character. The self-torturing that seems to us so revolting was to the Indians an occasion for cultivation of the spirit, for subduing the body until it was altogether governed by the higher faculties of the mind. The only regrettable feature of the sun-dances as they are conducted nowadays is the profaning of them into commercial spectacles for merely curious or irreverent onlookers.

LIFE IN THE LODGES OF THE CROWS

THE public officials of the Crow Indian tribal organization were: The chief, subordinate chiefs, chief medicine-man or religious leader, chief weather-prophet, camp chief, the camp criers or heralds, and the dog-soldiers. There was system in all of their doings. They had among themselves law and order more effectively prevalent than among any community of white people I have known. Their laws were few, but they were well enforced—or, better expressed, were well obeyed without need for enforcement.

Blackfoot was the chief of my band of the Crows —the Kick-in-the-Belly people—all during the time of my active life among them. The chief weather-prophet who held longest the office and kept longest the public confidence was Pretty Louse, a woman. The camp chief, or camp leader, who for several years held this office and who was most highly regarded, was Father of All Buffalo.

The camp chief was spoken of ordinarily as the "lucky man." He determined when the camp should move, and where. His proper position in such move-ment was at the head of the procession. Nobody ever should cross in front of him. He must have at all times an altogether unobstructed view of the country ahead of him. He chose the site of the next camp. He appointed his own assistants, and with these he allotted positions for the lodges of the various family clans, or he decided any disputes that might arise as to desirability of location. In fact, I never knew of any actual disputes of this sort that had to be settled by him. Official notice was given when it was determined that the camp should move. The comprehensive question of the desirability of movement was decided by a council of the old men. But having decided, the details as to exact time and conditions of movement were worked out by the camp chief. The weather-prophet and the chief medi-cine-man might be consulted, or either of these might interject his advice if the circumstances ap-peared to make it needful. The camp crier and his assistants—regularly, old men—mounted their po-nies and rode about the village calling out, for example:

"Raise up your bodies. Open your ears. Listen. To-morrow we move to Rotten Sun-dance River" (their name for Clark's Fork of the Yellowstone). "Our scouts have seen there plenty of buffalo. The wind is blowing right, and the weather-prophet says it will continue thus for many days."

In the movement, with the camp chief at the head, pickets always were riding out from the flanks, the front, the rear, to watch for enemies as well as for game. If game was discovered, the effort was to travel where the wind would blow from them to us instead of from us to them, so as to diminish the likelihood of their catching our odor in their sensitive nostrils and thus becoming alarmed into flight. "Keep watch of the wind" was a fundamental rule of action for scouting of this kind. If the atmospheric movement was so quiet as to be imperceptible to ordinary bodily senses, a handful of dust would be picked up and allowed to trickle from the extended hand while the eyes made minute observation as to the direction in which it might float as it fell to the ground.

It was against the law for any one willfully to chase game directly toward a moving band of people; a worse offense if the people were encamped. If such act were done, the presumption was that it had been willful, not accidental. A heavy burden of proof was put upon the defendant if he should claim innocent intent. Even if this result unintentionally ensued from any particular person's activity, this one had a penalty inflicted upon him.

I joined one time in mischievously chasing some buffalo into a camp. The animals tore up several tepees in their wild and indiscriminate efforts to get away into the open country. We sportive young men—two Indians and myself—dodged away and came into the camp from another direction; but we were found out. The dog-soldiers conducted us out and informed us we were to remain a certain distance outside of the camp's boundaries for the period of one moon—one month. It was a distressing penalty; but we stayed out. We should have received much worse treatment had we violated the order. We often hungered for food as well as for society. A few times our sweethearts slipped out at night and placed food where we could find it, but they too were watched and were subject to penalty if discovered, so this could not be depended upon as a regular comfort to us. In addition to our ostracism, our people had to pay fines by gifts to other people, particularly to the families whose lodges had been damaged. My adopted father had to give away many ponies as a consequence of my indiscretion. I never again entered upon any such adventure.

The dog-soldiers were the police force, or regular army, of the chief of the band or tribe. Each body of dog-soldiers had its chief, and he acted often upon his own initiative. Even the individual dog-soldiers occasionally took measures of law enforcement without waiting for orders. But they all were under the general direction of the tribal or subordinate chief. These policemen enforced all camp rules or rules of the march. They restrained anxious ones who might rush prematurely forward when a body of hunters was stalking game. They held back, likewise, whatever warriors in time of battle might put the general plan out of adjustment by hasty or inconsiderate action in an effort to gain personal glory or advantage. In every way the dog-soldiers were the immediate directors of conduct.

Such dog-soldier bands were a feature of every tribal organization among the old plains Indians. The Sioux, the Cheyennes, the Arapahoes, the Piegans, the Shoshones, all of the tribes that I knew, had them. Historians have written of these tribal policemen, used for internal government, as though they were fraternal organizations or warrior organizations, such as the Elk Warriors or the Crazy Dog Warriors of the Cheyennes, or the Kit Fox or the Red Stick societies of the Crows. Some writers have made reference to "dog-soldier bands" as having been the most desperate and fierce and bloodthirsty of all the old plains raiders. It seems the term "dog-soldier" hit the writers' fancy as implying the utmost of wild ferocity, so the orderly home policemen had attributed to them, especially, many of the gory deeds done by the Indians who resisted the movement of emigrants across the plains. In fact, though, any certain dog-soldier might have been either ferocious or gentle, either a great warrior or one whose mental make-up inclined him to peaceful life. Anyway, that was the Crow Indian dog-soldier situation.

I enjoyed always the movement of camp. We had no wagons. The travel was on horseback or afoot, with the camp paraphernalia loaded upon or into frames or sagging skins supported by lodge-poles attached to the sides of horses and having the rear end dragging along on the ground. Bad roads made but little difference, as this hindrance does when wheeled vehicles are used. The facility with which Indians might go anywhere with their lodge-pole transports postponed their use of the wagons which the Government issued to them.

I liked to have children with me on a march of moving Crows. And it appeared they liked to be with me. Many a time as Cherry and I would be getting ready to go, some boy or girl would call out to me: "Wait for me, brother! I want to go with you." Sometimes actual jealousy would be manifested concerning my attentions to them. I've seen them throw sticks at each other because of the ill feeling aroused by competitive desire for our approbation. It was an occasion bringing me special enjoyment if I should kill a deer or an elk along the way. It is a recollection held in a favored corner of my memory, this event that brought a swarm of little Indians to do the butchering for me. Oh, how lively they were in this work! How rapidly and efficiently they could skin and cut up a deer!

Fifteen miles in a day was a good march for a big camp of Crows. They could go faster, but usually they did not do so. When the camp chief had located the exact site for setting up the lodges, all were notified, or the leading ones were followed. Most of the camping-places were specially favored and were occupied on each occasion of travel along the trails. In such case each lodge was set up on the same space it had occupied on previous occasions. If there had been recent camping here or if repeated campings had befouled the land, a new position was chosen or assigned, either for the individual lodge or for the entire camp.

The same positions with relation to each other were occupied by lodges at each of the camps. Near relatives set up their tepees side by side, groups were made up of related families. My group was the Burnt Mouth clan. The arrangement thus was good public policy as well as agreeable to personal inclination. Relatives ordinarily will help each other in time of distress or shield each other in time of danger more readily than will mere acquaintances. Since the tribe was made up of clans and families and these were made up of individual people, whatever was good for individuals and families was good for the tribe as a whole.

Twenty poles, two of them guy-poles, made up the standard frame of a large lodge. Perhaps only eighteen poles in all might be used. The two guy-poles were the longest, these to shift the top opening as might be necessary to meet the variations of the wind and keep the interior heat and smoke circulating upward. The covering of the framework was of tanned buffalo-skins sewed together. In later times, other skins were used, and still later the use of canvas was adopted, this material being now the only tepee covering available.

The tepee opening faced the east. The whole encampment was in approximate circular form, so the individual east-facing necessitated that some of the openings were toward the outside of the circle, some toward the inside, some toward the neighboring tepee at the side. In every case, provision was made for convenient access to the interior of the great circle. The lodges were but a few feet apart, and brush was piled between them so as to make a fence enclosing the entire central camp space. Bar openings were provided at places for the driving of horses in and out. The lodges being so close to one another and the walls so thin enabled neighbors to talk together while each might remain in his own lodge.

The establishing of a lodge began with the selection of its central point on the ground and dumping out there the *pasflesche* containers of the luggage, the family household equipment and personal effects being put into a pile at first; but soon after the conical shelter was up, everything belonging inside of it was put into its proper place. When the luggage had been piled up, the first act of construction was to set up the household tripod out in front of the planned opening of the tepee. Upon this tripod was hung the shield and the medicine of the head of this lodge. These revered objects proclaimed to all observers the identity of the principal inhabitant of the shelter before which they were displayed. More important, they typified his reverent mental attitude toward the Sun—the substantial or tangible typification of First Maker, the Great Spirit—and they protected him and his family from harmful intrusion. The shield must face always exactly to the east, to catch the first rays of the rising sun. I have often seen a grumbling man readjust his shield that had been placed so that its face was not fully exposed in the right direction.

The shield was carried on the march by the wife or daughter. It was a special honor to be the shield-bearer. The tripod was set up by this same one or by her and some helper. The women ordinarily did all of the work of taking down and setting up the lodges. A man might help, particularly if his wife was not strong and the toil was heavy, but help usually was by exchange of work among the women. It was understood to be their business, and therefore they were more proficient at it than were the men. A man doing much of this or any other work among the women would be looked upon as one who was toiling thus among them merely to be in their company. By the women he would be regarded as a "softy," a shallow courtier whose presence was not desired.

The lower interior wall of the lodge was lined with tanned buffalo-skins, or in later times with muslin sheeting. Each occupant of the lodge had a special assigned floor-space for his bed and his special section of wall-lining at the head of his bed space. The wall-linings were decorated, the decorations in the case of men being by a painting or paintings upon the surface, depicting for each man his past commendable deeds. I had a lining that accumulated several paintings during a lapse of some years. One picture represented me at the battle of Pryor Creek, where we fought all day against the great body of Sioux. The artist was imaginative enough to show me boldly running afoot after the fleeing Sioux and just in the act of touching one with my coupstick. Another drawing exhibited me on horseback and driving rapidly before me a band of horses I had stolen—presumably from enemies. In yet another space on my wall was an area where nothing but horse-tracks appeared. This simple sketch told to an admiring Crow Indian world the whole story of my wonderful capabilities as a horse-thief. It cost me more than a trivial expenditure to get these paintings done. They all were Crow Indian work. But while all Indians are inclined to artistic drawing, not all of them keep at it long enough to become proficient. Hence, a good Indian artist got well paid for his labors.

We slept around the inner wall of the lodge, ordinarily about twenty feet in diameter, with our heads to the wall and our feet toward the center. Extra walls running from side to center usually were suspended at night to separate the segments of ground floor-space belonging to each sleeper. At all times the special *pasflesche* bag or bags containing the personal effects of the inhabitant of the compartment were kept at or beside the head of his bed. They served to weight the edges of the lining wall and thus keep it close to the ground so that wind could not blow directly in upon him. The beds of the head of the household and his wife—or his first or favorite wife—regularly were at the head of the lodge, the side directly opposite the flap opening. The old woman or household slave slept beside the entrance, to guard it. By the bed of the head man was kept always a pipe and tobacco, these lying on the ground or hung up, in either case serving as a continual invitation to smoke.

I slept clad in breech-cloth only, according to the Indian way. Bed coverings were used as needed. That mode of night undressing became with me a fixed habit that has not yet changed. In this and in other ways the Indians were like other people— some of them clean and careful, some of them not. I learned during those times how to keep away bed-bugs and lice. It seemed not all of the Indian people learned this, or they neglected to apply their knowledge. The simple procedure Cherry adopted was to keep always about our beds some mountain-mahogany leaves. The bugs avoided this odor, which to us was a pleasant one.

The lodge-fire was in the central space in winter, the smoke going upward and out of the open conical top. Much heat also went up, of course, but the camps always were set up where wood fuel was plentiful, so the lodge was kept warm even during the coldest weather. In summer weather the fire was made outside. Here or inside the utensil of first importance for cooking was the tripod. Its three legs were of wood, the upper ends tied together by a piece of chain or a broad strip of buffalo or other rawhide. Brass camp-kettles were mainly the cooking vessels during my camping days. They were very high in price, but the women preferred them because of the beauty of polish that might be brought out upon them. Everything was cooked in them, yet I never heard of any one having been poisoned by their use.

In the hunting periods we camped a week or so—maybe longer, maybe not so long—on one spot. Scouts went out and in as they sought the location of the buffalo. War-parties, mainly horse-stealing war-parties, also were sallying forth and returning. All skins, winter or summer, were tanned by the women. The winter skins only were salable as robes, because then the hair or fur was at its best. The summer yield was used for various purposes, mainly for lodge coverings. The deer- and elk-skins were the material that made our moccasins and our ordinary clothing. A buffalo-robe or a blanket served as an overcoat when needed, or often such article served as a substitute for an entire suit of clothing, with only the ever-present Indian breech-cloth under it. A buffalo-skin lodge might last several years, but each year there were many new lodges. The structures were of ample proportions. I have seen magnificent family lodges having a base diameter as wide as forty feet, with poles forty or more feet in height. I believe, though, the Mountain Crows had as splendid lodges as any tribe. One name for them as a tribe was "Large Lodges." By contrast, the Bannacks were known as the "Bad Lodge" or the "Worthless Lodge" Indians. In past times and to this day the Indian sign-talk gesture for designating the Bannacks as a tribe is made by shaping the fingers up for a conical tepee and then flicking them forward to indicate disdain.

Young bull buffalo-skins were preferred for *pasflesche* bags. They were tough, but were easily tanned. The big skins of the old bulls were hard to tan. They were held cheap in sales, hence their main use was for cutting up into straps for packing and for every purpose where a strap might serve well. The wool from the heads of old bulls was made use of in upholstering and as material for spinning and plaiting into lariats.

As food, the cows were preferred, although anything up to three years of age was acceptable. A three-year-old cow was the choice. The best meat was the tongue and the hump ribs. The back-fat was a much desired nutriment. I have stripped off this yellow back-fat four inches in thickness. The brisket, the tongue, the liver, the lining of the paunch, were eaten raw. The eating of raw liver was regarded as being good medicine for the eyes. To make the medicine more effective, some of the bitter gall was sprinkled over it. The bones and flesh of the cut-off lower leg were crushed and cooked, for their flavor, as soup. In the original butchering of the animal, after one side was skinned, the hump was cut off. This was necessary in order to roll the carcass for skinning the other side. It is a case for extraordinary appliances if one attempts to roll the body of a buffalo over. The tendency is to spin on the hump and fall back on the same side. Because of the hump, a wallowing live buffalo could not roll over.

Wild-game meat—buffalo, deer, elk, mountain sheep, with buffalo the first choice for regular daily use—was in those days the sustaining food of the Crows. It was eaten fresh or was dried in the sun and pounded into powder, after which it was stuffed into cleaned intestines or into rawhide containers. Wild berries or fruits might or might not be mixed with it. Hot melted fat was poured in last, to seal it so it would keep. When they discarded the beef that was issued to them during the buffalo days, they kept some parts of it—the tallow and brains for use in tanning, the long strip of sinew along the back for sewing. When cattle came first among them they considered these animals as half-way between the buffalo and the horse, from their resemblance to the buffalo in appearance and to the horse in amenability to taming. So the Indian sign-talk gesture for cattle became a composite movement. The sign for buffalo, the index fingers curved beside the temples, was made. This was followed by the sign for horse, the first two fingers of the right hand straddling the extended index finger of the left hand. Finally came a scattered tapping of the left forearm by the tips of the right fingers, signifying that the object under consideration was spotted. The composition was then translatable into the words, "buffalo-horse-spotted." This indicates the old Indian conception of cattle.

Dogs are supposed by many white people to be a food favored by all Indians. I can not speak for other tribes, but I know the Crows did not regard them as a delicacy. I myself never ate any except on one occasion. My second Indian wife killed and cooked a young dog as a special feast for some Sioux visiting at our place. In this instance, and doubtless in most other instances, the idea was a religious one rather than a catering to appetite. Dogs always were regarded by Indians as a special friend of mankind, as his reliable guardian while he slept, and to eat of their flesh was a sort of complimentary recognition of their virtues. The Indians always had and still have lots of dogs, of all kinds or any kind, just so they are dogs. They served in the old times a most useful purpose in giving warning of the approach of any stranger to the camp, like the cackling geese that once saved Rome. In yet earlier times, before the Indians got horses, the dogs were used for hauling the travois when traveling. Wolves and dogs mingled occasionally, I believe. I have seen them in peaceable association, and I have seen Indian dogs that evidently were half wolf.

But meat was not the only Indian food. They knew of many edible roots, and the women dug them and preserved them for winter use. They understood the procedure of drying and storing up plums, choke-cherries, service-berries, raspberries, and currants. Every woman had a root-digger. Usually it was a seasoned ash stick whittled to a point. It was two and a half feet long, the butt two or more inches in diameter, and at the end of the butt was a knob covered by buckskin that enclosed a wad of buffalo wool, this to protect the abdomen as the woman leaned against the end of the stick to shove its point under the root being pried out. I have seen women char their root-stick points in the fire, smooth them, and grease them. They said the treatment hardened as well as smoothed the point.

The principal root used as food was the one called by various names—Indian turnip, pomme blanche, ground-apple, white-apple. It grew on benches and side hills. It varied from three to seven inches in length, and a large one would be an inch and a half in diameter. The skin of this root was black, tough, stiff almost like the bark of a tree. They might be stored away with the bark on, or this might be peeled off soon after the digging or at times of leisure thereafter, in which event they were chopped up for drying.

Artichokes came second as an edible root. These were from one to three inches in length. They were washed, but not peeled, before being dried to store away for winter. They became quite brittle in storage. These as well as the other roots were boiled well before being eaten as food. The Crows did not use much the bitter-root which was and still is so popular with the Flatheads and other Indians. The meat of the Indian turnip is white.

Some poison roots were known and avoided. I knew of one young woman who died from such poisoning. A Bannack man visitor to us also perished in this manner. But this was not the principal peril of root digging. Many a woman, among all of the Indian tribes, was killed or taken into captivity by raiding enemies while she was out digging roots. Many a child intent upon these explorations for food thus lost its life or was taken away to grow up a permanent member of some other tribe. One of the police duties of the dog-soldiers was to keep watch of the women and children at these times and to restrain them from going out too far from camp or from other aid near by. But occasionally, there was lax guarding or thoughtless or disobedient wandering. In such event, look out for a tragedy!

Cottonwood ice-cream was one of the food delicacies enjoyed by the Crows. When the spring sap flowed upward, it produced this toothsome dessert. The outer bark of the tree was peeled off, then the peeled surface was scraped. The yield was a mucilaginous or jelly-like froth that tasted like ice-cream. The bigger the tree, the better the taste and the greater the result. This sap would keep in containing vessels for days, even a week or two, without special effort at preservation. Buckets and cans would be filled and friends would be invited to partake. Lots of young fellows would treat their sweethearts by peeling the bark from a cottonwood-tree.

Box-elder syrup was another sweet-tooth satis-
fier. This likewise was obtainable only when the sap
was running. Two notches would be cut into the
trunk of the tree and the flavored juice would be
sucked by the mouth or drawn off into containers.
Boiling it resulted in a syrup comparable to that
derived from the maple-tree. The Indian sign for a
box-elder tree is made by gesturing as if cutting two
notches and then applying the mouth to the cuts.

Yes, we had at all times plenty of food and a
variety of it. Everybody was well provided for in
the matter of both food and shelter. There were not
in those days any hoboes nor common beggars
among the Crows. Even now, I'd rather be penni-
less and disabled among the Crow Indians than to
be in like condition among any people of whom I
have knowledge. They were then and yet are, although now to a lesser degree, very generous in
scattering comforts among their own people.

Kinnikinick, the native material used for smoking, was derived from the red willows that grow
everywhere here along the mountain and valley
streams. As usual, the women gathered the supply.
They cut bundles of willow sticks and brought them
into camp. The outside red bark was stripped off at
once, while the sticks yet were fresh. This outside
covering was discarded. The inner bark then was

shaved off and laid out to dry and curl up in the sun. In hot weather it would cure fully in a day or two. It then was pulverized. In use it was mixed with tobacco, half and half, or in such proportion as suited the taste of the individual user. A beaded buckskin bag was the standard container for the mixture prepared for smoking. A slender separate compartment in the long bag held the pipe-stem. The pipe bowl was carried loose with the kinniki-nick. The pipe ordinarily was of red soapstone, but sometimes a blue pipe was preferred. The blue material was what the miners call serpentine. I know a mine of it near the present town of Red Lodge. The preferred tobacco was the plug, sweetened by the manufacturer for chewing purposes. Shavings from the plug were carved off as needed, a piece of board known as the tobacco-board being used as the base of operation. Such a board was a regular feature of the household equipment, and it had near one end a perforation through which a thong was tied so that it might be hung up when not in use. I have seen old, but treasured, tobacco-boards almost cut to pieces by repetition of the whittle, whittle, whittle, incident to shaving off on their surfaces the shreds from tobacco plugs.

Not many Crows smoked as a confirmed habit. The smoking usually was in moderation, and many of them smoked only as a religious rite. I never knew my wife Cherry to smoke. My second Crow wife did not smoke during her young womanhood; but as she grew older she became a medicine-woman, and then she smoked as a part of her professional activities.

The peeled willow sticks were held as being sacred, or as deserving of tender handling in their disposal as useless leavings. I got into trouble one time on this point. An old woman was working at peeling off the bark and had a pile of the stripped sticks beside her. As conversation was being carried on I unwittingly picked up one of them and broke it in two.

"Oh, my son!" she screamed at me as she grabbed for my hands. She then called excitedly for my adopted mother, who was in the adjoining lodge. The mother reprimanded and explained to me. She was in great fear of imminent bad luck for me. "You are likely to be hurt by your horse or in some other way," she warned me. "You must be very careful for a long time, and you must never again break one of these sticks." I felt ashamed, and I actually made unusual efforts to be careful, as she had admonished me. I believed what she told me.

I was adopted as their son by various elderly Indian couples during a long period of years. I was concurrently the son of different parents, sometimes in the same camp, but usually in differing camps. My wife and I also adopted some children, but only one lived altogether with us. It was regarded as productive of good luck if one adopted a child. In any case the voluntarily chosen parent and child felt tied together as such, and in their subsequent life they lent to each other such special comfort or assistance as might be needed. My fathers and mothers by adoption always were the leaders in holding me up in a praiseworthy light when any act of mine gave the least ground for praise.

Adoption was by initial request of the prospective foster-parents. It was a complimentary advance, and the favor was not often denied. After a feast and felicitations, the ceremony was ended by the new father sprinkling water upon the adopted one's head. A dance followed, and many presents were given away by the happy foster-parents, as indicative of their joy. Often it occurred that a child would be given altogether to the new father and mother, to take up its regular abode with them. Perhaps it would visit its actual parents every day, or spend much time with them, but its home was with the second parental couple. The burden of supporting a large family of children never was felt by any Crow married couple. They always could find some one else near at hand who wanted the children and would support them, perhaps some one living in a lodge regularly pitched right beside their own. It was a standing custom for the first-born child of any young couple to be given as a present to the paternal grandparents when it became about a year old and could be weaned. This child made its home always thereafter with these grandparents. Other children, if enough came to be a burden, could be disposed of in a like manner. This old-time practice was good for the young parents, it was good for the elderly foster-parents, it was good for the tribe, as it left physically capable young couples free from the worries of providing for their children and thus enabled them to go on producing others. Adoptions sometimes were made before the birth of some expected infant. The adoption-dance in the old times was a beautiful ceremonial movement. It was called the beaver-dance. It still is performed among the Crows. I am doubtful, though, about the clean propriety of the present-day beaver-dance, or the "hot-foot" dance, as it sometimes is designated.

The number of genuine-offspring children in any family was not easily discoverable. If one said, "This is my son," or, "This is my father," or made a similar declaration, the statement never was questioned. If any couple had several children when they apparently should have had but one, or if any had none or but few when it seemed they ought to have many, it was not polite to make reference to the situation. The fact that a woman carried on her back a baby was not proof that it was her own. Indeed, the young mothers ordinarily did not carry their own babies, this burden being assumed by old women or by elderly helpers who had but few children or none. It was bad luck for the natural parent to give a name to his or her own child. This service was performed by a special friend, upon request, or a name came spontaneously by reason of some peculiar event or some situation connected with the life of the named one.

The son-in-law of an Indian man was treated with most respectful consideration. The father-in-law ever was bragging about the high qualities of his kinsman thus connected. Perhaps back of this was the feeling of pride in his daughter, which impelled him to hold up her husband in the best possible light. At any rate, the son-in-law was addressed as "My son," and it appeared he received at all times more attention than the natural sons.

The mother-in-law and her daughter's husband never spoke to each other nor dealt directly with each other in any manner. Neither of them ever mentioned the name of the other. She spoke of him as "My daughter's husband," or "That man there," and he made reference to her as "This girl's mother," or by some other distant designation. Even though they were entirely friendly in feeling toward each other, doing for one another all sorts of favors that fittingly might be done, they never came into open association as acquaintances. I treated my own mother-in-law in this way. In fact, she would not allow any other kind of treatment. If she wanted to convey to me any message, she would address some one else in a way that would effect the result desired. She might say, "Tell my daughter's husband his food is ready," or, "Cherry, your husband's tobacco and pipe are ready for him," even though I were standing right there to hear for myself. She expected her message to go through the channel, though, and it always went through. I learned never to give the appearance of having heard until it got to me according to due form. Had I ever pretended to have received directly her communication, she likely would have denied having said anything whatever. But I never tried this.

The mutually respectful and dignified relations of the son-in-law with his wife's father was extended to include his brothers-in-law. These collateral relatives by marriage were fully considerate of each other, but they never became familiar, in the low sense. Brothers-in-law never joked each other; their communications were serious. Each of them might be disposed to vulgar speech in association with other people, but when they came into common company, all vulgarity was avoided. For one to tell an obscene story or utter any obscene remark in the presence of his brother-in-law was a grave violation of good manners. If such utterance were made, it was construed as an insult to the brother-in-law hearer, and he went at once out of his relative's company. However, I never knew of any instance where this act of rebuke was properly due. Had it been thus, the offending man would have been held in general contumely until he had wiped out his guilt by the indiscriminate giving of many presents, even to his complete impoverishment.

Care was needful in a man's conduct toward all of the wife's relatives. The entire two sets of family connections kept on particularly decorous terms toward each other. On my part, I had no blood relations in the tribe, so the dealing was a one-sided affair for me. It was not permissible for me to make joking remarks nor indulge in any sort of familiarity with my brother-in-law's wife, as well as with his immediate family. I could have playful times, though, with my wife's cousins. They were on the outskirts of the proscribed bounds, although not entirely outside. I stirred up various scandalous situations before I became well versed in the due etiquette of Crow Indian society. But the people were patient with me. It seems they believed I had in my heart the right disposition, and that, if I stayed long enough with them, I finally should become cultivated in mind and polished in manners.

The personal name of the dead was not spoken, except as this same name might be borne by a living person and spoken as applicable to this living one. The dead associate was referred to as "the man who rode the bob-tail horse," or as "the woman who made this beaded vest for me," or in some other descriptive way, as though the name were not known to the speaker. Speaking one's own name, in ordinary daily life, was avoided. Such act was looked upon as deprecable self-advertising. It was permissible, or even an indication of bravery, if one declared his own name in addressing himself to a known enemy. The theory was that he was altogether willing the enemy should know his identity and thus be enabled readily to find him when this enemy should want to fight. I got out and declared my own name—Horse Rider—on one notable occasion. It was when we were having the all-day battle with the Sioux, at the mouth of Pryor Creek. But within a few moments thereafter, I was running away like a coyote. Too many Sioux began shooting at me. I always was careful, not brave. Bravery is foolishness.

Oh, it was a great life. I had a good wife who made for me fine buckskin clothing, kept my hair in the best of order, kept me scented with sweet-grass, had my bed and my entire lodge always in neat condition, prepared for me the sweat-bath lodge whenever I wanted to use it, did everything that a woman can do to make a man comfortable and happy. I alternated at hunting and doing duty at the agency or in the military service, each a congenial employment and each bringing in plenty of funds to sustain us. At all times I had ample leisure for lazy loafing and dreaming and visiting. In summer I wore nothing but breech-cloth and moccasins when out in the camps away from the agency or the fort. As I idled and smoked, my wife sat by my side and did sewing or beadwork. She sat with her legs and feet drawn under and concealed by her dress, as was deemed proper for a woman. I sat with feet and legs projected in full view, as was permissible for a man.

Full clothing was worn only in winter. Or when hunting, the men put on leggings, to keep briers or brush from scratching the legs when either walking or riding. Also, if I moved about the camps at night, I always put on a pair of leggings, even during the hottest of summer evenings. This precaution of wearing leggings in night excursions was necessary in order to keep the dogs from biting my legs. The bare legs of a white man after dark, either from their odor or their appearance, always excited attack by the Indian dogs. They never bit the Indian legs nor did they assail a white man if he had on a pair of Indian leggings.

"Where shall we spend the evening?" Cherry might say. "There is to be a dance at Red Horse's lodge, but we do not care much for those people. Let us go and visit with my cousin in the next village."

Away we would go, half a mile or a mile, to the cousin's lodge. We would be seated at the head of the lodge, ever the place for welcome visitors. Water would be brought for us to have a drink. An hour or more of conversation followed. The Indians liked to hear of the strange ways of white people. They wondered at these peculiarities, the same as white people wonder at the customs prevailing exclusively among Indians. Supper would be served. Pemmican, doughnuts or "Indian bread," coffee sweetened always in the pot, some sort of dessert handed to each one in a spoon—most likely a wooden spoon made by the deft hands of a woman. The wife of the owner of the lodge was the servant of the "table"—the ground covered by a clean skin or a piece of cloth. Or the old woman who was attached to every household having its full complement would do the menial office. In either case one or more young girl helpers were likely to assist, under direction of their elder. The men were jolly, but never rude and brassy. The women were mirthful, but always decorously so. Somebody might give utterance to some such pretended deprecatory inquiry as:

"Cherry, how did you come to get this swift white man as your husband? You can not make pretty clothing for him; you can not cook his food right; you are lazy; you are entirely no good. Tell me—how did you fool him into marrying you?"

Oh, Sun, forgive me the renegade thought: I love with my whole heart the old ways of the Indian.

OLD CROW INDIAN CUSTOMS AND BELIEFS

A LARIAT rope was the first article of armament for a Crow Indian during the past days when they were at liberty to make use of it according to the fashion then prevailing. The choice lariat was one made of spun and plaited buffalo-hair. It hung tucked into the top of the breech-cloth or into an outside belt, continually accessible on instant notice. It never was absent unless the Indian were asleep, and then it lay beside him. He was ever ready to capture his own horse and mount it for a hurried ride, or if at any moment an enemy's horse came in his range of view, he had at hand the means of rearranging conditions so that the animal should belong to him. The lariat may serve as the best token of their constant pursuit, stealing horses. A good fighter was commended for his bravery, a good hunter and gatherer of skins was regarded as a capable provider for his family and a worthy man, but an enterprising and successful horse-thief was looked upon as both adventurous and thrifty.

Every full-panoplied warrior had a war-bonnet,

although there was not often an opportunity to use it, since fighting usually occurred on sudden contact. I had a war-bonnet and other equipment appertaining to mortal combat, but I never made use of them in the way they were intended to be used. The only pitched and long-continued battle I got into was when I was out on an errand from the agency and not expecting to meet with such a situation. I wore, though, an eagle feather sticking up from the crown of my head as a regular part of my everyday dress.

I counted personal coups a few times. This was done by touching the person of an enemy, either before or just after his death. The touch might be made by the hand or by some object held in the hand. A special coupstick, a slender rod well decorated, belonged in the equipment of the warrior, but it was for style rather than for necessity. The praiseworthiness of the personal coup lay in the evident bravery manifested by the full contact essential to its accomplishment. At the end of the battle of Pryor Creek, when we were chasing the Sioux over the hills, I counted coup upon one of their women. She was on a horse, but I outrode her and caught up with her. I lashed her once with my pony-whip and turned aside to go on. Just as I passed her she jerked up a pistol and shot at me. Although a coup counted upon a woman was not ranked highly, it seemed this one came near being very expensive for me. Coups upon prisoners taken were counted, but the acceptance of them as such was by mere technicality.

The captured gun of an enemy was a basis for a coup-count. A second coup could be counted by any companion who should grab the weapon and wrest it from the hands of the original captor. So, when such original captor might return to camp with a gun taken in warfare, there was a hurrying forward and a scuffling among the people—men, women, or children—to seize and get possession of the implement. Whoever got it kept it as his own property.

Horses brought back from a foray likewise were rushed after and led away as their own by people other than the one who had risked his life in their capture. He got acclaim, distinction, honorable mention, was serenaded, and perhaps his father gave away another horse or two in celebration of the glorious achievement of his son. Of course, this brave and cunning exploit and the generosity were kept in mind by the people, and afterward this one received presents of other horses or of such property as he might need. The point was, he proved that his motive for going out upon the hazardous undertaking had not been avarice, but merely for the honor of himself and the tribe. In allowing acquaintances to divest him of all his booty, he had shown full confidence in their dealing generously with him on some other occasion. And they did so. A man's wealth usually was according to the estimation in which he was held by his people. What he had was not what he had earned or obtained by personal effort. It came mostly from gifts by admirers. The Indians were not altogether communists, but they closely approached this social condition. While a man might have much property, it all was presumably at the command of any of his tribesmen who might ask for it. And pride prevented such asking except in case of actual need.

The finder of an object was not the keeper. If one were out alone and found something of value, it was his duty to retrieve it and bring it into the camp. But he must give it away to some one else, preferably to some one not a near relative. If two or more people were traveling together and if one of them saw some lost object worthy of recovery, he himself did not pick it up. He informed a companion, and this one took possession of the article as his own. It is easily comprehensible, knowing such rules of behavior, how an Indian can look upon the average white man as being one whose mind is ruled by avarice.

Scalpings and mutilations and torture at times

are chargeable against the old-time Indians. But on various occasions I have seen Crow men become nervous while cutting off a scalp. In two instances I saw the scalping victor grow nauseated, pause for a spell of vomiting, and afterward hesitatingly resume his hair-raising operation. I myself never essayed to scalp any head. It made me sick enough to look at another doing it. I never saw any torturing except in one instance when from a hiding-place I watched some members of another tribe slowly put to death one of my companion Crows whom they had captured. Young Crow people of to-day shiver in horror when I tell them this story.

The youths and the young men—that is, usually from fifteen to about thirty years of age—were the warriors. It was a warrior act to go searching for enemy horses as well as to go searching for the enemy in person. I know of a few instances where older men, forty or past, went out for horses. The oldest one I can recall was about fifty. He got one horse—and he promptly gave it away. I never knew of any certain rule among the Crows, such as existed among the Sioux and the Cheyennes, for fixing an exact high age-limit for warfare activity. But it actually was limited by age—about forty, I believe.

I have heard and read how an Indian always will stand by his friend to the uttermost limit of danger.

But they will not do any such thing. They will stay a while, but not to the uttermost limit. At any rate, my experience proved this to be an exception to their otherwise admirable traits. Twice—once in the hills north of the Yellowstone and once far up on Tongue River—Indian companions of mine ran away and left me in distressful circumstances when it seemed to me they should have tried to rescue me. In each case I got away by my own efforts. From this intimation of Indian superprudence I make one exception—Mitch Buoyer. I believe this Frenchman-Sioux would stay fully up to or beyond the essential needs. That was my belief about him, formed after many years of intimate association. It was confirmed irrevocably when, while serving as a pathfinder only, he remained with Custer and died with him, although that officer had released his guide from further compulsory duty.

Purchasing of brides was not a prevalent custom among the Crows of my active days among them. The young man gave presents to his bride. The brothers-in-law and others of her relatives gave many gifts to the couple, whatever they might need to set up their own lodge—blankets, robes, utensils, such things as would be useful to them. The gifts were comparable to a loan, as were all gifts among the Indians. Although there were no debts recognized as collectable by compulsion, honor led to compensatory giving, either at once or at a future time when the recipient became able to return the favor.

Visitors from other tribes received many presents and gave only a few. Our people got even by going at another time to return the friendly call. The hosts regularly were the free givers. Even an enemy, if he had come peaceably and openly as a visitor, might receive presents to take away with him. At least, it was unlawful to harm an enemy if his entrance into the camp was for peaceable purposes. Quite the contrary, though, if the invasion of the camp or its environs was for predatory action.

I stumbled once right into the borders of a Sioux camp while I was out for stealing horses. The horses snorted and lunged to the length of their picket-ropes, perhaps frightened more by the white-man odor than by my mere appearance among them. I dived into hiding in a little cave. I found there a she-dog and her puppies. The mother-dog likewise evidently did not enjoy my kind of aroma. She snarled and barked. I had to stay there, and I tried to soothe her. She kept on threatening me, but no attack was made upon me. Her continued racket, though, brought from a squaw in a lodge near by, "Shut up! Quit fighting your puppies!" And, after another spell of snarling, the woman shouted out, "Shut up, or I'll bring a club and beat you." Her scolding quieted the quarrelsome animal, or it learned I intended no harm to the brood. I stayed there about three hours, to be sure nobody had observed my presence among the horses and was patiently waiting for me to reappear. When I crept out, the first desirable thing that appeared in my pathway was a mule. I captured it and rode quietly away. Out from the camps, I flourished my buffalo-hair rope and looped it over the neck of a loose horse. It was a good horse. With the horse and the mule I returned alone to the home camp, as my original companions had separated from me when we first approached the enemy lodges and had gone away without any horses. At the home camp I was led about the village and made a hero. The horse and the mule were taken from me, of course, but for two or three weeks I had most of the girls there for sweethearts.

Ten or fifteen Sioux men came and visited a Crow village at the foot of the mountains east of the Stillwater River during the hostile days of the old Mission agency. Our camp scouts saw them coming and ran in to tell our people. We all went to the outskirts of the camp and shook hands with them. There were many repetitions of "How," "How," "How," the universal Indian greeting word, which they probably learned from white men. In Chief Blackfoot's lodge he introduced me to the Sioux as his son, saying, "Here is his mother," as he pointed toward his wife, who was born a Sioux and was captured during her early womanhood. She was yet so much Sioux that her Crow speech was imperfect. The presentation of me as her son put me at once into high favor with the visitors. One of them said: "These kind of men we have with us too. They have strong hearts. They are good, because they know us and also the white people. We like to have them, for they talk to the agent in our interest." They condemned the Indian white men who guided soldiers, who, they said, killed women and children without reason. Nevertheless, they said, "The soldiers have good hearts." They spoke of prospecting miners as being very bad men. "They kill us and cut us up," the Sioux complained. The conversations were carried on with Blackfoot, who knew fairly well the Sioux language, perhaps having acquired it from his wife. She listened to much of it, and at times she intervened as an interpreter. These Sioux were our guests three or four days and nights. The wife of one of them was a captive among us. She was returned to him on this occasion, and she went away with him. After a few years, though, she came back and stayed with the Crows. Notwithstanding I was officially their enemy for many years, both as a member of the Crow tribe and as a scout for white soldiers battling against them, I always liked the Sioux. They were terrible as enemies, but they were an amiable people as friends.

The Crows mutilated the dead bodies of enemies, the same as other of the plains tribes did. I have seen dead enemy Indians dragged about the camps by a rope tied around the neck. I have seen them after cutting and slashing had been done. On the few occasions where it appeared to me that mutilations were about to take place, I absented myself from the vicinity.

Quarrels serious in nature were infrequent among us. Incipient trouble ordinarily was smothered by the intervention of mutual friends. "Keep your heart good" was a first motto of conduct. It was ever "for the good of the tribe" that differences were adjusted by arbitration or by mutual forgiveness. I never had any quarrel with a Crow, but an Assiniboine visitor to us once vexed me to the point of blameful utterances against him. I was convinced he stole my saddle-blanket. I accused, he denied, I cursed him. Only a few minutes after the verbal altercation his wife came to the entrance of my lodge, tossed a rich blanket just inside, and said pleadingly, "White man, keep your heart good."

The Assiniboine and myself met thereafter as friends and never hinted of the dispute. I thought maybe his wife had stolen the blanket I had lost, but I never tried to find out.

A Crow killed one of his own tribesmen in one instance. The two were being pursued by Sioux and stopped at a little stream to get a drink of water. One of them, Blanket, shot the other in the back of the head as he was lying down to drink. Blanket came into camp, reported a desperate fight, his companion killed, and he was treated as a hero for his bravery and for bringing in a horse. Two or three weeks afterward a party of Sioux visitors came. It happened some of them had been in the pursuing party that had chased the two Crows. They told how the dead man had been killed, and our people were convinced they told the truth about it. Blanket was pony-whipped by the dog-soldiers, all of his horses were taken from him, and his relatives also were fined many horses. For many years after that, I knew him as a member of the tribe. He was barely tolerated, but nobody would associate with him.

Friendly relations between the Crows and white people were continuous from their earliest contact. When the Crows found roaming white men, these wanderers regularly were taken to Chief Blackfoot's lodge. "Take care of these men," he would order some one, "and turn their horses into our herd." Various Indians would offer to entertain the visitors. My service as interpreter always came into good use on such occasions. We would find out who they were, get whatever news they might have to tell, and we would inform them about the hostiles and how best to avoid them.

Three white men were brought in one day when the Crows were camped by Heart Mountain, on Clark's Fork of the Yellowstone, or Rotten Sundance River, as the Crows knew this tributary of the Yellowstone. They were prospectors, and they admitted they were lost. One was Ed Smith, or "Three-Fingered Ed," another had the nickname "Farmer," perhaps because of his clumsiness. The name of the third man has escaped my memory, but I recall he appeared to know much about the Bible and often quoted it in his conversations.

"You must stay here," Blackfoot told them, "or the Sioux may kill you. You belong to us, your horses will be cared for, and when we gather robes a few days longer, you shall go with us to the agency."

Their horses were too poor to hobble, so they were tied neck-to-neck in pairs. All three of the men appeared to be of good disposition, honest prospectors trying to uncover a mine that would make them wealthy. When we all set out for the agency a sixteen-year-old girl pointed out to me the man known as Farmer, and said:

"Tell that tall man I am his sister, so he must ride with me."

The man had a good gun and plenty of ammunition. He was an accurate marksman, and he killed two deer that day. The girl skinned them and packed the skins upon his horse. At the end of the day's march she requested me:

"Tell him to come to our lodge and unpack his horses with ours."

He accepted the invitation. He was given an honorable place as a son of the household and a brother of the girl. She made up a good Indian bed for him. Next morning she hid the bedding somewhere, in fear that he might take it and go away from the caravan or go to some other lodge.

The Crow word always used and still used to designate a white man, or a member of the white race, does not mean "white man," in literal translation into English. This word, or sequence of syllables, is, Mah-ish-ta-schee-da. The first three of these syllables, *Mah-ish-ta*, translates into "eyes." The two other syllables, *Schee-da*, describe a color, "yellow." So, a strict interpretation of the entire word is "eyes yellow." It seems probable that the first white man who ever appeared among the Crows was suffering at that time an attack of jaundice, or the natural color of his eyes was distinctly yellow as contrasted with the black-and-white colors of Indian eyes. Some Crow applied to him the descriptive classification, *Mah-ish-ta-schee-da,* "eyes yellow," and this same designation stuck as applicable thereafter to all members of the newcomer race.

Only one white man ever was killed by the Crows, or there was but one authenticated instance, so far as my knowledge or belief extends. This was at the time of the rebellion of a minor portion of the tribe, in 1887, led by Wraps Up His Tail, a medicine-man. The man killed was one of a company of soldiers making a charge upon the assembled rioting Indians. On another occasion, about twenty years before this, some Crows discovered what they believed was a Sioux camp. They charged upon it and shot into it. To their discomfiture, or embarrassment, they found it to be a camp of three white men, one of whom they had wounded. They took him to old Fort Smith, then located on the Bighorn River, where the army doctors attended him. The Crows gave him three or four good horses, several blankets, and other presents. He ultimately recovered fully from his wound, and he went away from the community praising the friendliness and generosity of the Crows.

Indian doctors received liberal fees for their services. Payment was in horses, blankets, robes, or other commodities. It was a basis for prideful boasting if a patient made liberal payments to his doctor. Moreover, since medicine practice and spiritual devotion were allied so closely as to be identical in many aspects, generous donations to the doctor pleased the Great Spirit. The people knew this to be true, because all doctors agreed in asserting it was so. If a patient paid but scantily or not at all, it was said he would linger in ill health or most likely would die.

I watched particularly some medicine-men engaged in treating a sick boy. Two of them worked alternately, it being the usual way to have at least two doctors, or maybe several of them. In this case, one of the medicine-men blew his powders through a pipe-stem over the face and body of the child. The other one used a pipe-stem to suck away the evil spirits. He made wry faces as the malicious invisible sprites came into his mouth, and he spat them out and crushed them in his hands. They both were uttering prayers, in humming songs and in ordinary vocal speech. One of them kept praying, over and over, "Let this little boy be up and playing to-morrow." Two days afterward I saw the little fellow out spinning a top.

Our official weather-prophet, Pretty Louse, was a medicine-woman. She was a trance clairvoyant and claimed to talk personally with the spirits. She was a very capable person, and in public matters her advice usually was good and was followed. She cured me of an earache and deafness. She made up and put into the ear some sort of tea. She received high fees and always had a herd of about a hundred horses. Often it would occur that some one would give her a complete buffalo-skin lodge, so she owned extra lodges. These she would trade off for horses. She was liberal, and she gave away lots of presents to needy Indians. The white people called her "the princess."

A favorite old-time place for the Crow Indians to go for devotional dreaming was on Pryor Mountain. While there was almost daily prayer and fasting and wailing by some one on some near-by hill, the pilgrimage to this lofty mountain resort was a special religious proceeding. A wonderful eagle dwelt there. It screeched in terrifying manner as if human intrusion were resented. Lightning-storms came there frequently during the summer season. The mysteries of the environment were attractive rather than repellent to the Indians. A certain great cliff in this region was held in special awe. This cliff is far up toward the head of Pryor Creek, at the lower end and on the west side of a cañon.

A legend belongs to this awe-inspiring place. Long ago, two lovers, a man and a woman, went up to Pryor Mountain for dreaming and prayer in expiation of sinful conduct. As they came down they stopped to sit and rest at the edge of the great cliff. The unappeased and angry Great Spirit kicked both of them over the precipice and they were killed. After that, the Crows who went there left rings, ear-ornaments, jewelry of various kinds, and other sacrificial presents, varying in character, to appease the First Maker, who had revealed His presence there. Many Crows still go there annually for this sacrificial offering. They say the rock is growing upward, which appearance is probably due to the washing away of surrounding dirt. In the old times they often stood opposite the cliff and shot arrows across upon it, as sacrifices. Old arrow-heads are plentiful there. From this practice the stream which our maps show as Pryor Creek received a long time ago a Crow Indian name, Shooting-at-the-Bank Creek.

The planting and harvesting of tobacco was a special annual procedure having religious significance. In the spring some chosen ones of a tribal band would select a piece of ground for the sacred crop. They would make a great brush-heap, would burn it, and would scatter and mix with the soil the resulting pile of ashes. The ground having been prepared, medicine-men and medicine-women would plant the seed, all the time following out a full ritualistic ceremony that uninitiated people did not understand. They built a brush corral about the patch and went away. When autumn came, all of the interested people returned there for the official harvest. They had a tobacco-dance, in which women were the special participants. Pieces of pressed pemmican food were laid beside the growing tobacco. Selected men and women painted themselves in due fashion for the particular occasion. While tomtoms were being beaten, the selected ones charged upon the tobacco-patch as though a concerted assault were being made upon some enemy. The pemmican first was seized, bites of it were eaten, other bites were brought as special favors to friends. Then the tobacco was gathered tenderly and respectfully. My wife Cherry served twice as one of the group of gatherers of the tobacco-crop. On each occasion she brought to me a piece of the revered pemmican.

Ceremonial smoking regularly was of the tobacco and willow-bark mixture known as kinnikinick. Any two or more persons using the same pipe constituted a friendship-cementing circle. If the smoking circle were in some one's lodge, the owner of the habitation proposed the smoke and presided over the ceremony. Or some other member of the family might take the initiative. The one making the proposition might go outside his lodge and call out the names of friends specially invited to come and smoke with him. The pipe was taken reverently from its receptacle, was loaded, and was lit by the owner. He took six or more formal puffs—one upward in reverence for the Great Spirit, one downward to propitiate the evil spirits, one to each of the four directions, east, west, north, south. Then he passed the lighted pipe to his right. If more than one participant sat at his right-hand side the pipe went from hand to hand to the last one on that side. Then it was passed back, each one along the way taking his puffs and handing it to the next, the passing being done always with the right hand only. It coming thus again into the possession of the chief smoker, he sent it in the same way to the extreme end of the left side of his circle, where it was smoked and started on its way back along this left side, to be again used by each one as the return journey was made. The receiver of the pipe held his hand passively open, the immediate presenter of it almost thrust it into this open hand, as though a gift were being conferred upon one not expecting it and therefore the more pleased at receiving it. Any associate in the circle might repeat the ceremonial puffs upward, downward, east, west, north, south. In any such formal action the stem of the pipe always was pointed simultaneously in the direction where the puff was emitted.

If a pipe was smoked out, it was sent along the line to the presiding man. He emptied the ashes out upon the ground—bare ground, not upon grass nor other vegetation which needed not the vivifying influence of the sacred refuse. He cleaned the pipe by use of the special cleaner, always a part of every devotional smoker's equipment. The bowl was allowed to cool, then it was loaded, lit, the six whiffs were repeated, the general smoking was resumed. It was permissible to break into a smoke circle without invitation, whether it were in a private lodge or elsewhere. Such breaking in was complimentary to the host in particular and a manifestation of friendly feeling toward all of the others. The newcomer belonged, though, in the array at the left-hand side of the chief position. If there was not suitable room there, he ousted some youth or boy and took his place. The young males ordinarily were tolerated in the circles when these were of a purely social nature and when their presence was not a hindrance to adults. They were not allowed to join any circle that was in the nature of a council or a business meeting. Women had no place in any smoking formalities.

My son-in-law, Little Nest, has now among his treasured heirlooms an old-time medicine-pipe. Accompanying it is a fossil rock, some buffalo-chips, and some buffalo fat, that necessarily must be fifty years old. These precious articles, with some beads, are kept in a special bag. About once a year, perhaps more often, Little Nest has the family ceremony of opening this bag and making religious use of the contents. A certain phase of the moon is essential to the proceeding. He notifies his people of the impending ceremony, and a feast is prepared. After the feast he calls into assemblage his family, including such acceptable visitors as may be present. Every one must keep very quiet; no one must go out; it is a solemn occasion. Finally, after a time of silent prayer or meditation he says, "I hear a voice from the mountain." Then he reverently opens the sacred bag and displays the contained objects. He fills and smokes the pipe. He sprinkles fragments of the preserved buffalo-chips upon the fire, and as the ensuing smoke goes upward he talks to it. My daughter, his wife, in recent years having become a medicine-woman, examines critically the

fossil. If there be flakes of it fallen away, she deter-
mines from these what children may come into or
go away from the family during the coming year.
She counts the beads, each year taking away one and
putting in its place another. I do not understand the
significance of all of this ceremony, but my daughter
knows all about it. I do not feel at liberty to tell
everything I have been told about it, since to them
it is an affair of the utmost sacredness. Furthermore,
I myself believe in it, to a considerable extent.

This honored medicine-bag used to be kept hanging at all times out of doors. But attempts were
made to steal it, so nowadays Little Nest keeps it
hidden away, or has it always inside his house. It
may be the attempts at theft were because of the
money it held. Small coins were put into it from
time to time. The accumulation was disposed of in
sacrifice. Offers have been made to buy the objects,
but no such offer has ever tempted the owner. I
know other old Indians who have antique religious
relics of this same nature. Some have been sold to
collectors of curiosities.

Red paint was the choice of the Indians for personal adornment, although other colors were used,
according to fancy, as garnishings. The preference
for red was said among the Crows to have come
from a long past event when four giants fought

among themselves in heaven. Their blood fell upon the earth. The people dabbled in it so as to become godlike. Thereafter, red was the favored color. It strengthened both the soul and the body.

Painting for death was not characterized by any special coloring. The only event that required a special color was the return from successful warfare, when black was used to indicate revenge accomplished and the fires of anger burned out to dead coals.

If one died in a lodge, it usually was abandoned thereafter, or perhaps it was given away or traded for a trivial exchange present, or possibly it was stored away or not used for a year, and then used again. If the camp was a stationary one, the ground under and about the last place occupied by the deceased was swept or scraped and the dirt all carried away. The burials all were on platforms built in trees or on scaffolds built eight or ten feet from the ground. At the old Mission agency, one time, I was requested by the agent to make a box and see to the burial underground of a child that died. I made the box, and Ed Williams and myself took the body out and interred it in a grave three or four feet deep. That night some Indians dug it up and put it upon a tree-branch platform.

The Fox society and the Red Stick society were

two competing fraternal organizations that used to exist among the Crows. They contested with each other in all sorts of ways—in warfare exploits, horse-racing, athletic contests, horse-stealing, in claims for the prettiest women, in rivalry as to the best-dressed and best-cared-for men, in every way that honorable competition might be aroused. The continual contest was keen enough to engender occasional ill feeling. Especially was this true if a member of one society should gain favorable notice from the wife of a member of the opposing group, which reprehensible situation occasionally flowed from the rival claims as to personal attractiveness. Among the lower competitive features was one wherein a man might induce the wife of a member of the other organization to get upon his horse behind him and ride about the camps. This was a strong proof of his winning ways. In such case the woman ordinarily had to find for herself a new husband. If the same mate took her again into his lodge, he was despised and ridiculed as a mental weakling, taunting songs or remarks would be hurled at him, perhaps his lodge would be torn down. As is customary among all peoples, the tempting man in the case was treated as a hero instead of being punished in any way. Notwithstanding this base and unworthy phase of their operations, these societies did much toward stimulating commendable conduct. I affiliated with one of them, the Fox society.

The Old Bull society was of a different nature. It was made up of the ultra-moral people, the up-lifters, the conservative and well-behaved element among the Crows. They condemned the meddling with each other's domestic alliances, the wickedness and the vicious habits in general. Their meetings were quiet, meditative, prayerful. I quit the Fox society and joined the Old Bulls. I liked it better. As an initiation fee I gave to a non-relative a horse. As we were at a dance I called out the name of my chosen recipient, tossed to him a stick, and he picked it up. It entitled him to go where my horses were being herded, choose one of my animals, and take it to his band. The giving to non-relatives at any time was looked upon as being a higher exhibition of gen-erosity than the giving to relatives, although gifts to any one were regarded as proof of a good heart.

Wives were proud of the attractiveness of their husbands. If many women or girls appeared to en-joy some certain man's company, the wife was greatly elated at this evidence of her own charms in having won him for a husband. She boasted of his good qualities when talking with these supposedly envious ones. She was jealous only if it seemed some one might draw the husband entirely away from her and keep him away. If two scratches were heard upon the outside of my lodge, just through the wall from my regular location in it, Cherry was pleased at this sign of some girl wanting to talk with me.

Sweethearts in every camp was the custom, either for single men or young married men. The hindrance was, it was rather expensive. As I now look back at the situation, I can but believe that many girls chatted and coquetted with me only because I usually had plenty of store-bought little presents to give away. It was customary to give presents to the fleeting entertainers. If one of my special friends from some other village came to ours, Cherry would say, "Your sweetheart is here; get some food and we shall have a feast." The friend would be invited to stay in our lodge,—perhaps so Cherry could oversee the visiting,—and maybe she would remain with us two or three days. At the end of the visit she likely would go away with presents from both my wife and myself. It was considered an accommodation for her to have assisted me in whiling away the otherwise dull hours when I was away from home in her camp. One girl on an occasion like this when Cherry and I were living at the agency brought us lots of choice buffalo meat as a present. When she went away we loaded her down with sugar, coffee, rice, needles, thread, calico, and candy. This girl's name was Buffalo Calf, or Bannack Woman, since she was a Bannack. She married a Crow and became permanently one of us. She was an unusually good woman, and she was one of the best tanners in the tribe. In fact, the Bannack women all were good tanners.

Bravo and I went together once to flirt with the girls of a band that had just come into camp near the agency. It was after dark, and we had blankets about us, partly to hide our identity and partly as a shield against dog attack. Bravo had five pounds of sugar in a package under one arm and he had candy in his pockets. I had some brass finger-rings and plenty of candy. We met a group of young men.

"Where are you going?" one of them asked us.

"Oh, we're just out to see the girls," Bravo replied for us.

"Which girl are you looking for?"

Bravo named the girl.

Swish! Whack! The questioner lashed Bravo with a pony-whip. "That's my wife!" he flared out. Bravo could do nothing but run away. The young man then turned to me.

"And who is it you want to see?" he queried.

I mentioned the name of a certain girl.

"Oh, foolish young man!" he laughed, and the group of them walked on past me.

I went on to the lodge of the girl I had in mind.

I stopped at its entrance and listened. The kind of talk I heard going on led me to take the precaution of peeping. There sat my prospective sweetheart and a young man on a robe pallet, goo-gooing and putting rings on each other's fingers. Discouraged, I hunted up Bravo and we decided the best place for us was at our own homes.

At another time a young man and myself went sweethearting in my own camp. We saw two female figures sauntering along under the cover of one blanket. Their manner indicated they were seeking congenial flirtation. We directed our course to catch up with them. When we had done so, I boldly pulled aside the blanket and playfully tapped one of them on the shoulder. When she lifted her downcast face I froze to death instantly. It was my brother-in-law's wife!

The next morning my mother—that is, my adopted mother—came to my lodge and asked, "Where is that pretty shirt you have?" It was in my *pasflesche* bag. She silently dug it out and went from the lodge. She took it to my brother-in-law's lodge and gave it to his wife, telling her to give it to her husband. I hated to lose that handsome shirt, but I was glad to do almost anything to square matters with these relatives. We two men entirely ignored the fact that an embarrassing incident had come between us for a short time. Whatever dispute there might have been about it, the women among our relatives settled it.

It was regarded as scandalous for one to engage in any kind of unnecessary conversation with his brother-in-law's wife or to notice her except in the most distant and formal manner. A brother and a sister grown up out of childhood were never to be in the same lodge together unless some one or more adults were with them, and the youthful brother and sister did not speak to each other except it were in some extraordinary situation, such as a word of warning uttered by one to notify the other of danger. Even among the Crows of the present school-educated generation, a brother and a sister during youth or young maturity do not travel in the same vehicle nor go on any journey together unless others be with them. If the brother is driving his team hitched to a wagon, his sister does not ride in the seat with him. Somebody else rides there, and she sits flat down in the wagon-bed behind.

A special wickiup willow-lodge shelter was a common appurtenance to every sectional clan region in a Crow Indian camp. This lodge was for married women only. At certain times a wife would say to her husband: "I sleep to-night in the willow lodge." She made that her shelter for a few nights, until such time as she might be ready again to take up her usual abode. A sweat-bath and incense purification immediately preceded her return.

At two different periods I had two Crow wives at the same time. In one of these instances I took the second wife on a promise made at a sun-dance. After a few days I persuaded her to go away, because of my fear of the agent's objections. In the other instance, Cherry and I were out with some Indians in a hunting-camp. A man came to me and wanted me to take his daughter, a relative of Cherry, for an additional wife. He wanted me to pay him by giving him a certain U. S. brand mule that I had stolen from the Sioux. I disparaged the qualities of his offered daughter, told him she was lazy, was not anything near the equal of Cherry, and so on, according to the customary way of dickering under those conditions. But after a while we agreed to trade on these terms. He brought the girl and her luggage, and I authorized him to take possession of the mule. Cherry was satisfied. Bigamy was a common condition. Polygamy prevailed in some lodges. Cherry now would be the first or sits-beside-me wife, the other would be the drudge of the husband.

These two wives got along well together. But their mothers quarreled about them. Each mother charged that the daughter of the other was worthless, and each alleged that her own offspring was the more diligent at bringing me water to wash in in the morning, at combing my hair, at making me fine clothing, at keeping my bed in good order, at taking care of me in general. One day when I returned from an absence I found exactly one lateral half of my lodge standing in place. The two mothers-in-law had divided it, and the mother of the second wife had taken her daughter and the detached half of the lodge and had moved them to her own domain. The domicile was of canvas and had cost me eighty-five dollars. Besides, they did at least twenty-five dollars' worth of damage to the decorative wall linings. The departing young wife's brother came and condoled with me. "This is very bad," he said. The next day he gave me six horses.

I believed myself to be popular with both the men and the women. The white men among the Crows mostly were desirable as husbands for the women. They usually had better business ability than the Indian men, and this ability drew women to them as being better providers. One drawback —the white men usually were liquor drinkers, and this the older Crows did not like. A few of the Indians would get drunk, but even these were not persistent drinkers. Often I have seen drunken Crows hog-tied by the dog-soldiers and their whisky bottles smashed. So it might be that whatever of favor I enjoyed was due largely to my almost total abstinence from liquor. I had this same belief during the times of my service as scout for the army. In fact, never in my whole lifetime has my brain been seriously befuddled by liquor.

WHEN GIBBON AND CUSTER CAME IN 1876

TEN years of association with the Crow Indians before the memorable military campaign against the Sioux in Montana during the summer of 1876 had prepared me for taking part in that eventful operation. During more than two months before the arrival of Generals Terry and Custer, a body of troops under the command of General Gibbon patroled up and down the north side of the Yellowstone valley in an effort to keep all of the Sioux south of the river while awaiting the arrival of the soldiers from Dakota and from the southward. It was my fortune to become connected with these Gibbon troops.

On the ninth of April Lieutenant Bradley and a detachment of about twenty-five men from Company E, Seventh Infantry Mounted, came to the Absaroka agency. The commanding officer of this company was Captain Clifford, but Bradley was in charge of this special detail. His business was to enlist Crow Indians as scouts for the soldiers. Colonel Gibbon, then acting as brigadier-general, arrived later with some other officers. The main body of troops remained at the mouth of the Stillwater River.

The army officers had a council with Chief Blackfoot and his leading men. Bradley, the industrious and painstaking recorder of events, jotted down memoranda as the talk proceeded. Pierre Chien, the aged, but competent, interpreter, served here in that capacity, with Tom Stewart and myself as checks. This checking of an interpreter often is useful. Even the best of them, such as was Pierre Chien, fluent in both English and Crow, as well as the Blackfoot and his own natural French, are not always able to transpose an idea expressed in one language into exactly the same idea when expressed in another language. However, Chief Blackfoot was a highly intelligent Indian and he had a way of talking that made it easy to interpret for him.

"You may mistake the Crows for Sioux and shoot them," Blackfoot objected.

Reluctance on the part of the Crows was manifested generally. But the old men agreed to talk about it among themselves, as Indians ever were wont to do before coming to irrevocable conclusions. I was on the agency pay-roll just then as a blacksmith, and although the prospect of adventure was pleasing, it seemed not wise to abandon my present appointment. That evening, though, Lieutenant

Bradley told me he would pay me, in addition to the small army allowance for scouting, one dollar per day for special service to him personally as a monitor in the lore of the country, the geography of it, and the ways of the Indians. He promised further that I should be the chief scout in command over the Indians, but subordinate to him. His offer decided me. I announced at once my intention to enlist. Bravo said he would go too.

The next morning General Gibbon tantalized Blackfoot with:

"You have been talking in the past about fighting the Sioux. Now is your chance to beat them, and you seem afraid."

"But the Sioux might come here when my young men are away," the wise old chief countered. "How long will they be with you?"

"They will stay with me," Gibbon declared confidently. Then he set forth that many other white soldiers were coming, that the Sioux would be beaten, that in future years the children of the Crows would read about their participation in the victory and would be proud of their fathers.

Bradley informed the chief that Bravo and I had agreed to go with him.

"You want them to be your eyes—your wolves?" Blackfoot asked.

"That is it," the general replied.

"If these two white men of ours are to go with them, I will let you know to-morrow," the chief temporized further.

But already some of the young Crows had signified their wish to join themselves with the white soldiers. Blackfoot gracefully yielded a tacit consent in his admonition:

"Take good care of my men."

The outcome of the conference is set forth in Lieutenant Bradley's diary:

Monday, April 10th. I completed the desired number of enlistments to-day, swore them in on the point of a knife— said to be a binding oath among them. . . . The detachment consists of twenty-three Crow Indians and two squaw-men —Le Forgey and Bravo—who have lived among the Crows. . . . (At Crow Agency, on Stillwater Creek.)

Except for the misspelling of my name, this officer's record is essentially correct. He administered to Bravo and me the regular oath, and we conducted the point-of-the-knife procedure in binding the Indians to the service. We lined them all up by the trader's store and gave to Bradley a list of the names and their ages. Most of them were in early manhood, twenty to thirty years old. But we had a few older ones, up to the age of fifty, these for wise counsel. We had also some very young ones, one of these being Curly, about seventeen years old. The youngest, I believe, was one known as Grandmother's Knife. I think he was not more than sixteen.

The Crows followed the soldiers away that afternoon. I lingered behind to adjust my blacksmith vacancy the best I could. I arranged for Cherry to have credit at the store. She declared herself as willing for me to go, but no women were taken with us, so she had to remain at the agency. She showed some grief at the parting, but at the last she cheered me:

"Do not shirk. Be brave. If you should be killed, it would leave me very poor; but if there should be a fight, I want to hear of you being in it. Come back with a good name, and bring me a good horse."

My delay in starting was also for the purpose of noting if any Crows recanted and turned back. Seeing no sign of this, I set out to catch up with them, which I did before they arrived at the main camp on the Yellowstone, twelve or more miles down the valley. Our horses trudged along the muddy trail, with wet snow covering much of the ground. The weather was damp, cloudy, chilly, and the usual wind was whistling along the Yellowstone. Nevertheless, the inauguration of our adventure saw us all in cheerful mood.

Mitch Buoyer had gone the day before to the central camp. He had been hired, not enlisted. His employment was as a guide, and his duty kept him at all ordinary times with the wagon-trains. At various times prior to this he had served in like capacity for both army and civilian travelers. As a reliable guide anywhere in this part of the West, he had a high reputation, and he fully deserved it.

He knew minutely every local region from the Platte to Bozeman, and he could talk Sioux, Crow, or English.

The first shock of army life came to the Crows when, on the next morning after their arrival, Lieutenant Bradley had them all line up for roll-call. There was difficulty both in getting them all together and in calling the roll after we did get them. I tried to explain to Bradley that they likely would do better and be better satisfied if left to follow to a great extent their own ways of scouting. It was hinted to him that Indians in general were shy, flighty, timid or fearful about new modes of procedure, and that they might try to get away if army rules were applied strictly to them. Some of the older Crows wanted to talk to General Gibbon, and the kindly commander assented promptly to a conference with them. When he had heard their complaints he promised he would talk to the lieutenant and see if some sort of more congenial arrangement might be made for them. Although the general kept mostly a grave countenance, he did not suppress altogether what evidently was his amusement at the idea of roll-call each morning for a band of totally untamed Crow Indians. But the omission of this formal "all-present-or-accounted-for" procedure was not a sufficient release from army restrictions. The red men chafed under other rules. They had bred into them and were accustomed to individuality in action. From time to time one slipped away during the night and did not return. Bradley's diary tells something of his troubles in this regard:

Monday, May 1. We now are minus six of our Crows. . . . This evening Bravo, interpreter, and one of the Crows, Little Face, were sent back to the agency, bearing a letter to the agent, who is requested to use his influence to get these six renegades to return. . . . Little Face's son is among the absentees.

The boldness of the hostile Indians is illustrated by an incident in early May. We were all the time on the north side of the Yellowstone, and the supposition was that our presence would intimidate them into staying at all times on the south side. But on many occasions they got over to our side. The first distinctly noticeable event of this kind is remarked in Bradley's diary:

Wednesday, May 3. We have found the Sioux, or, rather, they have found us. . . . It was discovered that Bostwick's horse and mule were gone. . . . As soon as the Crows heard . . . they rushed . . . where they had left their horses over night to graze, but every head was gone—thirty-two in all, gobbled by the Sioux. . . . The Crows had a good cry over their loss, standing together in a row and shedding copious tears, after which they set out to follow the trail of the robbers. . . . The Crows heard shots on the opposite bank. . . . Fearing to cross . . . turned back. . . . Of the seventeen Crows now with us, not one has a horse.

That record sets forth quite well the essential features of this raid upon us. To be specific, though, it seems fitting to correct the record by attributing the daring deed to Cheyennes. Information as a basis for this correction came to me many years afterward, in a prolonged conversation with Two Moons, a Cheyenne chief. He was the leader of the band who stole our horses that night. He told me various corroborative details that convinced me he actually was there. He described exactly the arrangement of our camp. He knew right where the tents of the officers were located. With a blanket wrapped about his whole body so that only one peering eye could be seen,—a mode of dress favored by Indians, and which makes them all look alike,—he idled a few minutes about these tents and stood looking into the opening of one of them wherein a group of officers were engaged in a game of cards.

The weeping of the Crows was not merely an effeminate yielding to emotions. They felt greatly humiliated, and they were vowing revenge. They themselves claimed high proficiency in the art of horse-stealing, and to be beaten so badly in this game, with white men observing their defeat, was hurtful to their pride. This was why they wept. Other horses later were brought from the agency, temporary loans were offered and accepted; but two or three of the Crows carried through their resolution to travel on foot until they could retaliate upon the enemy. An inkling of this feeling appears in the young officer's diary three days after the Crow loss:

Saturday, May 6. Mounted Half Yellow Face on my horse this morning and gave Jack Rabbit Bull a good mount also, and started them off on the Sioux trail. . . . The triumphant Crows . . . arrived early in the afternoon, proud of their exploit and three horses richer for it.

The soldiers chummed and joked with the Crows. The relations all during the campaign were good-humored and generally pleasant. Nicknames were formulated and applied to various ones of the Indian scouts. One became known as "Kelly." The appellation of Grandmother's Knife was changed into "Skookum."

We scouts all provided our own shelter. Although we were not supposed to have any baggage except what we personally carried, the wagons hauled our sheltering equipment and some other extras. Each of us had a piece of canvas or of buffalo or other hide. Sometimes we utilized as covering the saddle-blankets also. At each place of camping we made housing frames by bending over willows and tying together their tops. Often we combined into pairs or groups and occupied larger structures covered by our united canopy material. At every stop for more than a day or so, we built one or more sweat-lodges, of bent-willow frames and blanket or skin coverings. We had many councils of our own, where we would smoke according to standard rites and would talk about and give serious consideration to matters appertaining to our duties. We were a distinct little army of our own, with problems that could not be solved unerringly except by our own unhindered efforts. We had lots of rainy weather that spring. In addition to the discomforts of the temporary shelters, the wet moccasins hindered us. We had not, as in our home camps, women to keep us supplied with dry moccasins and other clothing and to keep our lodges in good condition. There were no women of any kind with the entire Gibbon expedition, nor with any of its allied expeditions during that summer, so far as I ever heard.

Scouting on foot was the regular Crow mode of movement for about a month after their horses had been stolen by the Cheyennes soon after we had joined Gibbon's forces. Many attempts were made to get horses from the Sioux, but most of these attempts resulted in failure. Two or three Crows would swim the river at night, taking with them their lariats. Early in the morning they would return, usually empty-handed. These forays always were undertaken with great secrecy, even as among themselves. That was the regular Indian way—to slip out on this kind of enterprise without informing anybody. They were influenced, too, by their "medicine," by the weather conditions, by superstitions of numerous kinds that no white man ever could comprehend. An Indian might go upon a foray at a time when nobody would have expected it of him, while at another time when it might seem to some one else that all of the conditions were most favorable, he would sit stubbornly in his lodge and smoke and meditate. This was not because he was totally unwilling. He simply wasn't ready just then. So when some officer might propose, "Now let's have the

Crows make an organized effort to-day for getting some Sioux horses," he was likely to be amazed and disgusted by the utter failure of his proposition. The intelligent and educated white man's misunderstanding of the Indian mind—or his erroneous notion that he has penetrated successfully into and disclosed entirely the Indian's thoughts—is illustrated in Bradley's diary wherein he records:

The general had a conference with the Crows to-day and tried to induce them to go in search of a Sioux camp, but they declined.

And elsewhere in his notes:

An effort was made to induce the Crows to form a war-party to go to the Sioux village after horses; but after deliberating a while they decided that the moon is too bright— that is, the nights are not dark enough to conceal their movements.

My horse was stolen when the hostiles got away with the mounts of all the Crow scouts. Mine was a pinto, a good runner over long distances, particularly useful as a buffalo-horse. Cherry's brother, Hairy Robe, had presented it to me as a war-horse when we left the agency. Cherry sent to me another horse when report of the loss reached the agency by messengers who were going back and forth all the time, but I already had bought from Lieutenant Bradley an extra saddle animal he had and had offered to me at a low price. I liked best this mount, and thereafter I used it at all times. I gave my other to one of the Crows.

We scouted on both sides of the river after we got down to Pease Bottom by the mouth of the Bighorn River. I went with some soldiers during the early part of May on a long excursion to the southward. We followed the Bighorn River up to the mountains. We crossed over to the headwaters of Lodge Grass Creek,—or Greasy Grass Creek, as the Indians called it,—traveled down this stream to its discharge into the Little Bighorn, moved on down this valley to the Bighorn, then on back to and across the Yellowstone. On the whole trip we did not see any indications of Sioux in this region. At this time those who were in Montana were on the Rosebud, Tongue, and Powder rivers. Many who a few weeks later were among the opposers of Custer's attack were now on the Dakota reservations or were just leaving there. We rode along over the ground where a month or so later was Sitting Bull's great camp. We passed by the hills where Custer and Reno afterward were to meet with disaster. But there was then nothing about these places to draw our attention.

Matt Carroll was in charge of Gibbon's wagon-train. His troubles were as burdensome as they could be, it appeared. Wherever the soil was such as to make mud when mixed with water, he found plenty of mud. In the course of traveling, his train could cover at times only eleven or twelve miles in a day. About the longest distance they made on any day—an unusually long day of movement—was twenty-five miles. Of course, on some days no attempt was made to move the wagons, even when movement was on the program. Our base camps were kept longest at places opposite the mouth of the Stillwater, opposite the mouth of the Bighorn, at the mouth of Big Porcupine Creek, opposite the mouth of the lower, or larger, Rosebud Creek, and on down to Powder River and back. But in our scouting we had been to and below and across the river from the Rosebud camp long before this became the base of operations.

We scouts often had our own minor base camps, these on down the river ahead of the coming main base. At various times Captain Clifford, the immediate superior of Lieutenant Bradley, brought detachments of infantry with him down the river in boats and camped with us. In a day or so they would return, perhaps after shifting the soldiers so that

Bradley had left with him and us a different group of soldiers for aid in the scouting.

Bonus payments were granted for finding any Sioux village. This stimulated explorations into the country on the more dangerful south side of the river. While the main plan of the campaign was to keep the Sioux south of the Yellowstone, and while this involved the necessity of hunting for them on the north side, so as to fight them back if any were found, the best opportunities for bonus money and fame—and also for death—were presented among the hills and valleys to the southward across the broad and swift stream that separated us from the hostiles. It apparently was deemed important to discover, if possible, the strength as well as the location of the Sioux. We were not expecting just then to go over and fight them. But we were gathering information that might be useful when came the proper time for engaging them in actual combat.

The "skull butte" or "painted rocks" below Billings aroused great interest in the mind of Lieutenant Bradley, the inquiring and studious young officer who commanded our scouts. I had learned from the Indians the entire story, and Mitch Buoyer and I had visited and examined carefully the place during the summer of 1873, when we were on a hunting-trip in this region and while Custer and Stanley had their soldiers encamped farther down the river while they guarded the Northern Pacific's advance engineering corps.

The drawings and carvings on these rocks depicted the main incidents of a smallpox epidemic that had visited the Crows during a previous generation. The pictures showed people dead and others about to fall over dead. Friends were abandoning the fallen ones and fleeing in all directions. Two Indian men were shown standing upon the edge of a cliff and holding their hands upward as they looked downward. The Crow legend here set forth was that only two men were left alive from what had been one of the large villages. These two men discussed between themselves their forlorn situation. They had suffered the disease and had survived it, but why should they want to live longer, with their friends all dead? They agreed upon a double suicide. This they accomplished by jumping off the very cliff whereon was inscribed now the story of the great disaster.

I found an old Sioux man alone one day when I was off by myself from Bradley and some of his soldiers. This was on the south side of the river. Near him were signs of several lodges having been there recently, but just now there were no indica-

tions of any Indians except him. I rode a wide circle
to find the trail of the departing Indians and saw
that they actually were gone, all in a body and leaving a plain trail. When I came back to the old Sioux
he was about to run away from me, but I signed him
to keep quiet, that no harm was intended.

"Are you going to kill me?" he asked, by signs, as
I rode up to him.

In sign-talk I asked him how it happened he was
here alone. He responded that he had been here
with some young men who were hunting buffalo, but
who had seen soldiers on this side of the river, had
become frightened, and had run away. They had
taken his horse and he was trying to make his way
afoot to some Sioux camp. I asked if he had any
children. He informed me he had, but that they had
quarreled with him and ousted him. Instead of killing him, I gave him some bacon, some hardtack,
and a piece of tobacco. I expressed to him a wish
that he might get back in safety to some friends;
but his feeble condition indicated he probably would
perish there alone in the hills. I never reported this
incident to Bradley. In fact, many signs of Sioux
that we scouts discovered were not reported. To do
so might have caused merely a fruitless sally of
troops—or, worse, a disastrous encounter. Our observations convinced us that there were many more

Sioux in the country than our present forces could handle.

Mitch Buoyer and I carried on an oral and sign-talk conversation across the river with some Sioux one morning while we were in camp opposite the mouth of the Rosebud. In general purport they said to us: "At the agencies they took away our horses and our guns. We then could not hunt, and as they did not give us enough food, we were starving. So we got other horses and guns, and now we are out hunting for food. Many of our women are walking because we have not enough horses, and our children are hungry. We do not want to fight the white people, and we wish the soldiers would stay on the north side of the river and leave us here. We will stay here and kill buffalo, where they are plentiful. Fighting takes away our energies that ought to be given to hunting for food and robes. Tell this to your chiefs." They asked us to give them some ammunition, said they would send one man over the river for it, but we had to refuse this request. I told Lieutenant Roe, Gibbon's adjutant, about this talk.

Some loose horses standing at the edge of the water and drinking at the south side of the river one evening about sundown attracted the attention of Mitch and myself. This was when we were in the base camp at the mouth of the Big Porcupine. We watched them a little while. They stayed grazing in that vicinity. It was growing dusk, and we decided to go over and make a capture. We stripped to breech-cloth and moccasins, mounted our horses, and swam them through the waters of the lively Yellowstone. We made our crossing about a quarter of a mile below the position of the animals in view. When we landed, our mounts were left at this point while we crept, guns and lariats in hand, toward the objects of our movement. We saw there were a black horse, a colt, and a little mule. We went first for the horse. But when we arrived within twenty or thirty yards of it we saw that it was staked out with a picket-rope. This condition at once decided us to retreat, and to retreat as hurriedly as the circumstances would permit. We did not then want any horses. What we wanted most was a safe return to our own side of the river. This no doubt was the saddle-horse of a Sioux doing picket duty on the bluffs, and if his horse had begun to move away from where he knew it ought to remain, one or the other of us might have been killed.

Six or seven Sioux lingered one evening by an ash grove across the river, as though they intended to camp there. Mitch saw them and told me about it. We agreed here was an opportunity to do some-

thing bold and to get some horses. We told the officer of the day about our planned enterprise, so that
he might instruct the picket-guards of our camp
to be on the lookout for us. A boat was comman-
deered and the voyage across was accomplished
without eventful incident. It was anchored on the
other side, and we two crawled and sneaked in the
direction of the ash grove. A horse-bell guided us
to the exact position of the coveted booty. We got
our ropes about the necks of four of them and
started back. The odor of kinnikinick smoke was
floating on the breeze into our nostrils. We were
making fair progress toward our boat when some
one, apparently off a little way from the camp, called
out in Sioux: "I don't see the horses." That hurried
us, and perhaps the sounds of our hurrying reached
the keen ears of listeners. The Sioux were right after
us, shooting at us. We let loose the horses, sprang
into the boat and paddled away into the stream. A
bullet or two splattered upon the water pretty close
to us, which was thrilling, but not injurious.

Mitch was a guide, not a scout. His regular place
was with the train when it was on the move, but
when a base camp would be established he would
go out at times with us or with soldiers, perhaps
as a guide, more likely for the pure love of adventure. He was my regular choice associate when we

were together in the same camp, as we had been friends and companions on many an adventure and at the home places during ten years preceding this time.

Sioux warriors came often into view on the hills opposite us, particularly when we were at the camp at Big Porcupine Creek. They would shake their guns and lances at us. Every indication was that always they kept pickets hidden on the hills across from us, to give warning of any movement we might make over the river into their territory. We saw about as many or more Sioux when we were not hunting for them as we did when we were out actually in search of them. Notwithstanding our supposed vigilance, parties of them often crossed over to our side. We often found signs of them here, and sometimes we saw the Indians themselves.

We found a raft one day ten or fifteen miles down the river from our camp and on our side of the stream. Three or four Crows were with me. In the vicinity were tracks of adults and children, some made by bare feet, some by moccasins. All indicated an ultimate movement to the northward away from the river. It appeared they were two or three days old. No horse-tracks could be found there. Near the raft we discovered a broken arrow-shaft— broken exactly in its middle and evidently laid upon the ground with particular care. We all wondered about it, then we sat down for a smoke and a council about the entire strange situation. We went out severally upon various high points, made observations that resulted negatively, then assembled again in council.

"The broken arrow means, 'I have quit fighting,' " one of our older men, Little Face, explained.

But who had been the people thus declaring their decision? One theory was that they were Sioux who thus gave notice to subsequent observers of an intent to desert the hostiles and return to their reservation in Dakota. But it was considered that the crossing of the river to its north side at this point was a diversion from the way to Dakota. Moreover, the arrow appeared to be not of Sioux origin. It finally was decided, to the satisfaction of all of us, that the traveling people were northern Indians, probably Gros Ventres or perhaps Assiniboines, who had been visiting with the Sioux, who had allied themselves for a time with the Sioux cause, but who now had recanted and were on the way to their home tribe. The barefoot tracks were not construed as indicative of distress and lack of moccasins or material for them. Indians liked to go barefooted when they could. Perhaps every barefoot track we saw there was made by some one who had a good pair of moccasins, or more than one pair of them, tucked under his belt.

Our blacksmith and three soldiers went out into the hills from the base camp one day to hunt antelope. One of our Crows posted himself on a hill as a sentinel lookout. Some other Crows were riding about at random in that vicinity. Our scout camp was on the outskirts of that side of the main soldier camps. After a while the Crow lookout gave an alarm signal. It spread quickly to us, and we scouts all mounted our horses and galloped away toward the point whence the alarm had come. In the distance we saw a dozen or so Sioux on horseback running away over the hills and toward the river below our camps. We turned our horses toward them, but soon we came upon something that attracted all of our interest. We found the dead bodies of all four of our comrade antelope hunters. Every head had been scalped. Their horses were gone. By the time we had learned they all were beyond need for our help, the Sioux probably were swimming the river back to their own regions. This being the case, we loaded the bodies upon horses and returned slowly to camp, where I reported the situation. Lieutenant Bradley promptly ordered me under arrest. The charge against me was that I had taken out my scouts without first notifying him of the call for aid and receiving orders from him.

General Gibbon had me taken to his tent. He had me tell to him the entire story of the call and our response. After he had listened to all I had to say he advised me not to worry, that he would present the case to Bradley, and that it was likely the lieutenant would ignore my breach of discipline, since the circumstances were of so unusual a nature. Evidently my offense was pardoned. Nothing was said thereafter about it.

Lieutenant Bradley was a clean and fine young man, held in respect by all who had anything to do with him, but it appeared to me he often interjected too much red-tape formality into situations where the contingencies of Indian warfare rendered the tedious procedure an actual hindrance to efficiency. I think he underestimated the capabilities of the Crow scouts. Or, better expressed, he did not understand the character of their capabilities. His feeling about us, as expressed at one time in his diary, was this:

The carelessness of these fellows at times is simply amazing. One would think the Indian's life . . . would make caution . . . so much a habit that he would never lay them aside; but it is quite otherwise. In my scouts with the Crows

I was compelled to watch them constantly to prevent the doing of some foolish or foolhardy thing that might have betrayed us.

But a joke at the expense of this earnest lieutenant came up while we were in camp across from the mouth of the Rosebud. Soon after dark one night a picket-guard mistook a floating log for a swimming Sioux, and he fired at it as it drifted past him. Of course, the camp was aroused. Bradley called out the scouts and hurried us all over to the river's bank. He had us all lie down and creep here and there through a brushy and reedy area where we knew there was an abundance of mosquitoes, frogs, and snakes. He himself was scurrying back and forth while giving orders to us about the proper mode of locating the enemy. He peered into brush-piles and out over the waters of the Yellowstone. The joke was that all of this time he was carrying in his hands a lighted lantern. In due time it became settled that an inanimate log had caused the alarm. I think our Crows enjoyed as much as did the soldiers the ensuing talk about the humor of the situation—a well-educated army officer using a lighted lantern at night in a hunt for hostile Sioux.

We located a big Sioux or Cheyenne camp on the Rosebud during one of our scouts. Lieutenant Brad-

ley and some soldiers were along with the Crow
scouts. We had crossed the river in boats, leading
our swimming horses, and our course was directed
into the heights of the Wolf Mountains. White
Man Runs Him and myself were doing the "wolf-
ing"—that is, the distant hilltop scouting ahead—
for this little expedition. We signaled back our discovery, and the entire body of soldiers and scouts
came cautiously to our point of observation. Indian
lodges were strung along the Rosebud for a distance
of two miles. It appeared the valley and adjacent
foothills were solid with grazing horses. We saw
various old women come out to the lower hills and
cut cedar-wood. Bradley jotted down memoranda,
as was his usual way. While we were spying upon
them, it seemed some sort of alarm was spread
among the camps. At any rate, all along the array
of lodges men hurried out and began herding in the
loose horses. It was apparent that some of their
outpost guardians had seen us or had seen our trail.
We at once began our retreat back to the river and
to the main camp. On other subsequent days we kept
watch of that body of Indians, until finally we found
they had moved elsewhere.

A Sioux village on Powder River was discovered
by a few Crow scouts accompanied by Mitch Buoyer
and myself. We had been gone several days and

were a hundred miles or so from the army base. During the first part of this excursion into the enemy's country, we had seen a band of a hundred and fifty to two hundred Sioux crossing the Yellowstone from the north to the south side. We tried to follow their trail, but there were many complicating trails, so we merely kept ourselves going in a direction that seemed most likely to take us where were most of the people. The trails evidently were mainly those of visiting Indians or new accessions of a few travelers in groups, not trails made by large buffalo-hunting parties. About the mouth of Powder River, or a little above this point, we discovered one morning the wisps of smoke curling upward from many tepees. We had done our full duty—had located the position of the enemy—so we set off on the back trail. This was the most extensive scout I made during that series of operations. When we reported our find the whole command moved down the river and set up the base opposite the mouth of the Rosebud. At the time of our having seen the Sioux crossing the river I had gone back the short distance and reported. Just after this, and while I was again with our scouting-party, the steps toward making the base move were inaugurated.

At one time General Gibbon decided to cross the Yellowstone with his whole body of troops and pursue the hostiles until in a general engagement they should be defeated and chased out of the country, back to the reservations where it was considered they belonged. Every arrangement was made for this enterprise. But the swift and treacherous Yellowstone hindered us. One man and eleven horses were drowned in the first efforts to cross the stream. The difficulties became so evident that the general curbed his anxiety and abandoned the attempt. Perhaps this hindrance alone saved him from the utter calamity that a few weeks later befell General Custer. Indeed, during the entire campaign, there was among all of the military leaders an underestimate of the numbers, the ability, and the determination of the hostile Indians in this region.

The crossing of swift rivers was accomplished more easily by Indians than by white men. General Custer's official report of his battle with the Sioux at Pompey's Pillar, in 1873, reveals this to an analytic reader of it, although it appears he did not design to point out particularly this feature of their superiority over his forces. His whole document was a song of victory, of commendation for his command, as ordinarily are the official reports made by commanding officers. He relates that the savage forces "crossed the river" and attacked his soldiers. He mentions that "the Indians outnum-

bered us almost five to one." He tells how Captain
Moylan's squadron "charged them and drove them
pell-mell for three miles." But, "my entire command
was disappointed when the trail showed that the Indians had crossed to the other side." The disappointed soldiers bivouacked there over night, and
they spent all of the next day in efforts at getting
across the Yellowstone in pursuit of the Sioux. Lieutenant Weston and three men are commended for
their brave, but futile, effort to go over on a raft
and carry with them a cable made of lariats.

The next day a body of the Sioux appeared on the
banks of the stream across in front of the Custer
soldiers. Some fighting occurred by long-distance
shooting over the waters. While this was going on,
it was learned that Indians were coming again, both
below and above the troopers, through the flood of
which, in his report of his own failure to conquer
it, General Custer wrote:

The current here rushes by at a velocity of about seven
miles an hour, while the depth of the water was such that
a horse attempting to cross would be forced to swim several
hundred yards.

It was found that already a body of the red warriors had come across the river and had formed on
the hills behind the white soldiers. The courageous

cavalrymen attacked them, beat them, chased them away, notwithstanding "the number opposed to us has been estimated by the various officers engaged as from eight hundred to a thousand." The flight before the pursuing soldiers ended when, in the language of the general's report, "they were forced back across the Yellowstone." So again a thousand skulking and cowardly Sioux got away—fled across the Yellowstone to perfect safety—from the white man's lame efforts at pursuit.

Grandmother's Knife, Push, and myself went out one day to hunt for certain roots we liked as food. Along up Big Porcupine Creek we came upon the bodies of two buffaloes that had been dead a long time. One of the carcasses attracted our special attention. We investigated it. Inside of the chest cavity we discovered a pair of rotted and fragile Indian leggings, a cut-off calico shirt such as the Indians ordinarily wore, a pair of earrings, and two brass armlets. We inferred that some Indian had hidden these articles, expecting to return for them, but had been prevented from doing so. There was in the vicinity no remnant of human remains. We were satisfied with our conclusion and went on our way.

Several years afterward I heard from the Piegans a story that fitted exactly into the missing parts of this one. Two Piegans had gone out from their camp on the Judith to invade the land of the Crows and steal some horses. In due time one of them returned, having with him two fine animals as coup-counting results of the enterprise. He bore the sad news that his companion had been killed. Some variation and some incongruities in his rehearsals to different people led to doubt and then discredit of his statements. He was pressed with cross-examining inquiries, and finally he confessed having murdered the missing Piegan companion. A body of his people backtrailed him, verified his confession, and recovered the body of the dead man at the edge of the waters of a creek where he had been killed while taking a drink of water, as the miscreant had told. The clothing was not found, and since the murderer had been disposed of in summary fashion, it never had been learned what became of it. This evidently was what we had found in the carcass of the dead buffalo.

A quarrel arose between two of our Crows when we were at the Bighorn base camp. Some of them had been out stealing horses. Upon their return, two of them got into a dispute about the ownership of a certain horse, a fine sorrel animal. Half Yellow Face intervened to help settle the argument. While he was inquiring into the circumstances of the capture, one of the disputants suddenly whipped out his big sheath-knife and buried it to the hilt in the breast of the horse. It plunged, staggered away a little distance, fell, and soon bled to death. The two men shook hands shortly afterward and conducted themselves thereafter as being on the same friendly terms as they previously had been. Half Yellow Face was instrumental in bringing them to this amicable basis. He was regarded as a great warrior, was a man of quietude and wisdom, and he had a strong influence over his companion Crows.

Military discipline among the soldiers was rigid. That is, it was likely to be rough when applied. I recollect clearly one instance that will typify the conditions in this regard. I was out scouting for a detachment of soldiers on the south side of the Yellowstone, along the Tulloch's Fork, three or four weeks before the Custer battle. As we were nearing the river on our return, one of the soldiers was jerking his horse in a manner displeasing to the officer in command of the detachment.

"Tell that man to dismount," he ordered a sergeant.

The order was obeyed. The officer then had the horse given to some one else for leading. The offending trooper's hands were tied to the stirrups of another soldier on horseback, and in this strained and most humiliating plight the fettered man walked

the rest of the distance, about a mile, back to the
Yellowstone. Still, the soldiers in those times were
hardy men, and perhaps hardy corrective measures
were needed.

The first man we saw of the Terry-Custer forces
coming from Dakota appeared as we were moving
our base camp from the Rosebud on down the valley. The Crow scouts all were ahead with Bradley's
troops. We were scouting the front and the hills
adjacent to the trail along the valley. Myself and
two Crows were far to the front. We saw a steamboat coming up the river. It landed. Some men got
off and walked about on the shore. One man walked
away alone, and he directed his course toward us.
As we approached he hailed us. He was a tall and
fine-looking man, dressed in army uniform. His
speech was quiet, but full of cordiality. He asked
who we were, who was coming after us, and put
other questions relative to the move we were making. In due time Lieutenant Bradley came, not long
afterward some other officers arrived, and before we
proceeded on our way I learned that the capable-
looking and pleasant man we had met was General
Terry. The steamboat was the *Far West*.

When Major Reno came, our first glimpse of his
cavalrymen was when we saw some one on a hill
by the mouth of the Rosebud and looking across the

river at our camp through field-glasses. A corporal from General Gibbon's headquarters wigwagged signals and received replies. General Gibbon wanted some one to take a despatch to the newly arrived major. Bostwick, a white-man scout, who had come from Fort Shaw with Gibbon, tried it, but he got cramps and had some difficulty in even getting back the short distance he had gone into the water.

"Have you an Indian who will try this?" the general sent word to our section of the camp.

Yes, we had. His name was Bull Rabbit. He tied the despatch into a bandage about his head and stripped to his breech-cloth. He probed carefully about a heap of driftwood and finally selected a dry chunk that seemed exactly to suit his wishes. Then he plunged boldly into the rushing flood of the eighteenth of June. He swam to the south side without apparent great effort, placed his chunk of wood in a secure place on the bank, and disappeared into a crowd of soldiers who were there to receive him. After a while he reappeared, picked up his wood buoy, and unhesitatingly attacked again the chilling and racing torrent. We all cheered him as he worked his way back through the waters that appeared hungry for his body. When he landed, some one met him with a whisky bottle and treated him to two big swallows. This was an indulgence rather excessive for the abstemious Bull Rabbit. He could overcome the opposition of the Yellowstone, but he could not withstand well the onset of the alcoholic attack. Pretty soon he said, "My friend, the medicine makes me dizzy," and he went away to his willow-and-blanket lodge.

Mitch Buoyer had been sent down the Yellowstone to join Reno as his guide. He showed the way to this officer and his six cavalry companies as they explored the Powder, the Tongue, and the Rosebud rivers, before they came to the point just across from our base, opposite the mouth of the Rosebud. They had not seen any Indians, but they had seen the site of the village we had discovered on the Rosebud. Mitch noted that the trail from this place went in the direction of the Little Bighorn valley.

My friend Buoyer was designated as the guide for Custer's Seventh Cavalry when it was announced they would go up the Rosebud after these moving hostiles. Six of my Crow scouts were transferred to Custer. I wanted to go with them, but Bradley would not grant my request. Ten days or so before this time I had met with a disabling accident. On a scouting expedition into the hills on our side of the river, my horse was frightened by the sudden jumping up of a fawn antelope. When the surprised mount leaped sideways I tumbled off. The immediate result was the breaking of a collar-bone. The ensuing result was that I went into the field hospital for repair instead of going out with the dashing cavalryman and his soldiers. The remote result may be that I now am alive instead of having been dead more than fifty years. Perhaps I should have been by the side of Mitch Buoyer when he was killed with Custer.

The confidence pervading the whole body of United States soldiers—at least manifested by the officers—is evidenced by this writing in Bradley's diary a month before the coming of Terry and Custer:

May 17. . . . but now the enemy had been found and we were going over to whip them. . . . Among the most enthusiastic were the Crows, who had chafed under the disgrace they had suffered in the abstraction of their horses, and who now beamed with satisfaction.

Here follows a description of the difficulties encountered in the attempt to get our troops in a large body across the Yellowstone, which event has been mentioned in preceding pages herein, after which the lieutenant records:

And so we failed to march against the foe. . . . The Crows, who were the most jubilant, were now . . . the most crestfallen.

True, there were exhibitions of jubilation. True, there was an ensuing manifestation of great disappointment. But among the Crows, there was not unanimity of desire to cross over and stay there in a persisting and conclusive conflict. The soldiers cheered and afterward groaned, thus presenting the appearance of great anxiety to come to close quarters with the enemy. I do not know how they actually felt about it. I do know, though, that the Crows expressed many misgivings when talking among themselves. From past experiences they knew that, as the spring and summer progressed, this region —the Powder, Tongue, and Rosebud river country —regularly was increased greatly in its population by the invading Sioux and Cheyennes. Whatever confidence our scouts felt was instilled artificially by the airs of the soldiers, whose talk convinced these red men that white men professional fighters were invincible.

I did not see General Custer nor any officer or man under his command, except as I saw their general encampment across the river from us. The steamboat had come up again from Terry's base at the mouth of Powder River, and it moved back and forth across the Yellowstone between our two camps here. I believe it merely transported the officers or afforded a meeting-place for them for their councils.

When Custer's command moved away to go up the Rosebud, our Gibbon corps of cavalry and infantry, with infantry and artillery belonging with Terry, set off up the Yellowstone valley. The steamboat proceeded also upstream, carrying a load of troops and supplies. We all headed in at the former base camp opposite the mouth of the Bighorn River, on Pease Bottom, or at old Fort Pease, where had been in earlier times the free-trader location of the Major Pease who had been our Crow agent at the old Mission.

I rode this journey of sixty miles in an ambulance, as a hospital patient. It was not in any way a pleasant trip, covering two full days. My preference was to be on duty, riding over the hills. But this was impracticable and, of course, not allowable. At the resumed location I continued to be a patient in the field hospital. From there I learned, by hearsay only, the stories of the thrilling few days that followed. The character of the weather and the condition of the trails may be learned by reference to the diary of Matt Carroll, master of Gibbon's wagon-trains:

June 22. Roads bad . . . programme is now to go to Fort Pease, when the boats will join us and cross the cavalry over. Indians supposed to be on the Bighorn or . . . tributaries.

And, the next day:

June 23. . . . day warm . . . trouble crossing creeks . . . account of heavy rains . . . twenty-two miles . . . camped one mile Fort Pease . . . cavalry camped two miles above Fort Pease.

These fragmentary diary extracts throw collateral beams of light that illumine many interesting phases of that very interesting period in our frontier history. Some condensed abstracts from Bradley's writings fix attention upon features of military custom and procedure peculiar to the situation then confronting our forces. For example, recorded as we all were leaving the Rosebud base camp:

Thursday, June 22. . . . battery of three Gatling guns. They belong to Custer's column, but were detached . . . might impede his march.

Again, on the same date:

Thursday, June 22. . . . Throughout the campaign the general [that is, General Gibbon during the preceding two months on the Yellowstone] has allowed neither drums nor bugles to sound.

Hopefulness, utter confidence, with the consequent freedom from restraint that had been regarded as necessary theretofore, are indicated in Bradley's comment the next day:

Friday, June 23. The reveille of the cavalry bugles came sweetly to the ear this morning over the intervening space.

On the twenty-fourth of June I sadly watched our fighting men and all of my Crow scouts ferried over from opposite the mouth of the Bighorn to the south side of the Yellowstone. They became lost to my view as they moved away in the direction of Tulloch's Fork. Barney Bravo had my place as leader of and interpreter for the seventeen Crow Indians accompanying the troops.

General Custer has been charged with excess of zeal—or worse—in his movement up the Rosebud and on to the Little Bighorn. It has been pointed out that he marched so rapidly as to exhaust the energies of both his men and his horses, and thus made himself an easy prey for the Sioux, who had been resting and waiting for him to come. But the troops of all commanders in this campaign were hurrying. They were afraid the Sioux might get away! Custer covered a little less than a hundred miles between the mouth of the Rosebud and the site of his battle. An approximation of his daily travel during that time is this: June 22, fifteen miles. June 23, thirty miles. June 24, thirty-five miles. Early morning and forenoon of June 25, twenty miles. Total, one hundred miles.

Matt Carroll's wagon-trains moved along the Yellowstone, a distance of twenty-two miles on that June twenty-third when Custer's cavalry is said to have "rushed" thirty miles. And Matt Carroll records that on this day he had "trouble crossing the creeks on account of heavy rains." On the twenty-fifth, his wagon-train made twenty miles on the march up the Bighorn, notwithstanding the whole column became lost for a time in the rugged hills up Tulloch's Fork. If Custer's light-baggage horsemen and pack-mules were being urged into hurried movement, how about Carroll's heavily loaded wagon-trains accompanying Terry?

Terry's forces also were in lively movement, although they used up some of their energies by rambling off from the nearest and best trails. In his extensive record of the events of June twenty-fifth among the Terry troops, Bradley says, "The infantry, which had already marched twenty-three miles, were to remain in camp for the night." Further along in his notes of this day's movements he informs the reader, "Cavalry marched about thirty-five miles, my detachment about fifty-five." This was crowding more spiritedly than Custer was doing.

Furthermore, the Terry forces got up early in the morning and hastened, anxious to catch the Sioux, whom they knew to be not far away. On June twenty-sixth, early in the morning and before they knew Custer had been in any conflict:

Major Brisbin, who in General Gibbon's absence commands the column, roused me . . . ordered . . . scout at once . . . not any breakfast. I was vexed . . . did not get off until 4 a.m. Sent six Crow scouts an hour earlier.

It seems their activity and progress at least equaled that of Custer's command, and the advance of the Terry column must have been accomplished after greater effort, by reason of the fact that they had no well-informed guide, while Custer had with him Mitch Buoyer, who knew so well the location of every creek and hill that no waste motion occurred while following his lead.

Custer himself was a tireless rider, and whoever served under him might have improved his own endurance in this regard. In his book, "Life on the Plains," telling of his Indian campaigns in the southern plains regions and published only a few months before his death, the energetic cavalry general mentions in various places the rate of travel by his troops. In a return to Fort Harker from one expedition they marched "about one hundred and fifty miles in fifty-five hours, including all halts." During that same season "with a larger command, I marched sixty miles in fifteen hours." Himself, two officers, and two troopers went back to Fort Harker in advance of the main body on one occasion, these five men "having made the ride of sixty miles without change of animals in less than twelve hours." He writes of his campaigning in the Kansas country that "our average daily march when not in pursuit of the enemy was about twenty-five miles." All of this, and more if it were worth while citing other figures, tends to disprove allegations that Custer made an extraordinary effort to hurry along the Rosebud trail and get to the Sioux first, when his maximum distance traveled in any one day was but thirty-five miles. I can but think that his men and his horses were very tired when they reached the Little Bighorn, and that their fighting efficiency was much diminished because of this; but it was his way, and on many previous occasions he had succeeded by reason of this same kind of dashing movements. Moreover, the Terry-Gibbon troops going up the Bighorn were almost exhausted, and this would have hindered them also if they had met and engaged the Sioux.

On Monday morning following my going into hospital at Fort Pease camp, as I rambled by the river I saw an Indian come on horseback to the opposite bank. He dismounted and set himself at building a fire, as if he would cook a breakfast. I watched him awhile, then I called across and attracted his attention. By sign-talk I learned he was one of my scouts, Curly, the seventeen-year-old Crow. He signed an inquiry as to the whereabouts of Gray Beard, their name for General Gibbon. I indicated he had gone up the Bighorn River on the steamboat. Curly mounted his horse and rode away in that direction. I supposed he had a despatch. He gave to me no intimation of there having been a fight. He told me afterward he was so sleepy he was thinking everybody knew all about it. He took the news to Gibbon, but this was not his special intent. He merely was looking for the Gibbon soldiers, to report for further duty. That same morning Bradley's Crow scouts sign-talked across the Bighorn River with the Reno and Custer Crows who were fleeing to the agency. From these escaping scouts the column of soldiers learned of the calamity.

All of Bradley's Crows joined the deserters and went to the agency. White Swan and Half Yellow Face were hemmed up with Reno. These two and Curly now were the only Crows we had. The deserters said afterward they had considered the war as being ended, but it was apparent they feared it had just begun. However, they had committed no military offense in having put themselves out of distance when the actual fighting began. Scouts were employed to *find* the enemy, not obliged to *fight* them. This latter activity was the duty of the soldiers. Lieutenant Bradley had reminded me of this on the occasion when he had me arrested for having permitted my scouts to go out and attack the Sioux who had killed our blacksmith and the three soldiers when they were hunting antelope. Mitch Buoyer, hired as a guide, could have gone away honorably into safety as soon as the Sioux village on the Little Bighorn was discovered had he chosen to do so. It is said that Custer reminded him of this, but in a challenging sort of way that brought from Mitch a retort that he was not afraid to go into any danger that the soldiers were regarded as capable of meeting. He is said also to have expressed to the general his conviction of the magnitude of his undertaking. This warning was the basis for Custer's sarcastic release of Mitch and the latter's stubborn refusal to accept it. Perhaps Buoyer's being one-half Sioux afforded ground for a feeling in the mind of the high officer that his good guide over the trails had a biased judgment when the fighting capabilities of the Sioux were under consideration.

I interpreted for Lieutenant Bradley when he

interviewed Curly, several ʻdays after the Custer battle had occurred. He was spoken of then as the "sole survivor" of the disaster. But he himself did not lay claim to that kind of distinction. On the contrary, again and again during the long examination of him by Bradley, the young scout said, "I was not in the fight." When gazed upon and congratulated by visitors he declared, "I did nothing wonderful; I was not in it." He told us that when the engagement opened he was behind, with other Crows. He hurried away to a distance of about a mile, paused there, and looked for a brief time upon the conflict. Soon he got still farther away, stopping on a hill to take another look. He saw some horses running away loose over the hills. He turned back far enough to capture two of the animals, but later he decided they were an impediment to his progress away from the Sioux, so he released them. He told me he directed his course toward Tulloch's Fork and came down the same trail I had come down on another occasion with Captain Ball and Lieutenant Roe.

Romantic writers seized upon Curly as a subject suited to their fanciful literary purposes. In spite of himself, he was treated as a hero. He took no special pains to deny the written stories of his unique cunning. He could not read, he could speak only a little English, and it is likely he knew of no reason why he should make any special denial. The persistent claim put forward for him by others, but as though it came direct from him, brought upon him from some of the Sioux the accusation, "Curly is a liar; nobody with Custer escaped us." But he was not a liar. All through his subsequent life he modestly avowed from time to time what he did to Bradley, "I did nothing wonderful; I was not in the fight." I knew him from his early boyhood until his death in early old age. He was a good boy, an unassuming and quiet young man, a reliable scout, and at all times of his life he was held in high regard by his people.

SCOUTING AGAIN AFTER SITTING BULL'S SIOUX

THE Sioux had left the Little Bighorn, at first moving away southward in a great body, but soon separating into bands. The dead bodies on Custer field had been discovered and buried there as decently as conditions would permit. Major Reno's wounded had been carried in litters borne by walking soldiers to the steamboat at the mouth of the Little Bighorn, where they were embarked and carried down the streams to Fort Lincoln, Dakota. The remnant of the Seventh Cavalry came under Terry's command and marched down to our base camp on Pease Bottom, at the mouth of the Bighorn River. A reorganization of all the forces took place and new military units were ordered from elsewhere into this region. The program was expanded. It was determined to hunt down and drive back to their reservations or to kill all the Indians roaming here without lawful right, or without what the War Department construed to be lawful right. To do this it was helpful to have scouts—Indian scouts preferred.

The Crows were most conveniently accessible and knew best the country. So it was decided to give them another trial.

Half Yellow Face, White Swan, and Curly were the only Crows I now had remaining of the twenty-three originally enlisted. Half Yellow Face and White Swan had been with Reno on his entrenched hill, Curly had been with Custer. All of the others had deserted and had gone back to Absaroka. General Terry sent for me to visit his headquarters. He asked about my injured shoulder, made solicitous inquiry about my general health, then put a question:

"Where are the Crows?"

I supposed he meant my scouts, and I replied to him that all but three were gone. He explained, though, that he wanted to know where the Crows as a tribe could be found. My information had been that they were at that time encamped at the mouth of Pryor Creek, one of their favorite assembling places, and I so informed the general.

"We are going to have a big campaign," he followed up, "and we want you to go and recruit for us as many of them as you can get for scouts."

General Terry stated that he would have me put upon the pay-roll as a quartermaster employee, thus adding materially to my compensation. This welcome news served as the stimulus he evidently intended it to serve.

My three Crow scouts and myself set out the following morning to find the tribal camp. We each had extra horses that had been given to us from the captured mounts found running loose in the hills after the Custer battle. I had two of them, which I was taking to give to Cherry. The horses counted for us as coups, according to the Crow Indian code of war. A man named McCormick was traveling with us. He had some canned goods in his stock of provisions. At a camp along the way, as we prepared the meal, we put upon the fire some of the unopened cans, to heat the contents. Curly and McCormick were attending to the cooking just then. Half Yellow Face and I were sitting down and leaning back against two trees beside each other as we alternated in puffing a common smoke from my little stone medicine-pipe. The terrible warfare that was only a week in the past was being discussed. We talked of what other warfare might follow. The country was full of Sioux, and they were in high glee and full of courage because of their recent great victory. They probably would be more bold now than ever, and—

"*Pop!*"

Curly and McCormick dived for a brush thicket.

Half Yellow Face and I both lay down quickly—or fell down—and went scrambling on hands and knees after our two companions. It was several seconds before we realized that the disturbing blast was caused by the explosion of one of the sealed vegetable cans being heated in the fire.

Arriving opposite the mouth of Pryor Creek, we saw the Crow lodges across on the south side of the Yellowstone. Oh, what a beautiful scene it was! And how glad I was to get back home! Half Yellow Face shouted across to the people, and we at once plunged our horses in for the swim. It so happened we landed right where Cherry and her people had their group of lodges. She saw us. She dropped from her hands a bucketful of water and came running to us. She had just come from a swimming-party in the river, and her hair was wet and flowing in bedraggled strings. Nevertheless, my mind just now conceives a picture of her at that moment as being the most beautiful woman I ever saw.

"Oh, are you hurt?" were her first words as she seized me and we exchanged embraces and mingled our tears of joy. My arm still was being carried in a sling, although I was almost recovered.

She led me to our lodge and put quickly into order a pallet of blankets and buffalo-robes upon which I might sit, as the head of the household.

My beloved son Tom wallowed all over me. Visiting friends crowded in to shake hands, to bless me, to ask about the great battle that had taken place on the Little Bighorn. I never in my lifetime experienced any day more full of domestic happiness. Cherry too was bubbling over with glad feelings. She had to tell me all about the bright sayings and doings of our boy, the same as white women do, and I enjoyed them, the same as other white men do. Her innate mirthfulness fully exhibited itself. She playfully informed me of various supposed sweethearts of mine who had been anxiously inquiring as to when I might return to camp. Meantime, the meat pot was boiling and special friends were invited in to join us in a feast.

My three Crow companions had receptions like mine. It soon became known why we had come. There was a hubbub of conflicting talk about what should be done in the matter. The subject was discussed in the home lodges that day and that night. The next morning Shot in the Jaw mounted his horse as a herald and rode all through the camps. Everywhere among them he shouted the announcement:

"Horse Rider has something to say in council."

The council of old men assembled. As a figure of importance just then, I was seated at the head of the council-lodge. Notwithstanding everybody in the village knew the purpose of our coming to the Crows at this time, after the usual tedium of a deliberate smoke and a prolonged silence I was asked the formal question:

"What is your present business with us?"

A mob of Crow Indians—men, women, and children—wrangled in tumultuous controversy all about the vicinity of the council-lodge. There were cheers, singing of war-songs, shooting of guns into the air, other cheers. Conversely, women declared their feelings, "I shall not permit my husband to go," or, "My son shall not go to be killed by the Sioux in protection of the white soldiers." "You have heard what happened to the white soldiers, and the same will happen to our young men if they go now to fight the Sioux," other peace-loving people argued. Old women stood here and there chanting of the deaths that were in store for foolish and adventuresome men.

One old man rode among the people and called out, over and over, "I want to get the ear of Horse Rider." He got my ear, as I could hear him urging the warriors to join in the movement. Some of them responded, "We shall go, and when we return our faces will be painted black"—that is, they would kill Sioux in revenge, and the blackened faces would be the token of their victory. To back up these willing supporters of the military honor of the Crows, a group of women carrying scalps on sticks serenaded them and came near to the council-lodge entrance and sang there in praise of my wonderful ability as a warrior. Chief Blackfoot committed himself only in, "Yes, they treated our white soldier friends pretty badly and we should not forget this." The council finally arrived at a decision. A herald was sent among the people to announce:

"Young men, we do not send you. But if you want to do so, you may go."

More than fifty enlistments occurred within a few hours. It appeared that the two or three good horses each of us returning scouts had brought with us had considerable weight in bringing favor upon our proposed new enterprise. We had been authorized to let women come along and live at the base camps if they should wish to come. A few of them attached themselves to the drove of men. Every individual had a saddle-pony and many had additional pack-horses. Cherry thought at first of going, but she afterward decided it would be much better for both her and our son to remain with her people in the tribal camp.

The enlisting Indians all boarded a steamboat that had come up to the mouth of Pryor Creek for them. The vessel had two decks. The horses were left on the lower level. The men and women favored the upper one, where the view was broader. There was much difficulty in keeping them from crowding too much in any one place on the boat, thus tilting it dangerously. A big band of special entertainers among them assembled on the upper deck at the bow. They beat their tom-toms and used clubs to pound upon the railings. They yelled, howled, sang their war-songs, the principal refrain of which was, "You killed our soldier friends and we shall have revenge." It was a continual pandemonium all the way down to the old cantonment on the north side of the Yellowstone opposite the mouth of the Big-horn, where we landed.

Preparations were made for moving on down the river. After a few days the whole section of the army located here were on the march. At this time I separated from Lieutenant Bradley, and this was our last contact. He was sent back to Fort Ellis or to Fort Shaw, and during the following summer he was killed in the upper Big Hole River battle with the Nez Percés. Since Mitch Buoyer had been killed, my duties included at times the position of guide, as well as scout and interpreter, although this special function of guiding was performed mostly by white-men civilians more familiar with the country on the lower Yellowstone and its tributaries there. We were located again opposite the mouth of the Rosebud, and from this base the search for hostile Sioux was renewed. General Gibbon still was in his same place of command, but the presence now of General Terry put this higher-ranking officer at the head of our local army. The waters of the Yellowstone had receded somewhat from the early-summer flood, and the crossing now was not so difficult.

An early military movement in this our second campaign was up the Rosebud valley. My scouts were kept scattered, as usual, upon and beyond the outskirts of the column of soldiers. One day some Crows farthest ahead saw dust-clouds in the distance to the southward. They signaled back, and the news of the discovery reached the army officers. It appeared we were about to come into touch with a band of the Sioux then roving here and there over this whole broad area of wild country. Orders were snapped out. The marching column deployed into front lines. A newspaper reporter who was with us hurried forward to learn what was going on. I remember he was somewhat corpulent, perhaps he might be called a fat man. I remember, too, how brave he was—or how brave he affected to be. He was mounted on a big horse, as properly should have been the case, and he rode along the front lines flourishing a rifle and declaring, "Boys, I'll be right with you in this fight." I did not observe any appearance of new confidence because of this announcement, but there was some noticeable amusement at the funny-looking fat man's dramatic proclamation. It developed, though, that the encounter was a peaceful one. The dust had been kicked up by the horses of the soldiers commanded by General Crook, who just then was coming again into the field after his repulse by the Indians on the upper Rosebud a week before the Custer battle.

I and all of my Crow scouts were transferred to General Crook. The Crows at once fixed upon this big-chief white-man the name "Braided Beard." Some other Indians knew him as "Three Stars." His supply officers issued to all of us a new and complete stock of ammunition. Along the borders of this unit army we worked back a little distance up the Rosebud, and then we crossed over the divide to the valley of the Tongue River.

On the Tongue River we had trouble trying to find good water. There was so much alkali in the water we could get there that an epidemic of digestive disorder raged among us. We had better luck after we crossed on eastward to the Powder River. Here we met Gibbon. I believe Terry also was here; but I am not sure of this. Anyway, there was a call for some one to take a despatch at once to Colonel Miles, who recently had arrived on the Yellowstone. The horses all were tired out, the men likewise wanted nothing more earnestly than a good chance to rest, so there was not any rush for the opportunity to ride at once the distance of about twelve miles. It seemed to be regarded as incumbent upon the scouts to provide the sacrifice, so Buffalo Horn, a Bannack serving among my Crows, agreed to go with me. When we were about to start, W. F. Cody, known as Buffalo Bill, announced his desire to go with us, which he did. He was at that time in service as a guide for General Crook.

We saw many criss-crossing and varying Sioux trails along the way, some of them freshly made. These were of small bodies of Indian rovers hunting, or spying upon our troop movements. Perhaps some of them saw us, but we did not get a glimpse of any of them along this journey. As we came close to the Yellowstone our attention was drawn to a broad patch of brassy, shimmering ground surface by the bank of the stream. We stopped to look closely, but just then we could not determine its nature. When we got down to it, though, we found thousands of bushels of corn scattered there. Steamboats had unloaded a great supply of this commodity, sufficient to fill the needs of a large army over a long period of time. The Sioux had found it there. They had cut open the sacks, had spilled out the grain, and had carried away with them all of the canvas bag material.

We three stayed at Miles' cantonment, since the troops we had left were to come on here. When they all had assembled, the officers had a council. It appeared they decided that just then they would do no more mass campaigning. The Sioux were rambling now in small bands, so it was thought that the mere establishing of a permanent base was the best plan. We now were at the mouth of Powder River. Miles was expected to go up the river and establish the permanent base, Gibbon and his forces were to return to Fort Ellis and Fort Shaw, Terry and the Dakota troops were turned back toward Fort Lincoln and Fort Yates. Our Crow scouts were released from immediate duty and told they might go to the agency, later to be discharged in due form.

A "free trader," or "whisky trader," as they sometimes were known, had come from Bozeman to Benson's Landing, where Livingston now is, and at this point he had loaded his goods into a flatboat and floated down the Yellowstone in search of soldier patronage. His main supply in the way of intoxicants was Jamaica ginger. He did not have to beat drums in order to attract customers. Barney

Bravo was one of the drunken results of the traffic. The Crows hog-tied him, hand and foot, and put him into his lodge.

We scouts all went up the river to the Rosebud camp, where we got our few women and their lodges and effects. Then we kept on westward. We traveled slowly, diverging to hunt along the way. At Pompey's Pillar we swam our horses and transported our whole caravan to the south side of the Yellowstone. We still moved in leisurely manner toward the Absaroka agency. Here we waited until Gibbon's troops passed up the river on their way to Fort Ellis. We followed them on to this regular post. Here we were discharged in due form from the military service.

Our women all went with us to Fort Ellis. When we got our pay the whole band of us went on to Bozeman. This was the most convenient place where we could get rid of our money. We bought blankets, provisions, tobacco, ammunition, calico, everything we could buy, as long as the money lasted. In that sort of life we had nothing to do with money except to spend it. Mitch Buoyer's widow was with Cherry on this journey. She received the pay due to Mitch. Cherry and I did what we could to cheer her. She was very sad.

Race-horses engaged the interest of the Crows at

Fort Ellis. Bozeman and Gallatin Valley white men had brought the animals there for this purpose. The Indians invested a large part of their funds in them, suited, as they were, either for sport or for hunting and warfare. When we got back to Absaroka these horses had to be tested thoroughly against all others in the tribe and against each other. Horce-racing was for a few weeks more than ever a leading feature of festive occasions.

I lived altogether as an Indian during the ensuing few weeks. Cherry and I still had plenty of money left to supply our simple wants for a long time, so I did not accept offered employment in the agency government service. That might come later, but just then I wanted to roam and do some hunting, without restraint of any kind. Word came of permanent military forts likely to be built on the Yellowstone and the Bighorn. This was comforting news, but to me it was not of paramount interest. One day at the agency, though, my mind became intently engaged upon the subject. This situation arose from the fact that Captain Hargus and a body of the Fifth Infantry from the new Fort Keogh arrived at Absaroka.

"I'm looking for you, Leforge," was the captain's greeting to me.

I was stunned for a moment.

"Sir, what am I supposed to have done?" I asked.

"It seems you haven't done enough," came the reply. He then went on to inform me that they wanted Crow Indian scouts at Fort Keogh, that General Miles had sent him to bring me and a band of Crow scouts, that the men could take along their wives and families and live there as their home place while doing scout duty in the surrounding country.

It required little or no effort to get enlistments this time. We had been treated well on the recent campaign, had been paid off, most of the money was spent, and the warriors had been back on the reservation just about long enough to be anxious to go out again in search of adventure. The advent of additional soldiers, the scattering of the Sioux, the oncoming of winter weather, all combined to overcome the former objections of fearful women.

We marched away down the valley two days afterward. Only a few women cared to go, but these were taken along with us. Again my wife expressed her preference for staying at the agency. Inside of a week we were on duty at General Miles' new base near the mouth of Tongue River and on the south side of the Yellowstone. It had been named Fort Keogh in honor of Captain Keogh, who had been killed with General Custer. To my astonishment, I was informed there by the paymaster clerk, George

Miles, that I had four hundred dollars due to me as a salaried employee of the quartermaster department. I had supposed this was discontinued after my discharge at Fort Ellis, but by the considerate action of General Terry I had been kept on the civilian-employee roll. I felt very grateful for this favor, and I am confident I tried hard thereafter to justify the kindly general in this exercise of his discretion.

A band of hostile Cheyennes had been seen east of our location. Major Brisbin, leader of the cavalry, was ordered to go out after them. The order was issued by General Whistler, temporarily in command during the absence of General Miles. I went with all of my Crow scouts to accompany Major Brisbin's troops. We crossed the Powder River, followed trails on toward Rainy Ridge, toward the Black Hills. Day after day we made marches that were utterly fruitless. On the Heart River we came into contact with Colonel Gibson. From here we began a return march.

Food became scarce with us. In fact, we exhausted our supply. There was no game. The country that had been so rich in buffalo and other wild creatures was barren of animal life. Indians and whites together had exterminated them from this region. We killed some mules, and the soldiers ate this meat. I ate a little of it. My Indians refused it. They preferred prairie-dogs, which were not difficult to obtain. I myself liked this meat. Prairie-dog tastes good when it is well roasted. Fuel also was scarce over much of the journey, and at many of our camping places it was not obtainable—no wood, not even the plainsman's convenient buffalo-chips, since these creatures did not inhabit this region any more. A little of the depletion of our meat stock was due to our using bacon-grease for oiling grass so that it would make a hotter fire for cooking coffee.

White Man Runs Him, one of my scouts, killed a little fawn as we came down the Little Powder River. He distributed it among his immediate friends, giving me some. But it lasted only one meal —or a part of a meal—for a few of us. Further along the march this same industrious Indian again eased our hunger, this time by finding considerable quantities of hardtack, bacon, and other food-stuffs scattered along the trail of a pack-train that had followed us out to bring us the provisions, but had lost our route and never did find us.

On this long and trying journey we never got even a glimpse of any hostile Indian nor saw the recent trails of any. We saw lots of old trails and found many places where there had been past encampments. At one place many lodge-poles had been abandoned, and at this same place there were numerous discarded plum-seeds, this indicating that the site had been occupied by a camp not long before, since this was in the latter part of the plum season.

Three Crow women remained with us through the entire expedition. They did no more complaining about the distressful conditions than the men did. I recall particularly that White Man Runs Him had with him his comforter in domestic life. I recall also that when we got back to Fort Keogh somebody there looked critically at me and asked what it was I had tucked under and dangling from my belt. I had forgotten to remove it before resuming association with civilized and well-fed people. It was a dead prairie-dog.

Cherry and some other women came down the river and joined us at the post. Myself and other husbands were gladdened by their presence. We had much social visiting in our scout camp. A few weeks of leisure followed our return from the long ride toward the Black Hills and everything was running along pleasantly until one day my Crow scouts spoiled all the fun. A band of them were out in the hills for hunting or for mere pleasure. They saw in the distance some other Indians. There were six of these strangers. The Crows watched closely from hiding-places and learned they were Sioux. Here was a chance to do something important. The Crows waited until the right moment arrived, then they charged upon the Sioux and killed five of them. The victors came whooping back to the post with the scalps of their fallen enemies. A few hours afterward they learned that their victims had been coming as delegates from a band of Sioux far up Powder River who wanted to surrender to General Miles.

The killing of the Sioux peace delegates frightened as well as shamed the Crows. This was a serious violation of the rules of war which even the Indians observed. According to the code, these Crow scouts now were outlaws, never to be recognized thereafter as entitled to any mercy. They had rendered themselves liable to be singled out specially and hunted continually to their death. They now were at the disadvantage always suffered by one who is in the wrong and knows he is in the wrong, in contrast with the advantage accruing to one who is in the right and knows he is in the right. They counciled about the situation and decided to go back to the agency. Various individuals who had not been in the affray determined also to get away as far as possible from the vengeance of the Sioux. Two nights afterward a big body of my scouts, with their women and their camp equipment, deserted and fled up the Yellowstone. I now had command of only myself and my wife, Half Yellow Face, Old Bear, and Buffalo Horn, the Bannack. This situation continued until the latter part of the winter.

A midwinter campaign was entered upon by General Miles. During late December he moved with a large body of troops up the Tongue River, whence reports had come of a big camp of the hostile Northern Cheyennes. As we came close to where Hanging Woman Creek empties into the Tongue River I located myself beside a rock on a high point to examine the country. Only a few hundred yards away, seven blanketed figures on horseback appeared suddenly. They were huddled up to keep warm as they moved along the bench-land in my direction. The Crows and myself opened fire upon them. They appeared uncertain whether to stand still or run away. We advanced closer, and finally we charged upon them. We discovered they were four women, two girls, and a boy. Although they were Cheyennes, one good-looking woman among them could talk Crow well enough to make herself understood in that language. She told us they were trying to find Bear Shirt, the name applied by them to General Miles, and that they wanted to surrender to him. This woman had an old horse-pistol. I took it from her.

I took the seven prisoners to the soldiers, who

were just going into camp for the night. Liver-eating Johnson, George Johnson, and some other white men serving as scouts joined us as we were escorting the captives. Yellowstone Kelley had turned back when we charged upon the unknown Indians and had steered his galloping mount to the main soldier body. When afterward he was twitted about this movement he claimed credit for the important act of having informed the troops of the encounter. However, he was employed as a guide, not as a fighter. His usefulness arose from the fact that for several previous years he had hunted game and had chopped wood for steamboats on the Missouri and lower Yellowstone rivers.

The captives were put into a separate tent and a guard was placed near its entrance. This precaution was not to protect us nor to prevent their escape. They were being shielded from the intrusions of soldiers. The boy and one girl had their feet frozen. Our medical officers attended them. The women informed us that other Cheyennes wanted to come and surrender.

I went out again with the scouts to watch for the approach of the other Cheyennes. We saw some Indians, but they rode hurriedly away out of our sight. We kept on going in their direction, but we spread out and went carefully, skittishly. Suddenly fifteen or twenty Cheyenne warriors jumped up from apparently nowhere and began to shoot at us. Yellowstone Kelley again dutifully dashed away to spread the news in distant regions. Myself and the other scouts fought back as we retreated toward our military forces. We all were on horseback, and we were about a mile away across the river from the main body.

My horse groaned and fell just as it was going down the last ridge to the valley. I was pitched forward head first. The last glimpse I had of any of my companions immediately preceding the fall was of Buffalo Horn forty or fifty feet from me, pausing there as he leveled his rifle to fire at the pursuing Cheyennes a hundred or more yards up the sloping bench. Half Yellow Face and Old Bear already had disappeared into the timber by the river.

The stunning result of my fall lasted only a few seconds, as well as I could estimate. My horse was dead. My rifle was not anywhere in view. The Cheyennes still were shooting in my direction. One of my legs was sprained and bruised, but this was all the injury to myself I could perceive. I crept into a washout gulch near me and stayed there close to the ground, or trying to imbed myself into the ground. I admit a feeling of fear. About this time Lieutenant Casey's troops had turned out and were firing Hotchkiss guns in the direction of the Indians. It was becoming almost dark, so the aim could not be accurate. The shots actually were falling beyond the enemy, which fact caused them to remain near me instead of driving them away from me. But this shooting kept them interested, at least, and therefore they did not trouble me further, or they had decided I already was killed.

I remained hidden in the gulch for two or three hours. The shooting had ceased long before this, but it seemed wise to keep quiet, since one never could know how patiently an Indian might wait to settle in his mind any doubt he might have as to whether or not he had killed his man. After having become fully satisfied that nobody was watching me, I carefully crawled out of my hole. Very soft treading characterized my sneak onward into the timber by the river. The solid ice afforded an easy crossing, and within a few minutes the heat from a wood-pile fire was thawing out my chilled body. Buffalo Horn told me he had taken a hasty look at me just before he had left, that he was convinced I was dead, and that he had reported this to be the case. Of course, my reappearance among them was as though the dead had come to life, so it was an occasion for joyful congratulations.

A new name, "Captured Seven," was conferred

upon me by my Crow associates. This name never did stick tightly to me, but thereafter it sometimes was used as a designation secondary to my regular Indian name, Horse Rider. The capture of four women and three children as they were coming in to surrender was not a feat that seemed worthy of boastful coup-counting, but my Crow Indian friends made the most of it. They reminded me that the capture of the pistol is always considered a distinct and separate coup. Anyhow, my exploit was greater than that of any one else thus far. Several years afterward I disposed of this second name in time-honored fashion. A Crow friend of mine requested me to set my mind at work and formulate a name for his young son. My mind worked rapidly, the appellation came quickly upon the tongue. This boy got the name "Captured Seven."

No other extensive operations appearing in the plans for the rest of the winter, myself and the three remaining Crow scouts were given a furlough of indefinite duration. The enlistments were for six months, but we were told we might go to the agency and stay there during the rest of the term or until called for by special messenger. So we set off up the Yellowstone. White Calfee, an old-time teamster who had been in the transportation department, traveled with us. Much of our journey was made on the solid mid-January ice, which made a smooth and pleasant road for us.

Cherry was failing in health. While she made the trip up the Yellowstone in her usual cheerful mood, it plainly was tiresome to her. As the winter began to break into early spring she grew weaker rather than stronger. The agency doctor did all that any medical man could be expected to do, but without avail. She asserted a belief that a certain Indian doc-tor could cure her. This doctor then was away with a band of Crows, including her own relatives, far to the southward, "beyond the mountains," as the region where they were camping was designated by them. She wanted to go to them. Some of our friends were about to set off for joining this band, so we agreed she should go with them.

I gave to her an ample supply of money for her use in case she should return to the agency when I might be away again with the soldiers. I let her take my discharge paper received at Fort Ellis, and I wrote also a signed letter stating, "This woman is my wife," etc., so that, in the event she might else-where come into contact with white people, she could be in possession of these papers of identification that might be helpful to her. At our parting she put her hands upon my shoulders.

"I think all the time of our happiness together," she consoled me. "The lodge that has pleased you has pleased me. We like our meat cooked the same way. We have not quarreled as some men and women do. Our paths have run side by side. But I am becoming afraid our trails must separate. My food does not nourish me. I grow weaker every day. Here—touch my breast, my arms, my shoulders. Feel that my bones stick out from the melted flesh. If I do not come back—"

I checked her. Yes, I shed tears—a flood of them. It appeared, though, that this move to her people and her favorite doctor was the only hope for her recovery. They were near some medicated hot springs well known to the Indians and in later times adopted by the white race. She took with her our son Tom and the older child, the daughter we had adopted.

That was the last time I ever saw my gentle and beloved mate. Her people told me all of the details of her last days. My letter of introduction and my Fort Ellis army discharge paper were wrapped in with her body on the burial scaffold. This disposition of the discharge paper inconvenienced me in later years. Yet every time such inconvenience occurred my heart was overwhelmed with joy. I could not feel otherwise but proud and glad that she trusted thus to notify the Spirit World that she had been the lawful wife of Thomas H. Leforge.

Cherry! Cherry! Often when I have been alone I have called out her name and have wondered if she could hear me. If it be that the best of hearts are of golden composition, surely hers was of gold—or of gold mixed with iron.

OLD FORT CUSTER ON THE BIGHORN

MITCH BUOYER'S Crow Indian widow and her two children lingered about Absaroka after her husband, my best friend, had been killed with General Custer on the hill by the Little Bighorn River. She often importuned me to help her to obtain some pension compensation for the death of her husband while serving the military forces. This woman was known to the whites as Mary Buoyer, but her personal Indian name was Magpie Outside. She was the same woman who at the old Mission agency had recommended Cherry to me and who had helped in bringing about my marriage with this girl. She was a year or so older than Cherry, and they had been all their lives on intimate terms, as Mitch and I had been close associates during the ten years of our acquaintance.

A mutual promise had been repeated many times between Mitch and myself that, if either should lose his life, the surviving one would see that the bereft family should not come to dire want. The most simple mode of performing this promise was by marriage to the widow. So Magpie Outside and I agreed that she should be my wife, second to Cherry. We felt confident Cherry would be satisfied with the arrangement, and the agent would make no objections so long as I had but one wife at the same time in my quarters. When the news came that Cherry had gone to the Unknown World, my wife Magpie Outside grieved with me. We became legally married then by the preacher, and thereafter she was my wife according to the white-man law, although, according to the law of her people, she already had this honorable status.

Lieutenant Doane, of the Second Cavalry, came to the agency with a detachment of soldiers early in the spring of 1877. He was originally of the Fort Ellis troops who had been serving under General Gibbon during the previous summer when the Custer disaster had fallen upon the military forces, but now he was to operate under the command of General Miles, who had established Fort Keogh at the mouth of the Tongue River. Doane announced to us at the agency that he was authorized to enlist as scouts all of the Crow men who could be obtained. About three hundred of them responded. I had been kept on the army-roll at Keogh during the period of idleness at the agency, so I went out again with the Crows as their immediate director in the scouting operations and as the interpreter for them in their relations with the military officers.

An early incident of this renewed service was the accompanying of Lieutenant Doane when he went up the Bighorn River in a canoe and chose the site for a new military post, to be named Fort Custer. We set out some marker stakes for the guidance of the coming pioneer corps of workers. Not long afterward I guided General Buell to the place, which was on a bench hill near the junction of the Little Bighorn and the Bighorn rivers, about fifteen miles down the valley from the site of the last stand of General Custer, after whom the post was to be named. I pointed out to the soldier workmen the stakes Lieutenant Doane had set for the road building. On this trip we killed some buffalo and many antelope.

The Crows were used as flanker scouts, mostly on the north side of the Yellowstone during that spring and summer. War parties from Sitting Bull's Sioux still were roaming in this region, and perhaps other Sioux in stray bands were wandering here as hunters and as hostiles off their reservations. Besides these, the Piegans, Crees, Assiniboines, and other northern tribes sent out parties of ambitious young men bent upon stealing horses, which was an act of warfare and often led to armed conflict and killing.

A terrible hail-storm during this summer of 1877 sticks in my memory as one of the most torturing experiences that ever befell me. We were out on the open prairie when it came upon us. Some of our horses were killed, several of them escaped from us, and perhaps these also were beaten to death by the icy pellets, since there was no timber shelter within twenty or more miles of us. We shielded ourselves as best we could by using our horses as buffers. Once before, when I had been out hunting with some Crows, I had been caught in this sort of storm, but this occasion north of the Yellowstone was the worst I ever saw.

We scouted for troops from Fort Keogh and also from the new Fort Custer, after some of them had been located at this incomplete military post. This took us to both sides of the Yellowstone valley. On various occasions during the summer I rode over the ground where Custer and his men were buried—or were lying scattered about. I had been there at times also during the autumn of 1876, a few weeks and months after the battle.

Many a grinning skull, ribbed trunk, or detached limb bones I saw on top of the ground or but partly covered up during the year preceding the visit of the reburial squad in early June, 1877. Many times I observed indications of wolves having been at the mutilated human remnants. Some of the bodies had been dismembered and otherwise hacked and cut up immediately after death, or perhaps as a part of the death-dealing blows. Even the best of the so-called "graves" were only a few inches deep, owing to the absence of digging implements among the Gibbon soldiers who discovered and made an effort to give decent burial to the dead men. A year of rain, sunshine, freezing, thawing, elapsed between the battle and the coming of the second group of their army comrades. All of these conditions combined created a ghastly situation. The mingled odors of decayed horses and humans permeated the air. Furthermore, the foul odors were not all gone for yet another year.

I went there with the reburial detail, a detachment of the Seventh Infantry, under the command of Lieutenant Nolan. My recollection is that the present General Hugh L. Scott, retired, who at that time was a captain, also was along with these troops, but not on duty as a director of their operations. The soldiers brought with them seven coffin-boxes— big and rectangular pine boxes, not standard coffins. The remains of officers were put into these boxes, or that was the effort.

I sat on the ground not more than ten feet distant and watched the soldiers respectfully go through the motions of disinterring and transferring to a box the body of General Custer. On previous visits I had become familiar with the locations of the bodies of the officers, which had been covered up a little more carefully with the sand and sage-brush and whose positions had been specially marked. Hence, I knew that at this particular place were the remains indicated as being those of the high officer. But they gathered up nothing substantial except one thigh bone and the skull attached to some part of the skeleton trunk. Besides these, the quantity of cohering and transferable bodily substance was not enough to fill my hat. This seems so horrifying and incredible a statement, so much indicative of a mere desire to shock a hearer, that during all these subsequent more than fifty years I have controlled my tongue in this matter. But I am now old enough to speak out without fear of browbeating reprimand. I was right there and looking, and that was all there was.* The body supposed to be that of Captain Tom Custer was less cut up than that of any other officer.

The exact location of an Indian ford over the Missouri about the mouth of the Musselshell was

* Leforge's story fits exactly with statements of old Cheyennes who fought in the battle. All of them say that none of the Indians knew anything of Custer nor of any other certain soldier there. The mutilations were without discrimination.—T. B. M.

wanted by General Miles, so a man named Campbell and myself were sent out from Fort Keogh to find it. When we had discovered the place and had returned, Lieutenant Kislingberry, who served at times at Fort Keogh and at other times at Fort Custer, was sent out with a mounted detachment of the Eleventh Infantry to watch this ford. I and about a dozen of my Crows went with them.

Signs of war-parties were plentiful. Indications of recent small camp-fires came to our notice in many places. We went into camp at the mouth of the Musselshell River. One day I got at shaving myself with a razor I always carried, for use about once a week. This task completed, I made for myself a cup of coffee. About this time Lieutenant Kislingberry came to my camp-fire. I lit up my little clay medicine-pipe and he joined me for a smoke. We sat there in conversation. In a little while this developed into a resumption of sign-talk lessons he had been receiving from me. About this time:

"Waoo-oo-oo-oo!"

It was a wolf-howl by one of my scouts on a near-by hilltop. He came running down toward us. The Crows in camp hurriedly built up a little pile of buffalo-chips. The incoming news-bearer ran up to them and kicked the pile into scattered fragments. It was an act as significant as the touching of the point of a knife. It meant he considered himself on oath to tell the truth.

"They are coming—afoot!" he panted out.

Soldiers and scouts deployed out and crept through the sage-brush to the rising ground. From here we saw six or eight Indians coming afoot in our direction. They all were carrying chunks of meat slung over their shoulders. When they got within range we fired upon them. One was killed, the others all dropped their burdens and ran away. They plunged into the near-by Musselshell River and got among the logs of a heap of driftwood. It was then growing almost dark, and we had to abandon further attack. We could hear one of them crying, so we decided he was wounded.

The Crows scalped the dead victim. Kislingberry had forbidden any further mutilations, so such customary additional indignity was omitted by them. With the scalp they included one ear, with its earrings. These were of little white shells coupled together. From them we could determine that the wearer was a Sioux. In a pocket of the jacket worn by the dead Indian was a note addressed to "The blacksmith." It directed him:

The bearer of this is Little Big Toe. You will fix his knife.
                                                      AGENT.

The escaped Sioux went on down the river. We learned later that they stopped at the place operated by "Happy Jack," a whisky trader. He knew them. He told them of our plan to guard this ford as a hindrance to the invasions of hostiles. They crossed the Missouri somewhere below his trading point and went northward.

As autumn progressed toward winter, the scouts all were released and sent back to Absaroka agency. Within a week or so, though, we were visited by Sergeant McFall and a squad of soldiers from the new Fort Custer. He informed me I was wanted at that place. The summons was obeyed promptly, and the beginning of winter found me on duty there and quartered with the Crow scouts in a buffalo-skin lodge at the foot of the hill below the post and by the Little Bighorn River.

Magpie Outside came later in the winter. She brought with her my two stepchildren—the offspring of Mitch Buoyer—and our own just born son. When she arrived I was given a slab house as living-quarters, but this structure also was down by the river, where were the tepee lodges of the Crows. My wife insisted upon giving our infant son the name Tom, notwithstanding that Cherry's son, now past six years old, had this name. Cherry's boy was living with her people, so I assented to the duplication of name. Among the Crows it made no difference, since each child had its Indian name by which it was known. The white-man name was not used by them nor by the mothers. The Indian name of the older Tom, Cherry's son, was "Takes the Pony-Whip." That of Magpie Outside's little Tom was "Born in Another Place," this name coming to him by reason of his birth having occurred after I had come to Fort Custer and while she still remained at Absaroka. I was not looking forward then to a time when my two sons, having the same white-man first name and surname, might meet in their manhood an occasional confusing situation. In time, though, Cherry's son became known as "old Tom Leforge," and Magpie Outside's son was "young Tom Leforge." This was not altogether clarifying, though, since I, the original "old Tom Leforge" of that community, returned to spend my last days among the Crows after an absence of many years.

My specific position at Fort Custer during the entire nine or ten years of my service there was as the fort interpreter. But I went out as a guide and as a scout on almost every occasion where this kind of help was needed for the soldiers, and I went on many despatch errands and on other official journeys. There also was ample opportunity for hunting or for other recreation. On many occasions I guided officers out after wild game. Wildcat hunting was with them a favorite kind of sport.

The Crow scouts were allowed to go out on hunts just about whenever they wanted to do so. It was required, as a regular thing, that only a few be kept about the fort at all times, to respond to a possible sudden call for scout service. It was considered that while the Crows were hunting, their observations would be useful, equivalent to what they might be if they were continually scouring the country under the exact direction of somebody. Furthermore, this loose-rein system was the only plan acceptable to them. Continual restriction to daily going and coming according to orders would have found us without any Indian scouts as soon as the term of enlistment might expire, or even before. This term was for six months at a time. About three hundred of them was the usual number enlisted. Some of them repeated year after year, some dropped out, while others came in. Their families lived with them all the time, in lodges at the foot of the hill whereon the post was built.

We had Indian dances, adoption feasts, councils, ceremonial gatherings of the various kinds, about the same as the Crows were accustomed to have when living merely as Indians on the reservation. In summer we lolled in the shade with nothing on but breech-cloth and moccasins, or we went swimming in the Little Bighorn River. Men, women, and children played in groups in the water, the women always clad in calico dresses.

The soldiers came down from the hill every morning and every evening to water their horses. They fraternized with the Indians. There would be greetings of, "How, Jim," "Hello, Sissy," "Good morning, Mary," and so forth. The soldier swimming-place was in the Bighorn River. They would go in ambulances or on horses.

Emigrant travel along the Bozeman trail was greatly increased after the military mobilization and the clearing out of the large bands of raiding Sioux. But there were horse-stealing parties always on the lookout for emigrant horses. The Crows themselves were not altogether guiltless of this kind of hindrance to the travelers. Our scouts were expected to keep watch of our own people in this regard as well as to guard against intruding Indians from elsewhere. In the performance of this duty of guarding these emigrants from our too enterprising young men, I was out one day along the Bozeman trail with Red Wing, one of the Crow scouts. We saw a group of wagons and we rode toward them. As we arrived at a distance of twenty-five or thirty yards from the vehicle nearest, a voice rang out:

"Halt, you blank-blank-blankety-blank-blank!"

We halted. A grim-looking old man had his rifle cocked and leveled at us. He was about sixty years old, was tall, lean, was wearing long gray chin-whiskers, was chewing tobacco, had his trousers tucked into the tops of his big cowhide boots, had his old faded, black felt hat pinned up on both side rims—was altogether the picture-book type of unsophisticated, but arrogant, determination. It was evident he was crack-brained enough to shoot on suspicion only.

"Throw down yer guns and git off them horses," he commanded.

We could do nothing just then but obey him. Once dismounted, though, I began to explain that we were friends, that we had been sent out from a military post for the special purpose of helping emigrants to traverse unmolested this uncertain territory.

"But what's that Injun doin' with ye?" the stern old crank cross-examined.

"Why, he's an army scout, the same as I am."

"He's a spy, the same as you are, that's what he is," came the startling charge. "You're jist here to spot us out and go and tell the rest of 'em. But you kaint cut 'er this time. I'm goin' to kill both o' you."

But somebody interjected a plea for further investigation; other people crowded to the scene. It finally was agreed that we should go along as captives to their camp for the night. Here, after our case apparently had been discussed in many conferences wherein we were not present in person nor by attorney, an old woman who was of the type of hard-of-hearing person who himself speaks loudly pointed out a tent and shouted at us:

"You kin sleep thar."

The same old man with his same rifle still urged that we ought to be killed at once. I was glad enough to get out of his sight and into the tent. The woman had been mistaken when she told us we *could* sleep in this tent. She should have said, "You *may* sleep," etc. I slept only a little, if that much. All night we were guarded by armed men, three or four of them about the tent all the time. I was wondering every minute if the old man was there, and I was thinking every minute he might poke his gun into our prison and pull the trigger.

The next morning we were given a breakfast in the tent. When the train was ready to move, our horses were brought and we were permitted to ride them, although men with rifles in hand kept watch of us. As the forenoon progressed the situation softened and finally became entirely tolerable. I apparently convinced them of the validity of my claims. I was allowed to tie my horse behind the wagon of a fat and jolly man and ride with him. His name was Young. He had two daughters with him, and, as usually was the case with me, I soon got on pleasant terms with them. Another man in the train was named Lamartine. Before the end of this day of travel, Red Wing and I were released to resume elsewhere our hazardous vocation of protecting emigrant-trains. Years afterward, when I was residing in Livingston, I renewed acquaintance with Lamartine, who had located in that region and become a pioneer resident of the town.

A frame house equipped with stoves, bed, and other heavy articles of furniture became my family quarters after a flood had overspread the valley camping-ground one spring. This house was at the outskirts of the fort on the hill. The slab house we had been occupying was abandoned to the Indians, who continued to camp by the river.

A daily morning report at the adjutant's office was expected of me when on duty at the fort, both while I was living in the valley and in the frame house by the fort. The position of adjutant was held during practically all of my time there by Lieutenant Charles F. Roe, who afterward advanced steadily in rank until he became Major-General Roe, and who during recent years has been retired on account of age. My appearance at his office was due at the time of the regular morning guard-mount. Usually I was dismissed with the statement that no particular service was expected of me on that day. During a time when Captain Sanders was commanding officer he told me I might omit the coming each morning to headquarters, that if I were wanted, an orderly would be sent for me. I was allowed to go away hunting or for visiting with distant Crows at almost any time I might want to do so. On a few absences I went surreptitiously with the Indians on horse-stealing expeditions against the Piegans.

Some of our army horses were stolen one night when I was away from the post. The next morning a detachment of soldiers and a few of the Crow scouts went out to follow the trail of the thieves. Near the Rosebud, thirty miles to the eastward, they came upon our horses staked out by a camp of two Sioux. The two entrenched themselves on a knoll and fought back at the attacking soldiers and scouts. Finally the besieged ones quit firing. A Crow called out in Sioux language an inquiry as to whether they were dead or alive. The reply was that one of them was wounded. They were asked if they were out of ammunition, but no answer came to this question. The Crow then proclaimed to them: "We do not want to kill you. We will stop shooting at you if you will surrender." They did surrender, and they were taken to jail at Miles City. I believe they finally were released without punishment and sent back to their reservation.

Reports of Indians stealing cattle from the Nelson Story herds in the Lake Basin country, north of the Yellowstone, came to Fort Custer. Steps were taken to go on a campaign against the raiders, whoever they might be. Lieutenant Pearson took twenty-five mounted infantrymen and ten Crow scouts, including me, and we rode away into that region. We found the true situation to be that the Indians were stealing horses and were killing some cattle, but not driving away any of them. The killing of cattle during those special years was partly a wanton manifestation of resentment against white occupation of the country and partly for the purpose of obtaining food for the forayers while away from their home camps. As food, they preferred the wild game; but this source of supply was not so plentiful as it had been, so if a herd of cattle was discovered, some of them might be killed. Even then, only the tongues ordinarily were taken, or additional choice internal and external meaty portions might be cut away and used.

It was not essential that we have actual combat with raiding Indians and kill them when we went out on these expeditions. Of course, we tried to find them for fighting them, because this was an exciting and attractive sport as well as in line of our duty. But our mere presence in regions infested by raiders frightened them away, or was presumed to do so and usually did effect this result. Even if we did not see them, they might see us. Or they might find our trail and our camping places. So we might make a ride of several days or a week or so without plainly apparent success, yet the effort might have been an entirely successful one because of the fear instilled and the consequent flight of the hunted ones and their evacuation of the country.

We had only one lively incident on this particular excursion into the Lake Basin country—that is, we had but one fight, this of minor significance. Many other incidents but little less lively were scattered through the trip by reason of the multitudes of lizards and rattlesnakes inhabiting the territory traversed. We slept every night on improvised scaffolds, to avoid nocturnal companionship with these pestiferous reptiles. Thoughts of them helped us to get up early each morning of the long summer days. But I always liked to be up early, especially in summer. I am in this regard a true sun-worshiper. Red Wing, Three Irons, and Scratch His Face were regularly with me as the first ones up and stirring about when dawn came.

One morning Red Wing and I went soon after daylight to a hill to look over the surrounding country, and incidentally to indulge in the Indian morning spiritual exercise of watching the beloved sun return to enliven and fructify the otherwise cold and inanimate earth. The scouts of the evening before had reported no evidence of other people anywhere in this vicinity. We sat there smoking, meditating, exchanging occasional brief words of conversation. Red Wing told me of a recent dream of his, wherein an unusually wise and wary wolf imparted to him much useful information. "A scout is like a lone wolf," he said the dream animal had told him, "that must be looking, looking, looking, all the time."

A white horse far off across the prairie plain attracted our attention. It came galloping in our direction. We soon saw that an Indian was mounted on it. The animal evidently was very tired, as though a long ride had been made. The rider directed his steed to the border of the lake beside which was our camp. The stop was made about a quarter of a mile from us. I watched the man and horse while Red Wing ran down to inform our party. The horse drank as though it had not seen water for many days. The man dismounted and splashed water upon his naked body. He unbraided and rebraided his hair.

I hurried to capture and mount my horse. The scouts had been withheld by the lieutenant until all were ready, so by the time we started for the lone horseman I was at the head of my scouts, who were at their regular position in the lead. Five or six of us got close enough to charge upon the man before he discovered our presence. We were only a hundred and fifty yards from him, and we gained upon him some more while he was mounting and getting his animal under way. Our rested horses soon overtook him, and we surrounded him. I had a needle-gun. I got up close and fired, but the movements of my horse as well as his prevented good aim, so I missed. He dashed toward me. Our knees locked, both of us bareback on our horses. He shot at me with his cap-and-ball pistol, but missed. At once he shot again, this time cutting the fringe on the shoulder of my buckskin jacket. The Crows were afraid to shoot just at this time, since they might hit me. One of them, though, jumped in and counted coup on the enemy during the short period of the close contact. At the first opportunity a Crow shot the man, then others of them shot him. He tumbled dead from his horse.

I had grabbed his pistol as we struggled, and when he fell from his horse I slid off mine after him and thus got full possession of the weapon. It was a

Remington cap-and-ball six-shooter. This seizing and keeping of the adversary's gun was accounted among the Indians as a first-class coup. A second coup was allowable to whoever might wrest the object from the original captor. But I held off my Crow friends and presented this pistol to Lieutenant Pearson. Perhaps he still has it, if he yet is alive. I was at the first part of the encounter in some trepidation lest this solitary Indian traveler might have been some peaceable and friendly man on a lawful journey. But it soon became evident he was a Sioux, and members of this tribe had no business to be at this time in this part of the country. The earrings and the hair dressing identified him as a Sioux.

Our meat rations were exhausted about the time we set out on the return journey toward Fort Custer. Game was scarce there for us, the same as it was for illegally plundering Indians. Cattle were in view grazing over the grassy plains, the same as they came into the view of bad Indians whom we were chasing out of the country. We were hungry for fresh meat, the same as they became hungry for it. We scouts discussed among ourselves the distressing situation. Some of our number were willing to endure the hardship. Others said, "We are soldiers, and we have a right to take meat when we need it." I allied myself with these latter patriots. A few of us dallied along until we got far behind the moving troops. Then:

"Bang!" Down dropped one of Nelson Story's fine three-year-old steers.

I presented to Lieutenant Pearson some choice pieces of the beef. He did not ask where I got it, and I did not deem it necessary to tell him. We made camp that night at one of Story's regular cowboy locations. Here the cook gave us a supply of salt-rising bread, which was a pleasing change from our hardtack. Prudence prompted that nothing be said here about the butchering of the steer.

A family named Bessy were living on the Yellow-stone, at the site of Colonel Baker's battle there in 1873. As we approached this outpost of civilization the Crows opened up on their war-songs, fired into the air their guns, waved the scalp of the Sioux man, dismounted and danced a victory movement intended to comfort these friends with this assurance that we were successful protectors of their home. The blackened faces of the Crows helped to instill a feeling of horror rather than of thankfulness in the minds of the family. Nevertheless, Mrs. Bessy set out for us all the buttermilk and sweet milk she had on hand, and we all helped ourselves to a drink of good water at their well, using the windlass to draw it up.

Our Indian reception at the Fort Custer lodges was all that such an event customarily was when victorious warriors returned. One scalp afforded a basis for about as much noisy demonstration as a hundred of them might have created. Plenty Coups, the young chief who during the past fifty years has become a decrepit old chief, was at his lodge just across a creek from the main scout camp. He sent some one over to tell Magpie Outside and the other people that we were coming. She was out to greet us with cheers, along with the rest of them, when we arrived. Tom and Phœbe and Rosa, our three children, gazed in admiration upon their hero father. He had killed a man!

The people in the fort on the hill heard the Indian celebration in the valley, and some of them came down to witness it. After a while the commanding officer sent word down to have the scouts march up to and into the fort, there to proclaim their feelings and to receive official commendation. To go to the fort I blackened my jacket instead of my face, but the Indians all kept the black paint on their faces. The commanding officer had a cannon salute fired in honor of the returning soldiers and scouts combined. We scouts fired a volley from our rifles, and then Pearson's and other troops lined up and fired a responsive volley. The band played several pieces of music. Wives of officers and enlisted men came and treated the Crow scouts to cake and jelly and like delicacies. It was here that I presented to Lieutenant Pearson the captured pistol. I dismounted, removed my hat, walked forward, and held the weapon out toward him. He accepted it and thanked me. The commanding officer gladdened my heart with his complimentary utterance: "Leforge, you did well."

The Sioux and Cheyennes were not the only troublesome hostiles. In fact, as time passed on they almost disappeared from our regions patroled from Fort Custer. But the northern Indians, especially the Piegans, often harassed us. They operated mainly north of the Yellowstone, but occasionally they came south of the river to or beyond our military post. They were old-time enemies of the Crows, the same as the Sioux had been. Hence, our warfare against Piegan raiders was entered upon by the Crow scouts with enthusiasm. On the part of the Piegans, they were willing to take any horses, but they liked to capture Crow horses in particular.

At one certain period about twenty Crow scouts and their families were in camp by the river below the fort. Fine place to camp, splendid trees, good stream for bathing, good shelter for winter, delightful shade for summer. There was plenty of feed, winter and summer, along the valley and on the adjacent rich bench-lands. It was a Paradise for a plains Indian. It seemed designed especially for peaceful abode. Home amusements prevailed here. The people slept every night with a feeling of security.

One morning these Crows awoke to find that only a few of their horses were in sight, these close to the river. The big herd all were gone. The fort officers were notified. Lieutenant Fuller and a detachment of mounted infantry were sent out, accompanied by the entire body of Crow scouts then present, about twenty of them. We had no difficulty finding the trail of the band of horses. We came in sight of them on Tulloch's Fork, there being hurried to the northward, to be taken across the Yellowstone and on into the land of the Piegans. We spurred forward to catch up with them. The thieves saw us coming. They abandoned the herd, jumped from their own mounts, and all ran afoot toward a certain butte·whereon were old Indian stone ramparts that likely had been used many times in past years by differing tribal warriors. Such buttes having such simple fortifications were in existence all about this country in those times.

We encircled the butte. Soldiers and scouts were deployed in the thin line just out of shooting distance. The Crows all had their war-bonnets, and they began to don them for the fray. I had not mine with me. In fact, I never did take out my war-bonnet at any time of going on the war-path. It always was kept at home, for show only. In earlier days I was in the habit of taking my special "medicine" object, one that Cherry had made for me. It was in the form of a certain bird which fluttered along the waters of the higher mountain streams. The Crows knew this flitting creature as "the bird that dives under." But even this charm object was not mine now. I had let Cherry take it with her when she went away, so that it could exert in her interest whatever of good influence might emanate from it. It was buried with her on the scaffold, "south of the mountains." I had now only my eagle feather whirling from my back hair. But I had a special chant of my own. This was my charm. I sang it now.

We opened fire on the entrenched enemy, but we kept at a distance too great for our bullets to be effective. They had a little advantage of us in this respect, by reason of their being above us. A missile from one of their guns bored a tunnel an inch or two below the skin's surface and through a shoulder-blade of Lieutenant Fuller. Since we had them surrounded, with a ground surface almost bar-

ren between them and us, we were ordered simply
to keep up an occasional long-distance firing
and remain in our position. During the remainder
of the afternoon we stayed there. During the entire
night we divided the time, half of us on watch while
the other half slept. That is, this was the order,
but most of us were awake during much of the night.

The next morning we resumed the shooting. But
there came no responding fire. After a while we
drew our circle into closer range. This did not draw
any counter action. It appeared they were awaiting
the time when they could do the most harm to us
with the least expenditure of ammunition. Or maybe
they were out of ammunition. This was an encour-
aging thought. Anyhow, from time to time we tightened up the circle. Still nobody shot at us. From a
distance of about seventy-five yards we made a concerted charge upon the rude fort.

Not a Piegan was there! There had been fifteen
of them in the party that scrambled up into the
refuge the afternoon before. We found their tracks
at the foot of a ten-foot cliff where they had jumped
off. From here the footprints scattered in all directions. By some means every one of them had gone
through our line without any one of them being
discovered.

Oh, those cunning old-time Piegans! What admirable horse-thieves! How difficult to corner them! Slickest Indians in the whole West!

But on this occasion we recovered from them our horses even though we failed to get a scalp. No personal injury occurred to any of us except the wounding of Lieutenant Fuller. There was no indication of our having wounded any Piegan. They had come afoot on the expedition and they went away afoot, their preferred mode of traveling when secrecy of movement was desirable. It is likely that for two or three days they journeyed singly, perhaps to come together at some certain appointed place. Anyway, that appeared to be their regular practice.

White-men raiders also operated in this country. They did much stealing of horses and killing of cattle on the range, which was attributed to Indians. In the matter of cattle, the Indian took nothing but choice parts. The white-man took all of the meat, perhaps the entire carcass except the hoofs and horns. We trailed a good many such rustlers into white-men communities, or into lines of travel not then being used by Indians. Red Wing and I had one successful adventure of this kind.

A dozen of our army mules and as many horses belonging to contract teamsters about the post were stolen one night. The trail led up the valley, in which direction no Indians at that time probably would be driving stolen stock. Red Wing and I were sent out to ascertain the general course of movement and to report back, when a careful patrol search would be made by troops. In dealing with white people, we had to be cautious about legal red tape, whereas, in dealing with Indians, we merely needed to know they were off their reservation, which fact put them in the classification as hostiles and justified us in killing them for this reason only.

Red Wing had been dubbed "One-Eyed Riley," "Old Riley," and then simply "Riley" by facetious soldiers whose amusements all had to be found in the monotony of post life and who took advantage of every opportunity for fun. But they all liked this Indian. He was a capable scout—quiet, cool, good-natured, reliable, brave, but not foolhardy. Notwithstanding the loss of one of his eyes, Red Wing was an accurate marksman with his rifle, one who ordinarily is spoken of as a dead shot. For these various reasons I always was glad to have him with me on hazardous undertakings.

We tracked our lost stock up the valley of the Little Bighorn. We followed them all day and camped over night. Early the next forenoon we observed a camp-fire's smoke curling upward. This was about fifty miles away from the post. The exact location of this camp-fire was right where now is the Crow Indian race-track at Wyola, Montana. We kept watch of it, and in a little while two men rode away from it. Pretty soon they came back driving ahead of them our mules and horses. We observed the direction where they were heading, which was toward a trail going over the divide into the country at the headwaters of Rosebud Creek, to the eastward. We dug heels into horse flanks and galloped far around to their front. They were moving slowly with the herd, we could move much more rapidly, so this maneuver of ours was an easy one to accomplish. We kept on going ahead of them, but keeping ourselves away from the trail, where the dust might reveal our presence. At a place where the frontier line of travel passed between two hills we took our mounts far back from the gap and tied them. Then we located ourselves both together in a cluster of trees on one of the hills overlooking the trail. After not a long wait the herd came, with the two men following. At our chosen moment we both opened fire upon the drovers, both of them white men. One of them let out a yell, dismounted from his horse, and ran limping into the timber. The horse of the other one fell and stayed down. The rider went sprawling forward. He did not rise up.

Watching a little while to see if this one should move, we went down to him and found him dead. Red Wing wanted to scalp him, but I forbade him. He wanted then to take the saddle, bridle, gun, and clothing, but I would not allow him to take anything. We left the body just as we had come to it, only a few feet from the trail. We then headed off the herd and turned them back toward their home at the post. About midnight of the next day we arrived there. We corralled the animals, talked briefly with the picket-guard and some other soldiers who were awakened, and then we repaired to our sleeping places. The next morning Adjutant Roe sent an orderly to call me to headquarters. General Hatch, the commandant at that time, was there. He opened the talk:

"Leforge, I hear you had a successful trip."

"Yes, sir, we brought back the stock."

"What did you do about the men?"

"One of them was wounded, sir, but he got away."

"Did you bring the other one with you?"

"No, sir, we left him there."

"Why didn't you bring him in?" the lively little gray-haired general scolded.

This was an embarrassing question. Evidently the

high officer had not received full information. I hesitated. Finally I framed a significantly veiled response:

"Sir, the weather is too hot. I was afraid he'd fall into pieces."

"Go to your quarters, under arrest!" came the instant stormy command.

His manner, as well as my own original feelings, alarmed me. I had killed a white man, not an Indian. He had not attacked me, but was merely driving away property that belonged to my employer. I and my accomplice had fired upon him without first attempting peaceably to arrest him. While I remained in my quarters, as ordered, the seclusion was not a restful one.

The following morning Lieutenant Roe sent an orderly after me. At headquarters the lieutenant restricted our conference to the usual business relative to the Crow scouts. He ordered me out on another expedition of minor nature. Neither then nor ever afterward was any further official notice taken of the tragedy in which I had just participated.

But the dead white man had relatives living in the Rosebud and Tongue River country. For several years afterward I received occasionally from them an underground threat of retaliatory action upon me. This may have helped to keep alive the mild prickings of conscience that annoyed me. According to my mental training, the killing of a white man was of much more grave significance than the killing of an Indian, under any circumstances. Yet my judgment told me that in the law of the Almighty they stood equal. I never boasted of this assassin-like achievement, but meditation upon it during later years has convinced me that it was a necessary incident of the harsh conditions then confronting the pioneer forces of orderly and lawful conduct.

The Custer battle-field was my summer-resort place during much of the time of my long employment at Fort Custer. At times I camped there, to obviate going there and back so much, which duty was incumbent on me every time any visitors came to the post. From this camp location by the Little Bighorn River at the foot of Custer Hill I spent many hours roaming alone on horseback over the battle-ground and its environs. I saw human bones here and there several miles away from the field. I saw remnants of soldier bodies as far away as Rosebud Creek, twenty-five miles to the eastward. Rotted army clothing articles and an occasional fire-arm or ammunition-belt were scattered all about the region for ten or fifteen miles. These various relics showed what became of the forty missing soldiers at the time of the original count and burial by Gibbon's men two or three days after the battle. It was evident that many soldiers escaped from the immediate encirclement by the Sioux and Cheyennes, but it was evident also that they were pursued and killed, or some of them may have died of wounds and the hardships incident to solitary travel in that country, which then was wild. Much food for serious thought came to me as I discovered here and there among the hills the remnants of what once had been a daring and hardy cavalryman following the banner of Custer. In an old blue blouse I found one time a tintype picture of a young woman. I kept it. I never made report on any finds of the human remains. It was not expected of me. I was at times with soldiers when discoveries were made. We merely looked, wondered, conjectured, and went on our way.

We had some night-school instruction at Fort Custer. I had some also during the short time of my service at Fort Keogh. Different soldiers had different studies they were pursuing or had different kinds of lectures to listen to. In my own case the main points of instruction were as to the duties, powers, and limitations—principally limitations—incident to service as a scout or guide. Despatch writing and despatch carrying methods were discussed fully by the instructors. Questions were put as to what I should do under such and such circumstances in the matter of carrying a written or oral message across the open country. While I already felt well able to perform this sort of duty, and while my preceding life of several years among the Crows gave good basis for this feeling, the instructing officers brought out many good points that made my understanding of the subject both more exact and more comprehensive.

No serious quarrels ever occurred among the Crow scouts, nor, for that matter, were there ever any grave results from differences of opinion or interest among these people in general. But minor spats came up from time to time. While living in the lodges as scouts at Fort Custer, Red Wing and Low Horn got into a heated controversy concerning their claims for grazing-ground for their ponies. They blustered and frowned, and finally they came to blows. The blows were mutually administered by pony-whips. They lashed each other mercilessly. Children were frightened into flight from the scene. Women went into hysterics and shouted, "Part them!" But nobody intervened. Finally, the two men became cooled by their own exhausting efforts at striking and dodging. They both were stripped to the breech-cloth at the time, and they both had big welts, some of them bleeding, all about their bodies. Neither had said, "Enough." They simply had vindicated their honor.

The members of the two families hastened to compose the difference. Red Wing's people hurriedly gathered up some suitable presents to take to Low Horn's lodge. They met people from there carrying blankets and food to Red Wing's lodge. That evening the two men smoked together the peace-pipe. Such was the usual outcome of Crow Indian disputes.

Of the officers at Fort Custer, my direct relationships were mostly with Lieutenant Roe, the adjutant. General Hatch and Colonel Baker were the commandants at different times after General Buell had inaugurated the post. Major-General Hugh L. Scott, a few years ago chief of staff of the United States Army, but now retired, was in the days of Fort Custer and Fort Keogh a lieutenant and then a captain. Lieutenant Doane led more of the patroling scouts that I accompanied than did any other officer. He seemed not to know the feeling of fear. He was rough in speech, or gawky in speech and in general manner, but he was considerate of the feelings of the men under his command, and it appeared he was the best-liked officer at the post.

My pay as interpreter was fifty dollars per month during the earlier years of the Fort Custer service. An additional bonus payment was made from time to time for extra duty on scouts or as a carrier of despatches to Fort Keogh, to the Absaroka agency, even as far as to Bozeman. Early in 1882, upon my request and upon successive approvals through the military channels, the pay was increased to seventy-five dollars per month.

Ordinary living expenses had been small during all of the almost twenty years of my living with the Crows. Hence, as a scout, an interpreter, a hunter or a trader, I had opportunities for accumulating money. I used the opportunities. I set off early at buying cattle, one or two at a time. I had them moved from time to time upon ranges adjacent to my place of abode, and I kept them branded each year and under the surveillance of other cattlemen. It cost me practically nothing thus to care for them, since the cattlemen were accommodating to me because of my activities in resisting the invasions of hostile Indians. I accumulated horses too. Some of them came by gift from Crow friends, some were apportioned to me as spoils of warfare by soldiers as well as by our Crows, others came by my own personal efforts at depleting the resources of the enemy.

I built a log-hut ranch home on the Yellowstone, above the mouth of the Bighorn. I was allowed to spend much of the time there while yet on the duty-roll at Fort Custer. So much of my time was spent at the ranch that I moved my family there. By this time Magpie Outside and I had born to us a son and two daughters. She had also the son and daughter, Mitch Buoyer's children, who to me were almost the same as my own.

We raised plenty of garden vegetables at our ranch. No fence was necessary, except a flimsy enclosure of the garden. We got chickens, and I tamed two cows for milking. I went from time to time to the post, but usually I did not go unless sent for. By this time, in the progress of civiliation in this region, little or no necessity existed for guarding against Indian depredations. Sometimes when I was called for to go to the post, I sent some one as a substitute, devoting myself to looking after my ranch improvements, my cattle and horses.

Mining also interested me. In fact, since I first had arrived in Montana in 1864, a youth of fourteen, prospecting was often uppermost in my thoughts as a means of acquiring great wealth. My father had been infected with this fever. He had spent most of his later years in pursuit of an elusive Golconda, and our occasional contact when on a visit to him imbued me with the same feeling. While I yet was living at the old Mission agency, before having moved to Absaroka, in 1874, I had bought mining stock. I myself had prospected on the upper Boulder Creek on various occasions of vacation from duty at the agency. From year to year thereafter I revisited the region, still prospecting. I had been there for a while each summer or autumn while on duty at Fort Custer. I located and filed upon one mine in particular that looked to my optimistic mind like a world-beater. It but awaited my digging deeply into it. I was awaiting my opportune time. It would keep, I was not in any feverish hurry, but I was becoming anxious to get at the development of this rich mine. My mind was seething with thoughts of gold.

The great change in my course of life was precipitated when Magpie Outside hitched up to the wagon at the ranch one day, loaded into it our small household equipment, got some of the children in the vehicle and some of them on horses, and drove to Fort Custer, where just at this time I was detained for an unusual length of time for some special duty there. She declared her determination to live as an Indian, not as the wife of a white-man rancher. My own inclinations just then were tending more and more away from the Indian life and toward the businesslike life of the white race. I felt capable of competing in this kind of game. It seemed I had graduated in the Indian accomplishments, and they appeared to me now as trivial. I earnestly wanted to conquer a new kind of world.

I sold all of my cattle and most of my horses. I deeded the ranch to Magpie Outside. Although she would not live there, she later realized a comforting sum of money from its sale. I got my discharge from Fort Custer. My wife and children were taken to the Crow agency. Here I provided a lodge for them, provisioned them for a prolonged subsistence, and gave to her also what it seemed was a fair proportion of the money received from the sale of my stock. Then I set off alone to cast my fortunes with the people of the white race. Magpie Outside and myself had parted without ill feeling. She had been a true and good wife, but our notions as to mode of living had become so fundamentally different as to appear not adjustable. Although I had in mind an expectation of returning from time to time for helping her and the children, no definite statement of this kind was made to her. The returning visits would hinge upon the extent of my success.

I came back two or three months later. I found my erstwhile wife married to a white man named Jack who was employed about the agency. People who knew him said he was a steady and trustworthy man. I shook hands with him and with Magpie Outside, and we all separated with outward manifestations of friendly feeling. I enjoined the ex-wife to keep sending the children to school as long as she could do so. To her high credit, she followed fully this injunction. All of them grew up to be among the best-educated of the Crow Indian young people of their generation.

WHITE-MAN LIFE AS A MINING MAN

THE Boulder mining district, out southward from Livingston and Big Timber, became my field of enterprise. When I left Absaroka the last time I gathered together the few horses I had remaining in the vicinity of Huntley, where my ranch had been, and with these I set off again for the region where it appeared gold was fairly calling for some one bright enough to stop there and dig it out. My gradual savings throughout past years and my recent sale of stock brought my working capital up to more than seven thousand dollars. My confidence was so high that seven hundred dollars, or even seven dollars, might have been sufficient to turn me toward mining.

At Columbus, on the Yellowstone River, I stopped for a few days to rest my horses and also to transact some business. It developed that I transacted more business than had been designed. One of the first persons I met, at a hotel, was Mrs. Mary J. Clay, a modest widow having no children.

As was my way, I found out quickly her social status. As also was my way, I decided at once that I needed her for a wife. A mention of this decision to her, coupled with a statement of my present and prospective ability to care for both of us, brought promptly from her an affirmative response. The services of a preacher were obtained, and within three days after we first met, she was on her second matrimonial venture and I was launched out upon my third one.

My new white wife could ride a horse about as well as could either of my Indian wives. She rode with me and helped me drive my little herd on up the river to Big Timber. Here we set up our home for the oncoming winter. I made arrangements whereby my horses should be taken care of until spring, putting them in with the stock of an old acquaintance named Kent, who had family attachments with the Crow Indians. My wife stayed at our home in the village, while I spent most of my time at the mines up the creek during the winter days of this season, 1887-88. When spring came she moved out with me. She rode on horseback while our scant home furnishings were transported on pack-horses. We set up a home there, and she did fully her part in making it a pleasant one. She was the first white woman to locate in that mining-camp, which for several years during those times was a lively little village.

The King Solomon Mining and Milling Company was the holding corporation of my group of prospects. It was capitalized at one million dollars. I had enlisted with me some additional capital furnished by Livingston and Bozeman men with whom I had become acquainted during the preceding years. The Poor Man Mine was our most hope-inspiring one. As manager for the corporation I purchased and had brought from Butte a ten-stamp mill. I had teams to haul ore from the mine to the mill. It was rich ore, but the transportation was not altogether practicable at all times. At places along the short journey the snow during that winter piled up to a depth of twenty-five feet. In fact, the mill became snow-bound and inaccessible except on snow-shoes. I was discouraged, disgusted. When spring weather began to clear up the situation, I sold all of my stock in the corporation and retired. My stock went at slightly above par, and I was well satisfied with the sale. My wife, who also had some savings when we were married and who had invested her money likewise in the mining enterprise, held on to her stock. Some years afterward she disposed of it at a profit.

We moved to Livingston, where I bought a house.

But we remained in this town only a short time. It appeared to me that life on a ranch was most to my liking, and the wife agreed with the idea. We got a piece of land on East Boulder Creek and moved out there to enjoy the delights that appertain to farming in the Rocky Mountains twenty-five miles from town. I still had my horses and a few milk cows. We stocked up with other needful farming equipment. I built a house, a barn, and cut some wild hay during the first season. A brother of mine came from Idaho to visit me here. His visit was cut short by my falling sick. It appeared the doctors in Livingston could do me no good. My wife and I decided to go to Billings.

Typhoid fever was the diagnosis of the medical man at Billings. Developments confirmed his opinion. For several weeks I lay sick in a hotel while my wife nursed me. Then we moved into a furnished cottage, to remain there until my full recovery. The doctor who attended me here was one whom I had known as an army medical officer. One day, when I was almost back to normal health, my wife answered a call to the door. Pretty soon she returned to me with the information:

"It's an Indian woman, and she says she wants to see you."

"Tell her to come in," I said.

It was Magpie Outside! She had heard of my sickness, had come ninety miles in a wagon to see me, had found out my abode, and here she was. I at once informed my white wife who this Indian woman was. Magpie Outside extended her hand. My plump little present mate shrank back in evident fear of personal injury. "Tell her I do not want to hurt her," the calm Crow woman requested me, "that I am glad my husband has a good woman to take care of him." The wife readily accommodated herself to the embarrassing situation. But then who in the world but could trust Magpie Outside? Her countenance had stamped upon it the feelings that were dominant in her heart—benevolence, generosity, magnanimity.

My wife invited her to have some food. But the invitation was evaded on the ground that the husband was waiting somewhere for her return. Her husband? "Go and get him! Bring him here!" My wife and I joined in this urging. The husband was found and was brought into our house. We all had a feast here. My white wife prepared some of the fancy delicacies she could make so well. We had several hours of most delightful visiting before the couple departed to get ready for their return to the agency.

Farm life did not, after all, satisfy the longings

of my wife and myself. We disposed of the land and the appurtenances to it and moved again into Livingston. The livestock and implements were sold to Major Pease, who had bought the buildings of the agency at Absaroka, the official headquarters of the Crow reservation being just then on the eve of establishment at the present Crow Agency, on the Little Bighorn River, later to be on the line of the Burlington Railway.

In Livingston I lived in semi-idleness for several years. I still had all the capital which I had when I left the Indian life and entered upon the white-man mode of living. In addition, I had received a legacy of a lump sum of money, and was also receiving from this same source a monthly income of more than two hundred dollars. My wife and I joined lodges and social clubs. I bought drinks for congenial companions, although for myself I continued the habits of abstinence followed during the preceding years among the Crows.

I joined a circus that passed through the town. Myself, Liver-eating Johnson, and twenty-five or thirty Crow Indians—men, women, and children—tied up to them at Billings. They wanted us to show circus crowds what people of the Wild West looked like, and we wanted to see the world while getting paid for making the observations. We got paid—in promises. I still have these promises. They are stored away in my memory, and I suppose the others who yet are living also have theirs. We went as far as St. Paul. I had no great trouble getting back to Livingston, but my companions did. I believe the Government brought back the Indians. When Liver-eating Johnson returned to my town he told me he had walked all the way from Miles City.

I built some houses in Livingston, for rent. I dabbled in mining stock. This involved various explorations into the neighboring mining districts, including the Boulder region and the Emigrant Gulch diggings. But I did not do much original prospecting during these years. It seemed I had no need for doing any. I was doing well enough as a small capitalist and a speculator, or an investor, in real estate and mining enterprises. At one time, for a few days, I owned the whole of Hunter's Hot Springs health and pleasure resort. That is, the property was deeded to me by the owners, Nickey and Crow, and after a few days I and my wife deeded it back to them. It was an accommodation for them, and they paid me for fulfilling the trust. The entire transaction was through the management of Mr. Talcott, a pioneer banker there. I took a keen interest in local politics. National affairs did not engage me so much, but when the campaign of 1896 aroused the people of Montana into resistance against the machinations that would prevent the free coinage of silver at the ratio of sixteen to one, I put upon my coat lapel and wore continuously a Bryan button. I was a silver Republican, for free silver and protective tariff—not one, but both.

But my prospective millions to be derived from mining ventures around Livingston dwindled into thousands, into hundreds. My funds kept at a standstill during the ten years there. I wanted to increase my wealth. A letter from my brother George in Oregon fired me with a desire to prospect with him what he described as a rich mining region. But my wife wanted none of such foolishness, urging that we remain in our present location. About this time another letter came, this one from Major James C. Merrill, an army medical officer whom I had known while in the military service. My acquaintance with him had been as Captain Merrill. He was a diligent student of science, taking a special interest in ornithology. It appeared he was from a wealthy family in the East. When I had known him in the army his mother would send to him from time to time some new and expensive gun. He always had me try out his guns.

Yes, I must pay a visit to Major Merrill, who

now was stationed at Fort Sherman, Washington, near Spokane. My wife, whom I called Molly, was left at home in the care of our adopted son, who was an apprentice railroad employee and who later became a locomotive engineer on the Northern Pacific. I spent two or three weeks in the company of my friend of former lively days in Indian warfare. When time came for me to go I set off in the wrong direction. I went further away from home instead of toward home. Indeed, I altogether "forgot" to go back.

At Heppner, Oregon, my brother met me. As we lingered a few days in the town, men were enlisting for the Spanish-American War. I wanted to go, but my brother talked me out of it. Perhaps I should not have been accepted, since I then was forty-eight years old. At any rate, I waived this adventure for hazards of another kind. We bought a full outfit for prospecting and journeyed forth into the Blue Mountains. Nothing came from our several months spent in this region. That is, nothing of golden composition came to us. But it was to me a glorious change from the humdrum tameness of insipid domestic and social life in Livingston.

The Umatilla Indians helped me to enjoy the outing. They recognized me at once as one of the "people of the world," as all old Western Indians called themselves, each in their own language and all in the same sign-talk designating gesture. But they were a little too civilized to suit exactly my notions of Indian attractiveness. Only the old ones could make good sign-talk. The younger generation were becoming flippant imitators of the lower class of white people. Nevertheless, I got on very friendly terms with a pretty young Umatilla woman and gave some consideration to the idea of joining the tribe. But it developed she was married. My informant told me her husband was polishing up his guns to use on me. This was the finishing touch to my association with these people. It was time for me to go.

The Natches River region, in the Cascade Mountains of Washington, called me. Billy Meeks went there with me, and we spent several months in fruitless prospecting among those far-western highlands. Then my brother George and I started a brick-yard at Prosser, Washington. We operated this plant a year or more, sold out at a little profit, and went to Granger. Here we built on contract a brick-yard for Thompson Brothers.

My wife in Livingston had been writing for me to come home. I had been writing letters urging her to sell out there and join me in Washington. It appeared we could not agree in the matter. I got an attorney in Livingston to arrange for a divorce. We had no children other than the adopted son, so the arrangement was mainly one of financial adjustment. This was settled amicably. Each of us had a comfortable small fortune. She was a good woman, and I was sorry we could not agree on place and manner of living.

On a train I saw a woman who attracted me. I planned my movements so as to stir up an acquaintance with her. I liked her modest manner; she apparently liked my forwardness. We told each other our names and something of our past lives. Her name was Lola Lewis, although her friends had nicknamed her "June" Lewis. Her home was in Yakima, Washington. Good! Glad to hear that! Yakima was the very place I wanted to visit! A month later I landed in this enticing woman's town. My only business was to see her. The outcome was a wedding. June Lewis became Mrs. Thomas H. Leforge.

The Alaska boom was in progress. Of course, I wanted to go there. After a few months of happy domesticity, my wife acceded to a proposition that I try my fortune in the far North. She took up her abode with her parental family at Cowiche, Washington. I went to Seattle and there made preparations for the new venture. At Yakima I had paid nine hundred dollars for an Alaska mine owned by a man named Nixon, who had spent one season there. My purchase was quite speculative, based altogether on his description of the mine and the country in general. Now I was buying equipment for working it. I invested about six thousand dollars in provisions, tools, lumber, and two small boats for traveling along the rivers. These I had loaded upon the steamship *Santa Anna,* which vessel carried me toward the land of superabundant gold. In mid-ocean the ship caught fire. The flames were suppressed, but my cargo was damaged. In due time I was recompensed to the extent of six hundred dollars, the amount agreed upon. E. K. Woods, one time mayor of Seattle, was the claim agent who settled with me.

My mine was a placer digging. It was far up Fish River, on the Goose Creek branch of that stream, and about twenty miles above Council City. I hired some help and worked on my rich bar. It gave good returns, but it was in a marshy spot, which made drainage a difficult and expensive undertaking. I dropped it and went prospecting on Fox River. Here I found and filed upon some good prospects. But as autumn came on I sold out everything and left the country. My return was on the same steamship *Santa Anna.* The net result of this summer of gold-seeking was exactly naught, both ways. I got back home with just about the same amount of funds I had at the beginning of the enterprise.

A second trip to Alaska was entered upon in the spring of 1901. I knew then more about the country, and I was anxious to see what I might find there. Again the considerate wife willingly assented to the effort and wished me good luck. The sea journey northward was on the steamship *Nome City*. My principal operations were in prospecting in the neighborhood of Teller, fifty miles or so above Nome. Lots of gold there, but the land in this place also was marshy and hard to drain. On both sides of the marshy area the earth was frozen throughout the year. This frozen section contained gold in its graveled soil, but thawing operations were expensive. Nevertheless, I acquired here some latent wealth in placer mines by perfecting a few claims. I left them, though, and went into the vicinity of Kotzebu Sound. Here I rocked out a few hundred dollars in gold. The outcome of this season of Alaskan exploration was a slight financial loss. My return trip was made on the steamship *Senator*. I recall that as we came into Puget Sound we noticed black drapings on the buildings in the cities and towns. In due time we learned the cause of this general mourning. President McKinley had died.

My brother George came from Idaho to visit me at Yakima. "Tom, there's big money in the brick business just now," he counseled me one day, "and I wish you'd go in with me on it." I fell in with his proposition. I put my Alaska holdings into the hands of an agent, for sale. We went to Bellingham, Washington. My wife went with me and we set up our home there.

"Brickmakers wanted," was a bulletin that attracted our attention soon after the arrival in Bellingham. We sought out the promulgator of the bulletin. We learned that Harry Garrett wanted somebody to go in with him in building a steam-drying plant for brick. We had learned at Prosser enough of this kind of undertaking to render us capable of carrying through the enterprise. We went into a triple partnership and in due time set up the business. After a year here we sold out, at a slight loss. But we went into other brick-making ventures, these industrial efforts being continued over a period of several years.

My wife had been to Seattle and elsewhere in the Puget Sound country with me during these years. Her health always was better there, so we decided she might remain there, and I would join her as soon as I could get clear of the brick industry. My money being all tied up in business, she sold a piece of land she had and bought a home in Seattle. She took our two small daughters and moved there. I went back and forth to visit them and to attend to my business interests.

Contracting for the cutting of railroad-ties enlisted the minds of my brother and myself as a money-making venture. We got out of the brick-making business and entered that of cutting ties. We got two teams and made an agreement for clearing off forty acres of heavily timbered land near Granite, Idaho. We employed Swedes to do the chopping. We made some money here, partly recovering what we had lost while making bricks. Yet, when we had completed this contract, I lacked a few thousand dollars of having as much money as I had when this country came first into my view.

The white-man system of continual struggle for money began to pall upon me. My thoughts dwelt more and more upon the simplicity of Crow Indian life, where I had acquired moderate wealth without special effort, or by efforts entirely to my liking. In fact, among them, great accumulation of material wealth was not of importance. Nobody having an amiable disposition ever came to dire want among them. More than twenty years of absence from them and association with white men on a white basis served to accentuate the virtues and to condone the faults of the Indian mode of life. Fond recollections of their liberal-minded customs flooded my heart. It was submerged by the inundation. I would visit the Crows.

I think I loved the wife in Seattle. I know I loved our two little daughters. Notwithstanding, it seemed nothing could ameliorate my heart-sickness but a sight of the lower Yellowstone, of Clark's Fork, of Pryor Creek, of the Bighorn River, of the stately mountains to the southward of them. So I bought a railroad ticket for Billings, Montana.

AT HOME AGAIN WITH THE CROWS

Two Indian youths came into the dining-room of a restaurant in Billings where I was sitting at a table. When they took off their tall hats it could be seen at once to what tribe they belonged. The triple braids of hair and the cut-off and roached-up foretop identified them as Crows. They were shown seats at a table by the wall of the room and ten or twelve feet distant from me. They conversed in low voice, as Indians regularly do, but their intonations drifted into my keenly attentive ears. They were talking of a shipment of horses to market. The subject itself was of no great interest to me, but the vocal tones were enrapturing. What enchanting music that was!

After having enjoyed for a while the exchange of talk or the mere presence of these young men, I got up and walked over to their table. Their customary shyness in the presence of strangers left them when they found themselves addressed in their own tongue. I made inquiries about tribal affairs in general. Presently I put a question about some one in particular. This question appeared to puzzle my

informants for a few moments. Then one of them
fixed his eyes in steady scrutiny of my countenance
as he replied:

"He's dead—died a long time ago, when I was
a little boy."

It seemed I became suddenly many years older.
Doubtless others of my old associates were gone. I
feared to ask. The questioning was shifted to Fort
Custer. Who was in command there now? How
many soldiers were there? How many scouts?

Fort Custer? Why, there wasn't any Fort Custer
now. They had heard their old people tell many
interesting stories about the days when the soldiers
used to be here, but the white warriors all were gone
away. One of the young Crows came back at me
with:

"We do not know you. Who are you?"

Didn't know me! Didn't know Horse Rider! But,
come to think of it, neither of these now husky
young men had been born when I had left the reservation. Neither of them now was more than twenty
years old. One of them told me he was a half-breed,
that his father's name was Morrison.

Morrison? Yes, I remembered the man. My
acquaintance with him had been only a scant one,
but I recalled the time and the place when and where
he had married a young woman of the tribe. She

had been a relative of my wife Cherry, and I had known her since her small girlhood.

The Morrison youth jumped up and seized my hand for a warm and prolonged second greeting. We were of the same people. Nothing would do but I must go with him to the ranch-home of his father and mother. The two young fellows were traveling in a wagon, they had plenty of provisions and plenty of bedding, all of which was at my command.

Joy and sadness contended for supremacy in my mind during this wagon journey. The hills and valleys and streams were the same. Every cottonwood-tree and every clump of alder brush and each plum-thicket seemed to be answering back to me the glad salutations my thoughts were sending out to them. What pleasant thrills came when we met along the way some one I had known in the old times! What checks to the genial reminiscent current when a meeting happened with individuals of the younger generation who knew me not. The Indians as a tribal whole were not the same. Their lands had been allotted in part and some of the former exclusive residence of the Crows had been sold and was occupied by bustling white men. These irreverent newcomers were plowing up and utterly ruining thousands of acres of good grazing-land! They were paying no heed whatever to the fact that this,

only a few years before, had been the home of the
deer, the elk, and the buffalo. To complete the dese-
cration, a railroad now had its thundering trains
tearing along through the very heart of the old-time
rich hunting-grounds. People were looking from the
windows of the flying fire-wagons and were saying:

"So that's where General Custer was killed?
What fiends these Crow Indians must be!"

At the Morrison ranch-home I felt at first like
the stranger I was. The man did not know me. It
was suggested he have his wife come and look at
the unexpected visitor. Reluctantly, with the shyness or modesty characteristic of Crow women in
the presence of men not known to them, she responded to her husband's call. She looked, her vision
soon became intently fixed, she clapped a hand
against her mouth, then she burst out laughing. The
fit of laughter extended to almost hysterical proportions. When she had gained sufficiently her self-control she seized me by a shoulder and shook me. She
jerked me toward her husband and exclaimed:

"It is Horse Rider! For many years he has been
dead, but now he is come back into life!"

This place became temporarily my home. Morrison sent couriers to inform my daughters and to
invite them here to visit me. They came—Phœbe
and Rosa. Oh, how I loved these grown-up Indian

children of mine! And how they clung to me! "Our dead father came to life again," they repeated over and over. And they could talk English—good English. They both had attended the local schools and had been away to the advanced Indian schools.

With these two daughters I went to see the oldest child of my Indian family, my stepdaughter, the offspring of Mitch Buoyer and Magpie Outside in the long ago when Cherry had been my wife. My three sons came to see me. One was known then as "old Tom Leforge," the son of Cherry and myself. Another was "young Tom Leforge," my son born to Magpie Outside. The third was my stepson, Mitch Buoyer's son, known to the people as Jim Leforge.

My six Indian children and I counseled together about the propriety of a visit to Magpie Outside. Her white husband Jack had died, but for several years she had been and now was the wife of a fullblood Crow Indian, Cold Wind. I remembered this man Cold Wind, but our past acquaintance had not been a close one. I had no doubt, though, he was a good man, else Magpie Outside would not be his wife. Or her being his wife would make of him a good man. I was longing to see her again, merely to be for a little while in the company of this benignant woman, having no thought of putting myself between her and her present mate. In fact, I had forfeited altogether any consideration from her, but I believed she would be glad also to see me. Furthermore, my mind now was made up to stay here with the Crows, and it would be almost impossible to avoid a meeting at some time. So why not go boldly forth and seek a friendly interview? When we arrived at her abode the daughters went inside and informed her of my presence beside the wagon a little distance away. She came out, bringing her husband Cold Wind with her. She stopped six or eight feet in front of me and stood there looking at me. Her countenance beamed forth the same old goodness of heart. I never saw a more sublime sight than she was when she lifted up her hands and solemnly invoked upon me the blessing of the Sun.

"I am glad to see this grand day when my children's father has come back to them," she said as she shook hands with me. "I see you are looking well, but you have grown older," she continued. "I too am older. But we both can be helpful yet to our children and to other people."

Yes, she was the same Magpie Outside. It seemed she never did love anybody exclusively, but her love included all human beings. She was the special friend of every orphan and decrepit old person in the tribe. During her lifetime she lived with four different husbands, and I have not the least doubt that to each one in his turn she was altogether faithful. She and her husband and myself kept on friendly terms, but of course I arranged my own affairs so as to be out of their vicinity except on unusual occasions. When she died several years later her husband and I mourned together her loss. Since then Cold Wind and I have been associates and friends.

My oldest daughter, Mary—that is, Mitch Buoyer's daughter—is married to Little Nest, a full-blood Crow. She now is a grandmother. She is a medicine-woman, as had been her mother during her later life. Mary Little Nest is in some ways my favorite child. Although I am not her blood father, if some one should ask her about the matter, she would say, "Horse Rider is my father," and no amount of cross-examining by any merely casual inquirer would elicit from her any other reply. She and her husband live in comfort in a good frame house, but on festive occasions they set up the old-time tepee of Little Nest's clan, the lodge having the conical top blackened. Little Nest's great-grandfather had a dream in which he was enjoined to keep blackened the upper segment of his lodge. Since that time all of his male descendants have kept up this distinguishing feature of their Indian lodges. Mary took no interest in school education, so she has only a scant knowledge of the English language. But as an unusually capable woman in all practical affairs and as a good wife and a wise maternal guardian, she possesses the high qualities of her mother.

"Old Tom Leforge," Cherry's son, received good school training and served many years as official interpreter at the present Crow Agency. He was Cherry's only surviving child. Her people kept him after her death. In his early middle age the scythe of the merciless reaper swept him from this life. Jim Leforge and "young Tom Leforge" are prospering as Indian farmers on the reservation. Phœbe married a full-blood Crow. Rosa married Charles Dillon, a half-Sioux. Both she and her husband were graduates of Carlisle. In his college time, Dillon was a great football player. Rosa served several years as bookkeeper at Crow Agency. She and Dillon visited Washington just after their marriage. There she met General Miles, and through her he sent to me a pair of fine buckskin gloves that I treasure. I had to suffer, though, another great bereavement. Early in 1927 my beloved Rosa succumbed to the dreadful Indian tuberculosis.

My two white daughters living on Puget Sound have become proficient in music and other educational accomplishments. Both are contented in marriage. I visited them a few years ago. They wanted me to stay there, but I like it best among the Indians. At any home of my Indian children I am welcome. An advantage to me is that I have the assurance they all will remain residents right here. My white children might move here or there about the world. I am too old now to be moving house. Moreover, here is the special part of the world where I can find most of mental peace and contentment.

I worship the Sun and the Bighorn Mountains. The towering range just south of my present home is to me both father and mother. During the most fondly recalled years of my life, their offspring lands and streams provided me with an abundance of good food and rich raiment. I'd rather sit upon the ground at their feet than to loll in an uphol-stered chair. My stomach craves meat cooked in the Indian way. I trust I may live yet longer than did my white-man father, who died in Bozeman at an age closely approaching a hundred years. The way I feel now, I surely shall do this unless I should meet with one of the three killing elements that to me are most fearful—heavy hail, lightning, or an angry bull elk.

I was born an Ohio American. I shall die a Crow Indian American. My last white wife, in Seattle, got a divorce from me, because of my desertion of her.

She was a good woman, but I could not live any longer the life of a white man. When comes the time for me to leave this earth I want to dwell wherever are the spirits of my wives—my Indian wives—both of them.

I like all American Indians I ever have known. Next to the Crows, I like best the Sioux. They were wicked, but brave fighters. I used to hold our Crow tribal enmity toward them, but this feeling now is gone. I have enjoyed rehearsing with some of them the old-time struggles. I appreciate now that those deadly combats were a sportive game more than a killing because of hate.

I have a few papers preserved from past times. Many others that might be of interest are gone. Among the remnant reminders of the old frontier army days is a set of official endorsement letters pertaining to my application for increased pay while on duty at Fort Custer. Perhaps these will help to present a portrayal of the conditions then existing:

Fort Custer, M. T.,
July 1st, 1881.

Lieut. C. B. Hoppin,
A.A.QM. 2nd Cav.,
Fort Custer:

Sir: I would respectfully ask that my salary as interpreter may be increased from July 1st, 1881, to $75 per month.

I make this application on the ground that my duties take me away from the post for days at a time among the Crow Indians and my present salary of $50 is not enough to defray my expenses.

Very respectfully,
(Sd) THOMAS LEFORGE, Interpreter.

1st Endorsement.
Office of A.A. Qr.Master,
Fort Custer, M. T.,
July 7th, 1881.

Respectfully forwarded to the Chief Quartermaster of the department (through Commanding Officer Fort Custer, M.T.).

I would respectfully recommend that the pay asked for be granted, as this man is a good interpreter and the pay now allowed is entirely too small for the duty he is required to perform.

(Sd) C. B. HOPPIN,
2nd Lieut. 2nd Cavalry, A.A.Qm.

2nd Endorsement.
Fort Custer, M.T.,
July 17, 1881.

Respectfully forwarded approved. This request seems to be reasonable, as the interpreter not only has to act as such, but makes outside trips, in other words acts as both interpreter and guide.

(Sd) G. K. SANDERSON,
Capt. 11th U. S. Infantry.

4th Endorsement.
Headquarters Department of Dakota,
Office Chief Quartermaster,
Fort Snelling, Minnesota, Aug. 1st, 1881.

Respectfully returned to the Adjutant General of the Department. The appropriation for incidental expenses for the present fiscal year will not admit of any increase in the salaries of interpreters employed in this department.

Employees ordered away from their stations on public business are entitled to per diem and actual expenses of transportation under provisions of G.O. #97, A.G.O. of 1876, and #25 A.G.O. of 1879.

WM. MYERS,
Deputy Qr.Mr.Genl.U.S.A.,
Chief Quartermaster.
(Sd) R. P. HUGHES,
Capt. 3rd Infantry, H.D.C.

5th Endorsement.
Headquarters Department of Dakota,
Fort Snelling, Minn., August 3d, 1881.

Respectfully returned to the Commanding Officer Fort Custer, M.T., inviting attention to preceding endorsement of the Chief Quartermaster of the Department. By command of   BRIGADIER-GENERAL TERRY,
(Sd) SAMUEL BRECK, A.A.Genl.

A true copy:
CHAS. F. ROE, 1st Lieut. and Adjt. 2nd Cavalry.

Office of A.A.Q.M.
Fort Custer, M.T.,
Dec. 28, 1881.

The Adjutant,
Fort Custer:

Sir: I have the honor to request that steps be taken to render effective my recommendation for increased compensation for Thomas Leforge, at present and for the past two years a scout and interpreter at this post. He has been in the government employ about twenty years, rendering important and valuable service always. Officers without exception place the highest value upon his judgment and reliability in all the attributes of his office.

Serious questions threaten to arise between the Government and Indians in consequence of encroachment upon the latter's reservation. In such event the worth of Leforge's presence and assistance can hardly be too strongly stated. His present compensation is fifty dollars a month and a ration, and is barely enough for his support. His relations with visiting Indians necessarily make demand upon his hospitality.

I therefore respectfully submit that Leforge's compensation be increased to one hundred dollars a month.

Very respectfully your obedient servant,
(Sgd) D. C. PEARSON,
Lt. & R.Q.M. 2 Cav. A.A.Q.M.

Fort Custer, M.T.,
Dec. 29, 1881.

I think this man deserves greater compensation than he now receives. He has been faithful in his duties as scout and interpreter and is invaluable in both these capacities. In addition, he has more influence with the Indians than any one I know, and I believe will eventually be a great instrument in finally civilizing the Crow Indians.

> (Sgd) A. J. ALEXANDER,
> Lieut. Col. 2nd U.S.Cav.

Fort Custer, M.T.,
Dec. 29, 1881.

I believe this increase of compensation is due Mr. Leforge, and for his past services would be glad to see it given him. There is always a call upon him by Indians visiting here that of necessity absorbs some of his pay.

> (Sgd) G. K. SANDERSON,
> Capt. 11th U.S.Inf.

Fort Custer, M.T.,
Dec. 29, 1881.

I strongly recommend that the compensation of Scout and Interpreter Leforge be increased to seventy-five dollars per month, the same as the interpreter at Fort A. Lincoln, as he is a very valuable man.

> (Sgd) JNO. P. HATCH,
> Colonel 2nd U.S.Cav.,
> Commanding.

Hdqrs. Dept. of Da.,
Office of Chief Q.M.,
Fort Snelling, Jan. 9, 1882.

Respectfully returned to the Adjutant General of the Department, recommending that the pay of Interpreter Leforge be increased to $75 per month.

> (Sgd) WM MYERS,
> Deputy Q.M. General,
> Chief Quartermaster.

Headqrs. Dept. of Da.,
Fort Snelling, Minn., Jany. 11, 1882.

Resp'y returned to the Commanding Officer Fort Custer, approved as recommended by the Chief Quartermaster of the Department, in preceding endorsement. By order of
BRIGADIER-GENERAL TERRY
(Sgd) SAMUEL BRECK,
Assistant Adjutant General.

I have enjoyed greatly during late years the personal meetings with some of the officers and men who used to do Indian fighting in this part of the West. General Roe, General Miles, General Scott, and others have been very kind in the way of visiting me and writing letters to me. General Scott has been the most faithful correspondent. Some of his letters may show what a good Indian he is:

Fort Bliss, Texas,
May 7th, 1913.

My dear Laforgie:

I have your Crow names for Clark's Fork, etc., and would like that for the Mizpah southeast of Fort Keogh, and Sunday Creek north of Keogh. I am sorry I did not write down all these names when I was young, but I thought I would always live in that country and would not need to write down anything. I remember Pryor's Fork—*ma-po-ar-sha*—but not Fly Creek. Do you remember what name the Crows had for Lieutenant Doane and Jack Barnet? I remember they called you "Lame Man" after you cut off your foot. I have a great deal of material now about the sign language, but lack most the names of creeks and mountains in the North. I know a whole lot in the Sioux and Comanche country, because I have lived there later than in the North.

Well, I am very much obliged for the trouble you have taken to write me what you did and I know that it was a whole lot of trouble. I made out every word, however, and it was all very valuable to me.

Very sincerely yours,
H. L. SCOTT.

P. S.—I forgot to answer your other letter. I am not now at Fort Sam Houston, Texas, but at Fort Bliss, Texas, on the S.W. border of Texas, and no longer have the 3rd Cavalry, but have been appointed a Brigadier-General and have charge of the Mexican border of New Mexico and Arizona with the 5th, 9th, and 13th Cavalry and a battery of artillery.

About the scouts in 1876: I can not tell you, as I graduated at West Point, June 14, 1876, and did not get out on the plains until the end of summer in the 7th Cavalry at Fort A. Lincoln, Dakota, and was with Doane and E troop of the 7th DeRudio.

War Department,
Office of the Chief of Staff,
Washington,
February 16, 1916.

My Dear LaForge:

Your letter of the 9th was received this morning, and I was glad to hear from you. I see Camp every time he comes

East. He is getting up a great quantity of information about the Little Horn. Major Reynolds the other day sent me a photograph taken, I think, by Huffman, 'way back in the seventies. It has Quivey in it, Two Bellies, and Old Crow. I am having it framed, and think a good deal of it.

General Miles is here in Washington, and a letter sent to him, care of The Adjutant General of the Army, would reach him. General Frank Baldwin is in Denver, Colorado, where a letter would reach him. He used to be up with General Miles, you remember, at Tongue River.

I am very busy now, every day, or I would have some questions to ask you about old times. Some day I am going to drop in to see you, the first time I get a chance to go to the Northwest. How the world has changed since the old times on the Yellowstone! How the army has changed, and everybody in it! It seems to me that I like the old times best. Mountain Chief, chief of the Piegans, was here the other day. He brought me a pipe and tobacco-bag from Montana and sang for me one of his old songs for drawing the buffalo into the pound. I do not know whether the Crows ever did that or not, but I hear much of the Blackfeet and Assiniboines doing it.

I am glad that you are getting along well, and hope that will continue, and that the cold will not do you any injury this winter. With best wishes, I am,

Sincerely yours,
H. L. Scott.

Mr. Thomas H. LaForge,

Wyola, Montana.

War Department,
Office of the Chief of Staff,
Washington, D. C.,
January 13, 1917.

My Dear Laforge:

Your letter of January 6th just arrived to-day, and it gave me great pleasure, indeed, to hear from you. I hope that if the Crows come on here, you will go with them, when we can have a talk about old times on the Yellowstone. You know lots of things about the times before I came on the plains that I want to get from you.

Colonel W. F. Cody (Buffalo Bill) was here not very long ago. A photographer followed him up here and asked if he could not have our photographs taken together, which was done. I have just gotten a telegram from Colonel Cody's sister saying he was dead in Denver, and I am sending my copy of this photograph, which, I think, is probably the last photograph he had taken, to his wife.

Thanking you for the letter and wishing you every good thing for the new year, I am,

Ever sincerely yours,
H. L. SCOTT.

Mr. Thomas H. Laforge,
Wyola, Montana.

————

Headquarters,
Camp Dix, New Jersey,
December 21, 1918.

My Dear LaForge:

Your letter of the 26th of November arrived here to-day. I was very glad, indeed, to hear from you. So many of my old friends are dying from the influenza that I am glad to hear you are still on deck. We have lost over 800 men in this camp from influenza and more at many of the other camps of the country.

We have won the war now and are engaged in discharging men who are on this side. We have discharged and sent away from here 480 officers and 20,000 men within the past few days, and are still discharging at the rate of 1,000 per day. There is a great deal of work attached to the discharging of a man, as his pay has to be made up and he also has to be examined physically in order to protect both himself and the Government, all of which requires at least 48 hours to attend to, so you see we are all kept very busy. I have been told that I am to be appointed on the Board of Indian Commissioners next spring. This will give me an opportunity to go to the various agencies and report on conditions. I hope this is true and that I will be able to get out into your country.

I have been reading some of the books written by J. W. Schultz, who used to be among the Blackfeet. He has written a great deal about the Blackfeet, and his Indian books are the best I have ever read. I think that were you to write what you know about the Crows, you would be able to make a whole lot of money by it and build a monument to yourself that would be very enduring. I want to see you and ask you many questions about that sort of thing that will clear up matters in my mind. I will be dropping in on you the very first chance I get, possibly next spring or summer, if I can make it.

Hoping you will remember me most kindly to your

daughter I saw in Washington, and with best wishes to you both for a Happy Christmas, I am as ever,

Your old friend,

H. L. SCOTT.

To: Mr. Thomas H. LaForge,
Wyola, Montana.

———

Department of the Interior,
Board of Indian Commissioners,
Washington.
Princeton, New Jersey, Oct. 30, 1919.

My Dear LeForgey:

I have at last gotten home to settle down for the winter, and my thoughts go back to the time I had with you and the Dillons. The next time I go out my time will be arranged so I can stay longer where I want to. I went to Lamedeer, from there to Poplar, in Thackeray's car, and he brought me back to Glendive, and we stopped at old Fort Union at the mouth of the Yellowstone. There is nothing to mark it but a few holes. Joe Culbertson showed it to us. He lived there in 1862 and his father built it in 1832. Joe explained the whole lay-out as it was in 1862.

At Poplar I saw a Minneconjou Sioux who was in the Custer fight with the Sioux. He drew a map and gave a good account of the fight. He was quite old, but was the brightest man with the best memory I met.

I stopped to see Camp in Chicago, but he was away on a 20-day trip, much to my disappointment. I saw George Bird Grinnell on the Hudson River boat the other day. He is interested in you and all the old-timers. He went to the

Black Hills with Custer in 1874. I wish we were all young and back in those times again.

I asked after Dillon's father at Standing Rock, but did not see him. I am sorry, as I wanted to tell him about his boy. There is much more grass down there than on the Crow or Blackfoot ranges, more also at Poplar. It is getting a little cool, but it must be quite cold with you. I hope you will give my best wishes to Rosa, to Dillon and the children and my Indian friends with you.

With best wishes for yourself, I am,

Always your friend,

H. L. Scott.